AMERICANS
of
1776

AMERICANS
of
1776

Daily Life
in
Revolutionary America

by

James Schouler

CORNER HOUSE
HISTORICAL PUBLICATIONS
Gansevoort, NY   12831
1999

Corner House Historical Publications
14 Catherine Street, PO Box 207
Gansevoort, NY   12831

Most recent printing is noted by the number below:

10 9 8 7 6 5 4 3 2 1

ISBN: 0-87928-127-8   Soft Cover, 1999 Edition

The Corner House Historical Publications edition is an unabridged
reprint of the original edition published in 1906. This edition includes
an introduction about the author. Printed on acid free paper in the
United States of America.

ABOUT THE AUTHOR

James Schouler was born on March 20, 1839 in West Cambridge, Massachusetts, the son of William Schouler and Frances Eliza Warren. He moved with his family to Ohio in his youth. He attended Harvard and graduated in 1859. After teaching school for a very short period of time, he pursued his career in law. He married Emily Fuller Cochran of Boston in 1870. They had no children.

The outbreak of the Civil War in 1861 found Schouler and his family in a good position to prosper. He returned to Massachusetts and became active in the Republican Party. He received an appointment as Adjutant General of the State and found himself in a very influential and profitable position. He completed his legal studies and was admitted into practice. He served with a Massachusetts regiment for a short period before returning to his practice.

After the War, he and his father pursued claims for veterans and other cases making his fortune in Washington, DC. Schouler began to write extensively, primarily in the legal area. From 1871 to 1873, he edited for the *United States Jurist* and published a series of legal treatises and textbooks. This venture became highly successful. By 1873, the wealth amassed by the family allowed him to pursue his primary love, the research and writing of American history.

His first work was a two volume *History of Massachusetts in the Civil War*, started in 1868 and completed in 1871. Schouler also began work on a multi-volume *History of the United States of America Under the Constitution.* This monumental work totaled seven volumes, all of which were prepared and published between 1880 and 1913. From 1891 on, Schouler was a guest lecturer at Johns Hopkins University. He published some of his articles in a 1896 in a work entitled *Historical Briefs.* His book, *Americans of 1776,* published in 1906, is a compilation of his lectures on the Revolutionary War period while at Johns Hopkins. He died in 1920 at the age of eighty-one. [1]

1. *Dictionary of Literary Biography,* Volume 47, pp 257-259.

PREFACE

THIS book is not a new narrative history of the Revolution, nor a new arrangement of old historical materials. It is an original study of life and manners, social, industrial and political, for the Revolutionary period. Newspapers, magazines and pamphlets of the period, old letters and diaries have been explored, and the results of a personal investigation among hidden but trustworthy matter are here set forth.

The substance of the present volume comprises occasional lectures given by the author before the Johns Hopkins University (1901-1905) while the present study was in progress.

February 1, 1905.

NOTE

THE following abbreviations are used in the citations of this volume: M. G. for *Massachusetts Gazette;* E. G. for *Essex Gazette;* N. E. C. for *New England Chronicle;* I. C. for *Independent Chronicle;* P. G. for *Pennsylvania Gazette;* P. C. for *Pennsylvania Chronicle;* P. J. for *Pennsylvania Journal;* V. G. for *Virginia Gazette.*

CONTENTS

CHAPTER I

THE THIRTEEN COLONIES AND THEIR PEOPLE

CHAPTER II

FREEMEN AND BONDSMEN

CHAPTER III

CRIMES AND DISORDERS

CHAPTER IV

BIRTHS, MARRIAGES AND DEATHS

CHAPTER V

HOUSES AND HOMES

CHAPTER VI

THE CASUALTIES OF LIFE

CHAPTER VII

THE THREE PUBLIC VOCATIONS

CHAPTER XIV

COMMON SCHOOL EDUCATION

CHAPTER XV

COLLEGES AND THE HIGHER EDUCATION

CHAPTER XVI

RELIGIOUS INFLUENCES

CHAPTER XX

AMERICANS
of 1776

I

THE THIRTEEN COLONIES AND THEIR PEOPLE

THE glorious age of our Revolutionary struggle for independence has been well explored for setting forth the main incidents of that heroic strife and the illustrious deeds of its leaders, civil and military. But posterity as yet knows little of the American people themselves of that famous age. Something has been sacrificed in the review—too much, perhaps—to what may be called the dignity of history; and historians of the Revolution, led by the venerated Bancroft, have not only, as they should have done, given us a scholarly narrative of the chief events shaped out by those who directed from the heights, but there have mainly rested. Macaulay in his day took strong issue against such views of public narration. And our own historian, the late Francis Parkman, with one of those strong expletives characteristic of him, used to condemn, so his biographer tells us, all such over-devotion to historical dignity. "Straws," he would say, "are often the best material."[1] After his incisive comment, in which I strongly concur, save for the impolite expression, I purpose setting forth in these chapters some recondite material gained

[1] Farnham's Parkman.

from miscellaneous but (as should always be the case) wholly trustworthy sources, in the hope of bringing out some features of an heroic age and its people, which should interest posterity and yet are unfamiliar to us; and I leave in other respects the grand panorama of men and events in the Revolutionary era as former historians have so faithfully described it.

Looking back, then, through the vista of nearly a century and a half, we see thirteen subject colonies planted successively on our North-Atlantic coast; each population tending westward into the wilderness from its landing point, and yet gazing filially eastward toward the land of its origin, keeping close to the Atlantic seaboard and to the courses of those tributary streams and channels which alone in those earlier days could support a genuine inland commerce. Three million and twenty thousand souls this whole colonial population was roughly reckoned at by the first Continental Congress of 1774; but this, however, without counting Georgia, whose delegates did not appear until Congress reassembled in 1775, when the style was at length fully assumed of "the thirteen United Colonies of America."[1] "Three millions of people, armed in the holy cause of liberty," was the eloquent exaggeration of Patrick Henry, in his immortal harangue; but to speak more literally, those capable at the outset of bearing arms, out of so large an aggregate of whites and blacks, young and old, men and women, bond and free, numbered more nearly 600,000 freemen. The most populous State or colony of the whole thirteen was Virginia, earliest settled of them all; next in num-

[1] Am. Arch., 4th series, 396.

bers followed Massachusetts, which in that era included our extreme eastern province, known as Maine; Pennsylvania (with the Delaware counties) stood third; while New York, though progressive and promising already, was surpassed in population by both Maryland and North Carolina.

America possessed, when the struggle of these thirteen united colonies began in earnest, five leading centres of population (all seaports)—Philadelphia, New York, Boston, Charleston, and Baltimore. All the rest of her inhabitants—and much the larger part of them—were scattered about in smaller communities; each distinct for local self-government, with its town meeting throughout New England, but with county units rather in the Middle section and the South. There was, popularly speaking, no West. Were the combined populations of our present Philadelphia and Chicago[2] transformed, soul for soul, into men, women and children of America's united colonies of 1774, the total aggregate of that former era would be very nearly reproduced. Or were that transformation to take place, instead, from our present metropolis of Greater New York, some four hundred thousand of that city's municipal aggregate of 1900 would be left unchanged. The people of the present State of Texas alone number enough, and more than enough, by our latest census, to reconstitute and replace America's

[1]The basis of this first Congressional estimate of population is not easily determined. British Boards of Trade had made earlier computations, and certainly from time to time, in various provinces, a local enumeration of the inhabitants had been officially undertaken. Thus Massachusetts ordered a census in 1765, as also in 1776, both of which required that Indians, negroes, and mulattoes should be reckoned apart from the rest.

[2]See census of 1900.

whole colonial population as it existed in 1774. Philadelphia itself, the chief civic seat of all America, had
that year scarcely more inhabitants than Oshkosh, Wis-
consin, or Jacksonville, Florida, by our latest count; and
fewer, considerably, than now inhabit Canton, Ohio,
the home and final resting place of our late President
McKinley.

To utterly subdue a rebellious people, devoted to
local home life and home rule, and at the same time
thinly dispersed over so broad an area, was not easy.
Yet the "old thirteen" were not the only American
jewels of the British Crown. England had other colonies this side of the Atlantic that never made cause
with us. A map of "the glorious British Empire,"
published and sold in our leading continental towns
in 1769, pictured eighteen American provinces, stretch-
ing southwestward from the River St. Lawrence to
the Mississippi, and including the whole of Canada;
all this, too, without reckoning British islands of the
West Indies. As a matter of fact, our own thirteen
colonies, when uniting for resistance, tried to draw
British Canada to their cause; and the Articles of Confederation show our Continental Congress alluring, if
possible, those more northerly provinces to our perpetual league. But there were good reasons why this
should not be. Canada had lately been conquered from
France. Standing armies were a familiar incident of
both British and French occupation at the St. Lawrence, while here they appeared rather as a new and
startling menace to the people. Local legislatures, too,
of at least a single house, chartered privileges, partial
self-government had long been largely enjoyed in these

thirteen colonies, under a home policy of easy neglect. Hence opposition flamed at once when Parliament asserted here a sovereign right to tax; but in the Canadian provinces it had been quite otherwise. Our own America, too, was strongly Anglo-Saxon, intensely Protestant; so much so, that the tolerance shown by the British Crown and Parliament to these alien French subjects of Montreal and Quebec when they came under the yoke was a cause of offence and provocation to our own inhabitants, though just and politic in itself. Great here was the indignation because those French colonists in a region adjacent to Protestant New Brunswick and Nova Scotia were allowed their own French laws and the Roman Catholic religion to live under as before; indeed, in the Continental Congress of 1774 we see this "favor to Popery" among the complaints clearly specified in America's first united remonstrance to the King.

Americans—historical Americans of the age we are describing—though rude, perhaps, as a people, loved liberty. In the rugged verse of one of their own crude poets of 1772:

> "The freeborn Americans, generous and wise,
> Hate chains, but do not government despise.
> Rights of the Crown, tributes and taxes, they,
> When rightfully exacted, freely pay.
> Force they abhor, and wrong they scorn to bear,
> More guided by their judgment than their fear.
>   *   *   *   *   *   *   *
> Let France grow proud beneath the tyrant's lust,
> While the racked people crawl and lick the dust;
> The manly genius of America disdains
> All tinsel slavery or golden chains."[1]

[1] P. J., Nov., 1772.

This fling at France, by the way, was characteristic of that earlier date. For in our thirteen provinces, still nursing the animosities of the late frontier war which had ended with Wolfe's famous victory on the heights of Abraham, it was the popular notion that "the Pope and Devil were inseparably connected with French faith, French alliance, and French commerce;" and it took the exigency of our new struggle for political self-existence, ripening into a league against the mother country with our late enemy, to soften that impression.

Colonies are a crown to the parent country only when bound in filial ties of race, lineage, and affection, under a just and liberal supervision and discipline. Such colonies were fostered in the ancient time by Greece, and as Thucydides has said of them, "colonies were as free as mother cities, though less reverently mentioned because of their dependence." Some have asserted that it was a life necessity for our thirteen colonies to become independent; and looking back now through the vista of a century and a half, we may well believe it; notwithstanding our ancestors proclaimed at the outset that no thought of separation from Great Britain had ever been cherished by them until the despotic policy of making them dumb tributaries against their consent was entered upon by the King and Parliament.

"Everything which is, partakes of that which has been"—this was a favorite postulate of that sprightly and gallant Frenchman, the Marquis de Chastellux, whose book of travels during 1780-82 furnishes the first real trustworthy record of life in the new United States of America, as jotted down by a European sojourner. That acute observer notes, first of all, the fact that while all these American commonwealths, now practically unloosed from the British yoke, resembled one another in being democratic or representative in cast, yet traces of the original character of each separate colony still existed; and hence that the thirteen States differed somewhat in opinions and habits. Colonial society, while loyal, is apt to reflect, with however faint an image, the prevalent ceremonies, the passing fashions and tastes, of the parent country; and a people brought up in allegiance to a British sovereign must have transformed themselves but slowly, even if surely, into a democracy. Reverence for European institutions and traditions—a formal reverence at least—stamped these colonies from the outset; and class distinctions were everywhere accepted as part of the established order of things.

When the Stamp Act was repealed, our provincial assemblies vied with one another in humble thanks to the throne for its gracious assent, voting heroic statues to George III. and the Earl of Chatham alike. Observe, much later, the petition of our first Continental Congress, which besought a gracious answer from the King, and wished him a long and glorious reign; see how his sovereign regard is dutifully invoked by these distant subjects, as against the wrongs assumed to have been perpetrated by his agents, civil and military, and by Parliament. Thus far, it truly seemed, the King could do no wrong. It was only when the defiant instrument of Independence was published, nearly two years later, that our representatives spoke through their Congress to the monarch as to a fellow-mortal, and drew their indictment against George III. himself, as responsible author of all the wrongs that

had forced us to fight for freedom. During all those
trying years which preceded collision and bloodshed,
our colonists as a whole had bent with dutiful homage
at the footstool of royalty.

The ceremonious forms and expressions usual at
Westminster were familiar here, in the press and in
common speech, and were imitated, withal, in official
intercourse with the King's governors and vicegerents.
Men prominent in Great Britain, members of the nobility, had the honor to kiss the hand of his Majesty—
the high favor of an interview with their most gracious
sovereign. His Excellency the Governor, in Massachusetts Bay or elsewhere, was pleased to prorogue the
great and general court or assembly of the province.
On the birthday anniversary of the reigning King or
his Queen, and on the coronation anniversary besides,
our colonial gentry at the leading capitals, and members of the honorable legislature, would gather for a
banquet and celebration, under patronage of the Crown
officials; and toasts were drunk, framed sedulously in
the language of allegiance, leading off with his
Majesty, and next the Queen and royal family. Even
by the time that our Sons of Liberty had ceased offering dutiful toasts on such occasions, British army and
navy officers stationed in our forts would join civilians
of the Crown and good Tory citizens in setting the
pitch of loyalty.

Titles of nobility had not strongly prevailed on this
side of the ocean; yet the colonial press was full of
London tattle and gossip, and scandals were reprinted
touching certain peers and persons of quality, whose
title might be denoted by a dash between consonants,
where the printer meant to avoid prosecution and yet
to identify the individuals. Civil officers in these colo-

nies, and landholders besides, held posts and titular distinctions from abroad which our people dutifully recognized. Peers of the realm sojourned in America, now and then, officially or otherwise. Even aside from a peerage, Americans had ranks and social grades of their own, notwithstanding the strong approach to political equality in so many provinces. The Virginia "Tuckahoes" of the tidewater region used in the winter to flock to Williamsburg— "that toy capital," as one has called it—for the choice dissipations of a viceregal court; and between mean whites of the South and plantation owners, the social barrier was very great. In the simplest New England towns, where all congenial inhabitants came much into friendly contact, and joined in congregational worship and public discussions, the type of a republic was much like that of which Milton had approved for the English Commonwealth:

> ". . . Orders and degrees
> Jar not with liberty but well consist."

Massachusetts and Connecticut were great exemplars of ceremonial etiquette, and long continued so, as inherited forms of routine and processional programmes still remind us. Both at Harvard and Yale, college students were long arranged in the class lists according to their family consequence. Even our Revolutionary press indulged the prevalent taste of pompously announcing great public characters; thus, in 1776, "arrived in Boston from Philadelphia, that most worthy and patriotic gentleman, the Hon. Samuel Adams, Esq., a member of that august and united body, the right honorable the Continental Congress."[1]

Aside, indeed, from the British official set in these

[1] N. E. C.

colonies, we see much nice discrimination used between
"Mr.," "Esq.," "Captain," and the like; "Honorable"
being the appropriate prefix, and not superfluous, where
one had served in the legislature; while officers chosen
in town meeting were described with one such title
or another. "Deacon," though in common use, served
a less secular purpose. One often finds, to this very
day, more strife and heartburning in adjusting the
claims of petty distinctions like these, than over the
precedence of dukes or marquises; for the little things
of life seem great to little men. Colonial legislators
and writers for the press did not scruple to distinguish,
in their public expressions, those of good family, or the
upper class, from "the lower orders of the people." In
one of our chief seaports, in 1766, on St. Patrick's
Day, according to newspaper report, a number of Irish
gentlemen sat down to a dinner of roast beef and claret,
and celebrated the occasion as loyal and patriotic
Britons, "with decent mirth;" while at the same time
a number of Irish "of the lower order" dined at the
same inn, in an apartment by themselves; and "they,
too," it is added, "were orderly."

Pepys, in his inimitable Diary, discourses very
frankly of periwigs, laces and fine velvet suits, such
as men rising in public station, like himself, donned
for distinction from the vulgar; and he tells how, when
he and his friends entered a country church on the
Lord's day, the rustics all stood up and the clergyman
began his exhortation from the prayer book, "Right
worshipful and dearly beloved brethren." That typi-
fied England when Charles II. came to the throne.
American social life was much like that in the quiet
English towns; and change came slowly, here or
abroad, in such respects, during the century which preceded our Revolution.

II

INDIANS made no great figure in our colonial life after the French war was over. Fresh outbreaks were feared among the copper-colored, and commissioners for the Crown in America made pacifying treaties with various native tribes. Our aborigines had been much injured in morals by the white man's strong drink, but their indocile disposition saved them at all events from enslavement. Negroes, on the other hand, they "of God's image carved in ebony," were held to bondage, through all these thirteen colonies; and after South Carolina's repeal, in 1768, of a prohibitory tax upon their importation, the slave trade from the Guinea coast found a favorite port in sunny Charleston, whose rice and indigo were choice staples for a thick-skinned race to sweat upon. A press of 1765 mentions that in course of the eight months previous to July of that year, 5082 negroes had been brought for sale into Charleston port, with half that number of hogsheads of rum; and the rum and negro traffic went much together. More blacks, said the press of 1773, had been imported there for sale than ever before in a single month, and were sold profitably.

For more than fifty years the inhuman trade, once fully revealed with all its horrors to civilized Europe, had been denounced by some of the ablest and most influential of home writers and moralists; but Parlia-

ment and the ministry catered to the commercial greed
of London, and the traffic went on briskly, as before,
blacks on the coast of Africa being taken in barter for
the manufactures and merchandise of various European countries. More indirectly, slaves were brought
over to America from the West Indies, where the
culture of coffee and sugar kept them in brisk demand.
The Pennsylvania Assembly tried to discourage the
slave trade in that province by imposing a capitation
tax, but the Crown would not approve the statute.

Doubtless in fostering this traffic our colonists took
a large share of the blame, as their descendants have
borne the full force of the penalty. Colonial merchants
fitted out vessels and embarked with enterprise in the
trade; and, whatever might have been the casual pro-
test, silence or counter-argument on this continent encouraged the system to continue. Some, to be sure,
protested manfully in the local press.[1] But against
such, other Americans took boldly the cudgels, adducing
in defence of the institution some of those arguments
which became hackneyed and trite in our later century
of irrepressible conflict; while one, who styled himself
"a Southern man," showed in a Philadelphia newspaper, by a series of ingenious syllogisms, that negroes
had no souls.[2]

Emancipation on the parent soil of Great Britain was
another matter, however, and there a liberal home
sentiment might have its way without interrupting the
imports or imperilling the wealth drawn from these

---

[1]"Slave trading," writes a son of Boston, "is the abominable
thing that the soul of the Lord hateth;" and in 1772, we see a
Philadelphian inveighing against the system in a pamphlet entitled "A mite cast into the treasury—or observations on slave
keeping."

[2]P. G., 1769.

distant dependencies beyond the seas. It was in June, 1772, and only three years before Bunker's Hill, that "the great negro case" came up at the English King's Bench for trial on a writ of *habeas corpus,* where Lord Mansfield pronounced his memorable decision that the slave, Somerset, who had been brought to England by his master from an American colony, was thereby freed. Released in the court room amid loud applause, Somerset, with others of his complexion who had attended the trial, suppressed all signs of extravagant joy, and bowed reverently to the Chief Justice and assembled members of the bar while withdrawing from the court room, overawed; but two hundred British negroes with their ladies soon celebrated at a London inn, with a dinner and ball, the personal triumph of their brother from the plantations. It was to this famous case, and to the principle of "universal emancipation" which it so far established, that Curran, the Irish advocate, alluded in 1794, in one of the most eloquent and impassioned outbursts of oratory to be found in our mother tongue.

Yet why should the soil of the British Isle itself be deemed thus sacred, when British domains beyond the sea were willingly polluted by a system of bondage? Lord Mansfield's decision, so the London press predicted at the time, would make greater ferment in America than the Stamp Act itself, and most of all in the British West Indies, where now slaves were the chief chattel property. But such was not the outcome; and in our thirteen colonies, though a sense of the unrighteousness of slavery deepened with united efforts made for their own independence by the master race, that institution remained practically undisturbed, on the whole, while Revolution lasted. Massachusetts, solitary and alone of these commonwealths, shook off the curse by a determined effort, and deduced in 1783 from her own new State constitution and declaration of rights the boon for all of human freedom.[1]

That slavery practically existed in all America before and even after the 4th of July, 1776, is plain from contemporary notices in the local press. "Negro fellow" or "mulatto fellow" was the common contemptuous expression for persons of this race, North or South, when published as runaways or as the subjects of merchandise. "To be sold, a tall, likely, straight-limbed negro of twenty-four;" "a likely negro boy of seven;" "a negro wench about nine years old;" "a negro woman with a fine child three months old;" "two negro girls of sixteen for sale cheap"—such are among the current announcements in Philadelphia or Boston papers of that era. Sometimes we see negroes offered for sale on an execution against the master; or to close out an estate, as where among the assets offered by a Massachusetts executor in 1765 were two negro men, a negro woman and a mackerel sloop. A sale "on

[1] It seems that in October, 1773, a slave of the Massachusetts province, in Newburyport, sued his master in damages for detaining him in slavery. The jury returned a verdict in his favor, and the master appealed the case. M. G., 1773. But revolt, revolution and the disruption of provincial government soon followed; nor was it until 1781-83, when other test cases came up, of which the record has been preserved, that the Supreme Court of that now independent commonwealth decided that—however it might have been while Massachusetts remained a royal province—slavery had not now on that soil a legal existence. See 5 Banc. U. S. (last ed.), 418. In 1776-77, in Massachusetts, as I gather from the newspaper advertisements, negroes were sometimes offered publicly by their masters for their board and keep. After our Revolution and the treaty of peace, other Northern States took measures for local emancipation, by gradual means or otherwise; the New York statute dating 1785. 2 Fiske's Dutch and Quaker Colonies, 326.

trial" we see announced of "a likely young negro woman, a negro cook, who can make jellies, puddings, and whipped syllabubs." And again, sardonically, "to be sold very cheap for cash, a sprightly, clean and healthy negro woman, about thirty years of age, possessed of every domestic quality except taciturnity, which is the reason for disposing of her."[1]

It was not uncommon in these years to sell off a slave for the avowed reason, not of his fault, but the want of work for him. Yet other and more personal reasons might be alleged. "To be sold or exchanged for a negro girl, a strong and healthy man about twenty; the only reason for disposing of him, his habit of being out at night." "Negro crimes are many," complained a Boston paper in 1766, "and yet we still keep bringing in those creatures from Guinea; scarce one in a hundred of them good for anything." In various New England towns we see these servants out and about the streets and disposed to noise and mischief in the evenings—so much so that the selectmen would issue strict orders to the watchmen to take up all such negro, Indian or mulatto slaves as were found on the streets after 9 P.M., unless they carried lanterns with lighted candles and could give a good account for being out.[2] In 1741, various incendiary fires were charged in New York's metropolis as negro plots, and while popular excitement lasted that race suffered vicariously for the suspicion.

All the items here quoted are from old files of Northern newspapers, chiefly those of Pennsylvania and Massachusetts, during ten years down to and inclusive of 1776; and many more like extracts might be made.

[1]M. G., 1765, 1768, 1771, 1775; P. G., 1772.
[2]M. G., 1765.

So far as a Southern press existed thus early, a condition of slave traffic and slave labor still more repulsive was perhaps revealed; but while negroes were in the greatest demand for plantation life and the raising of great staples, their employment in Northern colonies was rather as menials and for petty farming and mechanical work, and of course it was less extensive, especially in New England.

But negro or mulatto slavery was not the only human bondage known in America in these colonial days. A large number of poor whites were in every province still held to labor and servitude by a tenure scarcely less degraded, during some stated term of years, whether for farm and menial service or as artisans. First of all were the redemptioners, so called, emigrating with unpaid passage-money from Europe. These engaged themselves and their families to the captain of the vessel or the ship-owner for a specific time after their arrival in the New World, that they might work out their dues. Many a poor Irishman or German came over from abroad upon such terms of carriage; and the hirer, when not paying down the full passage-money at once, would give security outright, so as to indemnify the vessel against loss should the bond-servant run away. The middle provinces were, now and later, most familiar with the system. A hundred, just arrived by the brig *Patty*, we see advertised in Philadelphia in 1772, whose time was to be disposed of at the wharf—men, boys and girls; among them skilled laborers, such as smiths, nailmakers, skinners, carpenters, grooms and farmers. Again, this same year, a load of hearty Irish servants of both sexes from Cork was similarly put up, varying in age from thirteen to twenty years, and suitable for serving "gentlemen, farmers or traders." And once more, "various redemptioners, maid-servants, boys and girls; coopers, weavers, tailors, shoemakers and hatters; their time to be disposed of by the captain of the vessel."[1] Besides these white temporary slaves of debt, British convicts were shipped to our colonies in large numbers to work out their punishment as bond-servants for such as might choose to employ them.[2] Nor were our thrifty colonial authorities indisposed to lighten their own local taxation and relieve their local jails by letting provincial criminals fulfil their penalties in servitude at private cost. Many condemned subjects had been brought up to some useful handicraft or occupation in which they were expert; and whether for household employment or as farm hands and journeymen, they largely supplied the labor market of our colonies. Political and military prisoners had sometimes been thus sent over.

Once more, indentured service in this era was protected by law; and needy men and women would bind themselves out to a master in consideration of board and wages during some considerable period mutually agreed upon; while parents in humble circumstances took it as of course to apprentice their minor sons by indenture to a trade, thus to relieve their own immediate burden. History shows us the parental Franklin, worthiest among Boston mechanics, disposing of his young Benjamin in this manner, and, after casting

[1] P. G., 1772.
[2] About 50,000, in the seventeenth and eighteenth centuries, is a trustworthy estimate. Between 1717 and 1775 not less than 10,000 were sent from the "Old Bailey" alone, chiefly to Maryland, Virginia and the Caribbean Islands. 2 Fiske's Virginia, 183.

about among other pursuits, binding him at the age of twelve as printer's devil to his own adult half-brother.

White convicts and indentured servants, young and old, of both sexes, figure largely in the columns of the native press of this era.[1] Fine, healthy, self-enslaved servants were offered—not manual laborers only, but sometimes schoolmasters or surgeons. Convicts seem not seldom to have been transported fraudulently from the mother country in the guise of indentured servants or redemptioners; and with the abundant influx of poor Irish, Welsh, Dutch, and other whites, who were put up publicly to be disposed of for specified terms, with negro slaves besides, it may well be apprehended that domestic service on the common-law equal footing of a contract of hire had no great prevalence in these colonies. Those cargoes of women shipped into Virginia for matrimonial purchase, of which we read in a popular novel of recent date, may well have belonged chiefly to the seventeenth century; and yet we find a load of white girls brought over from Europe and offered for sale (presumably for marriage) from shipboard at Philadelphia scarcely five years before the first Continental Congress met in that city.

Two impressive features of such white service in those latest years of British rule are observable, which ere the present day have ceased to be legal or customary: (1) The service was not undertaken simply as a personal relation of employer and employed, but was freely assignable to others while the term lasted; so that, with a pecuniary chattel interest in the master disposable to third persons at discretion, the servant,

---

[1]Thus, the *Virginia Gazette* of 1772 advertises an indentured servant thirty-three years old to be disposed of—a tailor by trade, with a stoop in the shoulders.

for the time being at least, might fare little better than a brute. (2) The specific service itself was often for a term long enough to be thought impolitic and unreasonable, as we should view the law to-day. For, to say nothing of a child's apprenticeship during his useful minority, a person of full age might have been put under a service contract for five years absolutely or even longer. An unexpired four years' term seems to have been frequently transferred in this era, while five years was a redemptioner's usual time, and seven years by no means exceptional.[1] Redemptioners, besides reimbursing their own passage, would sell their minor children or themselves into service long enough to get a knowledge of this new country before starting in life independently. A convict's penal term might, of course, be a very long one.

With thirteen distinct provincial governments in the vast and then impenetrable American wilderness, it is not strange to find these bondspeople, whether white or black, whether bound for life or for a fixed term of years, escaping from one colony into another and lost to the master's pursuit. No advertisements were more common in the press of this epoch—in the papers of Boston, New York and Philadelphia, as well as Virginia—than those of runaways whom the owner of his time and labor sought to reclaim. Usually a reward was offered to any one securing the fugitive in any of his Majesty's jails so that the master might have him again; shipmasters and others were warned emphat-

[1] One mulatto girl's time in 1769 is advertised in Philadelphia as having fifteen years yet to run; hence, I presume, she was no slave in the strict sense.

ically not to harbor or employ, under penalty of the
law. The captors, too, of runaways clapped in jail
upon suspicion and not identified would give public
notice that the person apprehended would be sold for
charges (like some runaway horse) unless claimed or
taken away by the owner. Even our peerless Washington, in April, 1775, is seen proclaiming a reward
in the *Virginia Gazette,* not for negro fugitives, but
for two Scotch serving-men who had just absconded
from Mount Vernon.

Announcements like these in our provincial press
were often accompanied by the rude wood-cut of a
tramp with a bundle of clothes borne on a stick over his
shoulder—the usual outfit of a vagrant travelling in
search of work; and sometimes, by way of general
warning, a two-horned devil was depicted in the act
of seizing him. A terse and graphic description of the
runaway—of the clothes worn, of his personal singu-
larities, traits of character, scars and malformations—
identified him in language more plain than elegant. If
an immigrant had lately come over the seas, it was
suggested that the peculiar odor of the ship might aid
in his detection. If the fugitive was a man, he wore,
most likely, a small, coarse, leather cap or uncocked
felt hat; an Osnaburg shirt; leather or perhaps hair-
cloth breeches, a homespun jacket, a snuff-colored or
cinnamon waistcoat; his head displayed his own short-
cropped hair, and was usually wigless. If a woman
servant, she had on a loose calico gown, a linsey petti-
coat and plaid stockings, while a brass ring adorned
her middle finger; her slattern attire was otherwise
inventoried minutely from headgear to stockings.
Many runaways were to be known by the marks of
smallpox: this one might be identified by a stoop in

the shoulders; that by scars of the whip upon his back
or by malformation of foot or hand from some early
injury. The publication of such traits and peculiarities
ran often into malicious libel and ridicule; and, positively or by insinuation, a fugitive would be charged
with stealing his master's horse or pilfering from the
family wardrobe before taking flight. The defrauded
master thus took out his revenge upon the absconder.
One indentured servant, a master of Low Dutch, is
described as speaking through his nose; a negro slave
as quite black naturally, "but when challenged and he
is going to lie, his eyes will twinkle and his face change
color." One refugee showed his teeth when he
laughed, or winked with the left eye; another, an Irish
servant girl, took snuff immoderately at the right side
of her nose, was much given to liquor, and "when in
liquor was apt to laugh greatly." Various of these
fugitives were "down-looking, dull-like fellows;" one
talked loud in discourse and was apt to swear by his
Maker; and very many were artful, pert, impudent,
smooth-tongued, turbulent in temper, in the injured
master's estimation, whether drunk or sober. One employer in 1772, who took the full humor of his loss,
published his Irish runaway lad in the *Philadelphia
Gazette* in doggerel rhyme, and his poem of thirty
lines—fugitive poetry—embraced the usual points of
such description.

Men of a master race holding others in obedience
may yet cherish a vigorous sense of freedom, and detest
all the more for themselves, from the contrast with
which they are familiar, whatever might reduce them
to the social condition of their vassals. "Britons never

can be slaves," was the burden of a favorite national song, still remembered; and a corresponding sentiment was shown in colonial appeals of this stirring epoch for liberty or death. "A vile system of slavery like that of Domitian is preparing for us," writes a patriot contributor to the press in 1775; "before God and man we are right." But New England's sons were nearest to a republic. What nobler type of yeomanry has the world ever witnessed than they who gathered on Lexington common at the roll of the drum, on the gray dawn of that eventful 19th of April, to seal as martyrs their devotion to the sacred cause of liberty and self-rule? Seventy minute-men drew up in line to withstand a royal disciplined force of more than ten times their own number, and the fatal volley, fired to break and scatter them, signalled to mankind the loss forever of European supremacy in this New World. "Stand your ground," said their sturdy captain, as the fatal moment approached; "don't fire unless fired upon; but if they mean to have a war, let it begin here."

III

CRIMES AND DISORDERS

NEITHER in England nor in these English settlements of America did the law relax its severity toward criminals while the authority of the British Crown lasted. Nor need we deem it strange that, in our far-away wilderness, crimes were committed of which a local community took peculiar cognizance to detect, punish and hold in check. While law-abiding people were greatly in the majority, respecting the lives and property of one another, there was throughout a drifting element of the lawless and reprobate, largely recruited from the runaway servants and convicts I have described, who roamed from province to province committing crimes—not to add those needy and disreputable vagrants out of caste abroad who had come over the Atlantic to better their chances in a new world, but brought with them vicious tastes and habits.

Such incidents are natural to the colonizing of a new country; and though there must have been little, comparatively, to steal where portable wealth increased so slowly, crime kept in practice. Footpads abounded, horse and cattle stealers, petty thieves and burglars, forgers and counterfeiters. A prudent freeman carried his loaded pistol as he journeyed with money about his person, and highway robberies committed after dusk in the lonely suburbs of Philadelphia were again and again reported to the magistrates. A threatening letter would be sent anonymously to some thriving citizen, commanding him to leave a stated sum in cash at a certain milestone just outside that city on a specified date. In one province or another the lonely traveller's purse was abstracted from his cloak or his saddlebags by force or cunning stratagem; a farmer's house was broken into and robbed on the Lord's day while all the family were at divine service. In 1769, as we read, thirty armed men at the suburbs of Philadelphia waylaid all passers-by, with their faces painted black. For heinous and alarming instances of highway robbery, the colonial governor or the town authorities made proclamation offering a reward; and the people of the neighborhood would pursue as a posse, eager to preserve good order against all disturbers of the peace. New Jerseymen by their own vigorous concert once broke up a gang of robbers in that province, whose accomplices were in New York and Philadelphia; and when, in 1774, near Westchester, footpads attacked a traveller, robbed him of his cash, silver buckles, surtout and coat, we are told that "his worship the Mayor of New York" sent out promptly a searching party which caught the culprits.[1] The hue and cry started against offenders in one colony would attract notice and induce co-operation in other colonies if the crime was atrocious or ramified extensively in its plot.

In 1771, a gang of thieves was broken up at Williamsburg, then Virginia's capital, whose confederates were in the various neighboring provinces, negroes and housekeepers being alike implicated. In 1772, the workhouse at Philadelphia was feloniously entered, and out of one of its closets was stolen a black walnut box, "a

[1] *Essex Gazette,* 1774.

little larger than a wig box," which contained valuable papers and money; for these were not the days of iron safes, even for public officials.   Brass kettles were purloined from housekeepers, as well as silver spoons and mugs, coins and bills of credit.   "Horse stealing is prevalent all over the country," complains a New Jersey farmer to the press in 1772; and by the time our Revolutionary disturbances began the ownership of all cattle became precarious.

Humane and discriminating treatment of crimes and culprits dates from our political independence; and Virginia's famous bill of rights gave the first grand impulse to criminal reform for our English-speaking race.   For while colonial relations lasted, capital punishment here, as across the seas, was visited upon many of the lesser offences, besides murder or treason. Abroad in 1777, two men swung from the same gallows at Tyburn—the one, a scholar and a doctor of divinity, for forgery; the other, a low-lived wretch, for highway robbery; and while jeers and ribaldry and the hawking about of a culprit's last dying speech were incidents less manifest here, perhaps, in America than in a London crowd, the common people yet flocked to see a local execution with a like morbid curiosity and a brutalizing sense of delight.   Men were hanged in various American colonies for robbery, for horse-stealing, for forging and counterfeiting, during those ten years that preceded the outbreak of Revolution. In Connecticut, one notorious and hardened offender, sentenced for burglary, was ordered to be loaded with chains, while a guard was placed over the county jail every night until he was executed.   In New York, four persons convicted of burglary and horse-stealing—a negro woman and three Irishmen—were all hanged

together *in terrorem*. Burning at the stake was in
England an infliction of the law upon one gross mur-
derer in 1765; and in New Jersey a similar sentence
was pronounced and probably carried into effect about
the same time; while in the West Indies, certainly,
roasting alive in the crackling flames was a penalty
for crime not seldom visited upon the black bond-
servant. Just as banishment to America was imposed
on convicts in the mother country, as a lesser infliction
than hanging, so here, occasionally, a province was
seen experimenting with that punishment, though perhaps to no more definite end than to ship a reprobate
out of the particular jurisdiction, to settle and annoy
elsewhere as he might.[1]

Of "cruel and ignominious punishments" which
stopped short of a death infliction or banishment or a
long imprisonment, there are many on record in this
country up to the very latest date of our royal establishment, and some of them were found effective, indeed,
for striking terror into offenders of the baser sort. For
"vagrant men" were a stigmatized class, and the usual
policy was to keep them so identified and separate from
the elect. Thus, burning in the hand was inflicted in
Virginia in 1765, and again in South Carolina in 1768.
A notorious burglar was in 1771 publicly whipped in
Connecticut; one of his ears was cut off besides, and
"B" was seared into his body with a hot iron. That
same year, in New Haven, a mulatto was branded with
an "A" in the forehead for adultery with a white woman.
In 1769, a Boston burglar was publicly branded in his
forehead, at King Street (now State), amid a crowd
of approving spectators. New Englanders, in fact,

[1]Watson's Philadelphia shows £25 allowed a sheriff for thus
clearing four notorious offenders from Pennsylvania.

about the time that Massachusetts broke with Great Britain, had complained much of the prevalence of thefts and stealing in that section of the country, and it was claimed that the greater severity shown in Southern colonies had driven many loose and lawless scoundrels thither, who expected, if caught, from the comparative lenity of New England law and the compassion of New England juries, a light punishment. New York was a province where, at this early date, for the smallest theft, a petty criminal was carted through the principal streets, that he might be publicly viewed and identified. Under a new sense of provocation, Rhode Island denounced banishment against all roaming miscreants of horse-thieves, besides full forfeiture of property (if he had any) and a severe whipping, and death was threatened to all culprits of that description who were ever caught and convicted in that colony a second time. In various towns of Massachusetts, Rhode Island and Connecticut, harsh sentences revived in these last days of King George; and the ignominy of cropping and branding was superadded to whipping, before thousands of the applauding people. Another torturing sentence applied in these days was that of causing a culprit to sit for an hour or more on the gallows doing public penance with a halter about his neck; and this sometimes while some worse malefactor was from the same platform swung sternly off into eternity.

Often these tormenting punishments were accompanied by the more usual infliction of whipping and imprisonment. And if the public disposition was to exempt one from infamous punishment on his first conviction, a second offence was likely to be unmercifully dealt with. And these, let us recall, were not the days of anæsthetics nor of the skilful knife of surgery; and some of the unhappy culprits thus mutilated bled so profusely as to endanger life itself.

Both in England and America, the whipping-post, the stocks and the pillory were instruments of petty discipline, in vogue for both sexes, until long after the Revolution.[1] A Boston woman took twenty-one lashes at the whipping-post for pilfering some stockings exposed for sale at a shop window; a Rhode Island man bore thirty stripes twice repeated for stealing two yoke of oxen; and at Providence, in 1771, an old offender had to stand in the pillory for two hours with a halter about his neck and the label "notorious thief." Six women at a time were in 1765 lashed for immorality in York County, Massachusetts, and the more hardened of them were sent to the house of correction, whose regular discipline required ten stripes specially by way of initiation. In Philadelphia, a woman who had been caught picking pockets in the market was exposed for two hours on the court-house steps, with her hands bound to the rails and her face turned toward the pillory; and when released she was publicly whipped. Watson relates that Philadelphians of the choice circles would send their stubborn servants to the jail yard for chastisement, with a letter of introduction to the jailer;[2] and a like custom certainly prevailed in some of our slaveholding towns at the South far into the nine-

---

[1] In the pillory the victim stood on a stool, with his head and hands fitted into holes, while stocks were for the feet, as one was placed recumbent. These long familiar contrivances were usually fixed in some public place. But the whipping-post was in New York made a perambulating punishment, the criminal, perchance confined in a tar-barrel with his offence placarded, being whipped at each street corner.

[2] Watson's Philadelphia.

teenth century. But colonial laws and procedure from
the earliest times fostered class distinctions; people of
quality were usually fined simply for the lesser trans-
gressions, while the poor and miserable had to take the
lash in ignominy.

"Benefit of clergy" was a privilege long conceded
by our common law to men of letters, so that they
might escape the block or the gallows. A book in
black-letter Latin was put into the hands of the convicted person, and if he could read and translate it like
a trained ecclesiastic—as "a gentleman and scholar"—
he was only burned in the hand; but otherwise he had
to suffer the death penalty. In 1769, a burglar tried
and convicted in Boston was seen invoking this privilege. But a stringent act of the next year's general
court denounced death for a capital offence in Massachusetts "without benefit of clergy," and in such phrase
did legislation come to exclude the plea in other
colonies. Compassion softened at times the rigor of
the law in imposing sentence. We read that in 1771
a young and beautiful girl under twenty was indicted
with some fellows in Charleston, South Carolina, for
stealing horses; she was found guilty with the rest,
but the susceptible court was so won by her beauty and
air of innocent distress that the judges let her go un-
punished. Persons under sentence of death got sometimes a reprieve or a pardon on the scaffold, the authorities not seldom contriving a torturing delay for discipline until the last moment.

When it came to imprisoning men for their politics
after these colonies rebelled against Great Britain,
rescues and jail-breaking became quite frequent,
whether on Whig or Tory side. Then again, we had
jails and the jail penalty for insolvent debtors in

colonial days, as in the mother country; and prisoners for debt did occasional business in their quarters. One quack doctor thus debarred of his liberty advertised his medicines for the liver in a local paper, and offered to supply all customers who chose to call at the jail or send in their orders through the keeper; another prisoner who wanted to dispose of 7000 acres of wild land on the west side of the Connecticut River announced an auction in his jail chamber. Revolution, however, stirred strongly the American heart against punishments for misfortune. After an anniversary dinner given in New York City[1] to commemorate the repeal of the Stamp Act, the remnants of the feast, with plenty of liquor, were sent to imprisoned debtors, the donors bearing their supplies in person; and that generous example was followed elsewhere. Our American States, their independence of Europe once achieved, led mankind in abolishing imprisonment for debt as one of the earliest of legal reforms. But debtors' prisons had been destitute of comfort; and a New York appeal in 1771 claimed that the prisoners of that city depended entirely upon common charity in the winter season for wood to warm them and· to dress their victuals, and that the bedclothing doled out to them was scanty.

The rude audacity of our populace was in constant evidence in the several colonies after the Crown once entered upon its career of arbitrary taxation. When, in 1765, the baleful Stamp Act went into operation, a Boston crowd, collecting after dark, pulled down the

[1]In 1768.

newly built house of the Secretary of the province, and broke into the mansion of Hutchinson, the King's lieutenant-governor, ruthlessly destroying his furniture and carrying off papers and private effects. Signs of riotous resistance followed generally in the colonies; and to hanging and burning in effigy, our Sons of Liberty added the coercion of those appointed to distribute the stamps. In Norwich, in New London, in New York City and elsewhere, effigies of these obnoxious minions of the Crown were borne about in nightly procession and then were left gibbeted or else destroyed in a bonfire. Such puppets were made up often with a boot fastened to one shoulder,[1] from which the devil was seen peering out. Maryland patriots made ghastly burial of a printed copy of the Stamp Act; a mock procession down in North Carolina bore solemnly an effigy of Liberty laid in its coffin, to the muffled drum and tolling of bells; and then, pretending to feel the pulse and finding that Liberty was still alive, they marched back to a lively quickstep. Stamp distributors were waited on in every colony by local committees and forced to resign under threats of personal violence. He who resigned or recanted by speech or writing was welcomed with huzzas, but whoever stood out obstinate was likely to be dragged through the town with a halter on his neck, while a patriot mob broke into his house and despoiled his goods. "Liberty, property, and no stamps!" was the cry; and majorities proved tyrannous, though always with some clear purpose to be achieved, and not often for wanton or promiscuous violence.

Such colonial riots were renewed when Parliament applied new methods of taxation, and the King sent

[1] For "Lord Bute," one of the grim puns of the day.

his troops to America for discipline and compulsion.
The scuffles between townspeople and the soldiery, which
in Boston caused the massacre of 1770, found their
counterpart in New York City; and Maryland had her
tea destruction on shipboard as well as Massachusetts,
and more openly. Besides the Crown officers, revenue
informers received rough treatment from the colonial
Sons of Liberty. Our Whig patriots handled roughly
the persistent loyalists, and were roughly handled in
return by British troops on opportunity. Tarring and
feathering made a feature of such demonstrations; the
victim was stripped down to his breeches, smeared
on the skin with the pitchy mixture from a bucket, and
then treated to the contents of a feather bed, after
which the drum beat, the procession moved, bearing
him in ridicule upon a rail or in a cart, savagely mal-
treated. "Curse you," said a sergeant of red-coats to
a Boston citizen thus seized upon, while the port bill
was enforced; "I am going to serve you as you have
done our men;" and we read, not strangely, of a woman
who died of fright as she saw a man borne riotously
past her window in that fearful garb of punishment. Personal suffering and disgrace were in-
geniously worked into the infliction of such riotous
penalties.

What we call lynch law, then, is no new product of
American life, but antedates the Revolution, and our
patriot forefathers gloried in it. Our Sons of Liberty
held many a secret conclave to discuss plans of local
resistance, and in the evening a bonfire made upon a
certain lot or common was the sign to gather for rebellious concert, often in disguise as well as darkness.
But whether by day or by night, a crowd came readily
together in those exciting times.

Downright and determined in their course of action, whether toward person or property, American commoners of that day, like their contemporaries of the mother country, were disposed when incensed to plain speech, coarse, forcible and vulgar, and withal to mischievous acts of violence. Duelling, to be sure, was not frequent among our common people, being rather an indulgence of the upper class, and fostered by the habits of military officers; but there were brawls in the coffee-houses and wherever elsewhere personal opponents came together. Smollett has familiarized us from his own youthful experience with the oaths and brutality which accompanied naval discipline on board a British man-of-war in his day; and the press-gang method for obtaining crews was long a disgrace to humanity. Nor were military officers of the mother country less overbearing than those of the navy; and, likely enough, Major Pitcairn, who marched the royal troops to Lexington common, not only ordered our rebel yeomanry to throw down their arms and disperse, but swore at them besides, as he was reported by eye-witnesses to have done. Coarse abuse, with profane or indecent expression, too often accompanied a civilian's act of violence, religious though so many of our people were in their general course of life. Colonial almanacs would print essays on profane swearing, and a printed colonial sermon against "that abominable but too fashionable vice" was recommended to families for the frequent perusal of young people. Yet blasphemy against God or the Trinity, swearing, and Sabbath-breaking besides, were all severely punishable under our local codes; and by some turn of expression that distorted the irreverent word or phrase into something anomalous, the vehement man of morals was taught to compound with his conscience or divert the denunciation of the law.[1]

Where our commoner had a personal altercation, he would not unfrequently resort to the local press by way of invoking a public opinion in his favor. One man advertised injurious reflections upon his neighbor's character; the latter would adduce proofs of his righteousness or else retaliate. The hirer of a horse who quarrelled with his letter over the recompense published as excessive the sum he had been forced to pay. A general offender forced to recant would do so over his own signature, and many a Tory was compelled to such penance. We see one countryman humbly confessing his fault through the press for having slandered another; he publicly asked the man's pardon and promised to be more careful for the future. For one would throw down his adversary in those days and then force him to eat humble pie. "Judge ye between me and my neighbor" was the frequent appeal, not to courts so much as to the community.

[1] E.g., "I swow," "I swan," "doggoned," "darn it all."

IV

I N no respect were Americans of this early age more admirable than in the home and family relation. Marriage was honorable, almost universal; and men and women paired to rear a family and give the genealogy of the race a new progression. Something of that same devotion to their wives which the polished Tacitus had remarked of those savage tribes, our ancestors, when the decay of Rome's degenerate empire supplied a classic but corrupt comparison, could be traced in these hardy Anglo-Saxons of the eighteenth century, who were peopling a new continent for a fresh example to mankind. At the pioneer home and fireside, Americans of all social grades received an early discipline that fitted them for free institutions and good citizenship. The household made somewhat of a tribal bond, and industry, thrift, learning, religion, patriotism and the social affections were all taught in the family circle. Marriage—nature's true companionship of the sexes, contrived for the whole human race—was the settlement for life in each commonwealth; a rugged, commonplace existence found in the home and helpmate, life's chief solace and recreation. Children, too, and the duplicated ties of marriage alliance and progeny to a remote issue confirmed one's hold upon the future and gave a personal zest to the coming years. Of the common wish then prevalent to marry and

settle in life, various reminders have come down to us.
And as the old churchyard epitaphs so often remind
us, marriage came, not to the single alone, but to
widows and widowers; for home was an institution so
essential to the well-being of the race that neither man
nor woman could well live comfortably without it.
Sports and recreations, too, which brought the young
and bashful of both sexes together turned largely upon
the mimic choice of a partner; the unmated one of the
game, the odd number, was the butt of a company.
And so did village ridicule pursue most keenly the
mincing spinster or the crusty old bachelor.[1]

Since labor found ready recompense in these days,
and simple station made simple social life, our
marriages were early and prolific. The young paired
for themselves and made love matches, struggling upward through poverty together. Unmarried daughters
remained and served in the parental abode; for women
found mostly their sphere in farm or household work.
Sons, however, shifted naturally for themselves, and
by subdivision of the paternal farm found place for
their own new homes; mating, multiplying and building apart, or restlessly seeking out new scenes, perchance to make new fortunes. Each town and community stood firmly banded in upholding God's holy
institution, though Protestants sternly denied the
Roman Catholic doctrine that marriage was a sacra-
ment, declared it a mere contract, and schemed already
a freedom both in making and dissolving the marriage
tie that threatened a future laxity. In general, marriage was celebrated simply enough, as befitted the

---

[1]In 1756, under pressure of the French and Indian War, Maryland levied a tax upon all bachelors of 25 years and upwards,
classifying the rates by their several fortunes.

social custom of the times; but station and circumstances made variations. In some leading centres, like Philadelphia, marriage feasting among the fashionable was thought extravagant; for hosts would send out cake and meats to neighbors who had not been invited to the wedding, besides indulging their guests. Complaint, too, was made that the married pair were kept too long before the gathered company, exposed to rough banter. It was common for the colonial press, when announcing a marriage in high life, to compliment the bride in set phrase as "a young lady of great merit, with every accomplishment conducive to the happiness of the marriage state."

The old common law of coverture adjusted thus early the rights and duties of the married life—a system, by the way, far less harsh of operation than is generally supposed, and tolerable enough where the husband does his part well as family provider, and little personal property is brought to the marriage on either side. Real estate, that only inheritance of dignity in earlier times, was fairly preserved to the wife's blood relatives by our English law where she brought land to the marriage and died childless. But the husband was head of the house, and ruled the family after the Christian dispensation as preached by Peter and Paul. For divorce from the bond there was little show, whether wife or husband had misconducted, nor was legalized separation frequent yet or easy to procure. Man's discipline, if stern and masterful, compelling wife and children to obey, might be just and considerate notwithstanding.

But infelicities occurred, as they always may in the marriage state, and now and then might be seen a husband publishing his wife in the local paper for

desertion, and refusing to pay a farthing of any debt
she might contract while absent. "She has left my
bed and board," complains one husband; "she has
eloped," says another; "she has been very unfriendly
to me," says a third; "she has behaved badly with other
men and unseemly," says a fourth, "and her im-
prudence has reduced me to great poverty and distress." One forsaken advertiser makes pertinent cita-
tion from 1 Corinthians 7: 10, 11; another threatens
the law against all persons who may harbor his runaway partner; while still another offers to reward any
one who will land the seducer in jail, so that he may be
prosecuted. The wife sometimes responded in print to
the husband's accusation. One fair spouse retorts that
the husband became an insolvent, and had used up the
whole income of her inheritance from her father before
she left him; another alleges sadly that she never left
his home until compelled to do so by his cruel and inhuman treatment in abusing and kicking her about.
"I never ran him in debt one farthing," responds a third
indignantly; "neither has he ever purchased me or his
infant child one article of clothing, except two or three
pairs of shoes, for almost two years." And once again
we see an unhappy wife publishing to the world that
she had left her husband because he deprived her of
the barest necessities of life and forced her to do servile
work, such as taking constant care of the cattle during
the cold winter months; and this one appends an affi-
davit he had made shortly before, which acknowledged
her conjugal goodness and obedience and his own fault
toward her. Thus again does the press of that century
show how prone were our people to invoke public opinion in their private differences. Reconciliation healed
happily some of such distressing feuds; while Christian

forbearance and a sense of duty, not to add the wish to keep up appearances (always strong in the feminine mind), checked or prevented many others.

Marriage in this simple and sincere age was not only stable as an institution, but remarkably prolific; and such must be the usual incident of domestic life in a new country where they who marry are robust, and an offspring builds up society and increases the common means of livelihood.   No advertiser figured more constantly in the local wants of that day than the wet nurse with a good breast of milk; and so popular was midwifery that one Mrs. Hallelujah Olney, a zealous anti-pædo Baptist and most estimable widow lady, who died in 1771 at Providence, after having practised her profession for thirty-six years, was said, in an obituary notice, to have introduced into existence upwards of 3000 children.   The midwife took commonly the place of a doctor; and one in New London was said to have delivered 1200 children in her day and never lost one. Franklin, it is remembered, was the fifteenth in due order out of seventeen children, and a son of his father's second wife; and we shall find various other marriages of that era equally prolific if we trace back the genealogy of almost any of the famous families among our early settlers.   For the first object of every new colony in the wilderness has been to increase and multiply, assuaging life's dulness.   Men started in life as founders, they lived to be patriarchs.   And the long-lived pioneer gloried in such distinction.   Of a worthy man who died in 1771 it was printed, first that he had kept a grist-mill for seventy-one years and never took more toll than the law allowed; next that he left a progeny of 108, in children, grandchildren and great-grandchildren. Another dweller in Massachusetts, a deacon, had died three years earlier, in his eighty-fourth year; "his life was exemplary, his departure in firm hope of a glorious immortality; his progeny were numerous." In fact, it was stated that this pioneer left 157 of his issue alive, including five great-grand-children. Another colonial veteran, older by ten years, dying about the same time, saw those of his fifth generation before closing his eyes upon the world.[1]

In spite, then, of all decimation by exposure to casualty and disease, Americans of both sexes in this era had strong constitutions and often lived—the men especially—until long after fourscore, witnessing the growth and spread of the families they had founded, and widening immensely their own personal influence through multiplied offspring and marriage ties. Many a New England Thanksgiving or a New York Christmas of that era must have brought a family reunion indeed—enough, one would fancy, to burst the rafters of the old dwelling-house and cause the very walls to bulge; and everywhere the buttress of a home community must have resisted all undue coercion from external society. Households were united, though not demonstrative always in mutual affection. The paternal head made his authority respected; sons, when old enough, were pushed out like young squabs from the nest, to fly and mate for themselves; while daughters found there a sure shelter and refuge against the

---

[1] "Died in peace in 1771, at Wilmington, Delaware," says a local press, "a pious, elderly matron, who had been mother of 16 children, all married and comfortable; 68 grandchildren, 166 great-grandchildren, and 4 great-great-grandchildren—in all 238 living offspring—survived her: the generation of the just shall be blessed."

possible ills and failures of life. Family discipline, if stern and repressive, was conscientious, grounded on Bible precept and example; and parents aimed honestly to bring up their offspring to lives of usefulness and honor.

Chastellux, visiting this country toward the close of the Revolution, was impressed by the comfort and simplicity of our domestic life—by that "sweet and serene state of happiness," so he styles it, "which appears to have taken refuge in the New World." And again, he observes, "there is no licentiousness in America." Surely, here were seen none of those Lovelaces of rakish inclination, such as Richardson and other novelists of that era portrayed so vividly for London, whose idle game of life seemed chiefly to consist in intriguing for the ruin of virtuous women. So much of the common concern, indeed, was absorbed in the domestic pursuits of life that social scandals related most to the mishaps of lovemaking. And for matches that turned out ill-suited and miserable, social compassion gave without cynicism its alleviating sympathy; while the aggrieved one sought first of all that medicine, more potent for the soul's lasting good than the surgery of divorce can ever afford—to make the best of things.

The whole tendency, then, of our primitive American life was to develop the natural affections and make people neighborly and helpful to one another, recognizing those common joys and sorrows of humanity of which all ages and conditions partook. Hence, and because, too, of the strong religious sentiment of a Christian people, much was made of individual death

and of paying last tributes to the departed. The hereafter, with its rewards and punishments, was the goal
upon which most had set their minds as readers of the
Bible and devout believers; and at each exit of life was
an earthly judgment to be passed in the little community, forecasting the Divine, with preaching of
sermon and exhortation, according as the example was
felt for good or evil. It still holds true in our remote
Atlantic villages that a funeral brings neighbors together more readily than any other private occasion.
We smile at the quaint epitaphs on tombstones of that
earlier century; yet the "amiable consort" and those
other high-flown terms of endearing expression were
set phrases of the day, and a certain elegiac strain of
tombstone expression took its usual pitch from a local
pastor's discourse or the conventional tributes of
friends and relatives in the newspapers. In that age
of sermonizing, funeral sermons preached on the
sombre occasions of bereavement were widely printed
and read; and obituaries dwelt much more than our
present fashion would commend upon the details of
death-bed suffering or of some lingering illness. Obituary rhetoric shaped its expression in prose or poetry
with intensity of seriousness:

> "Her hearse moved slow and sad to meet the tomb,
> While real sorrow sat on every plume;
> While many groans her dear remains convey
> To her cold lodging in her bed of clay."

One funeral sermon sets figuratively forth the dying
utterances of a good woman of the flock: "With these
words she closed her mortal drama; her next were
heard in Heaven." And, to quote the eulogy of a distinguished officer who died in Philadelphia in 1772:
"There scarce appeared a struggle between soul and

body at parting. The former in an instant took its flight to the realm of spirits, and the latter without a groan dropped down to embrace its kindred earth."

Press and the pulpit alike in colonial times made note of the death lesson to be inculcated upon the living. Seeing the remains was an important incident of every well-ordered funeral, as it usually is, perhaps, to this day; and in various presses the versifier was seen arousing his Muse "on seeing," or even "upon a supposed view of" the corpse. So important, withal, in a public sense, were these last functions of mortality, that funerals in the winter time were sometimes announced to take place on a certain date with express reservation as to the weather.

Mortal sickness, with, if need be, its long-drawn ailment and suffering, was met in this age with fortitude and Christian resignation. A suicide was sometimes seen reported, but self-destruction was then very rare. The sane and prosaic routine of life, incessant industry, the manifold family ties—all aided conscientious views of a hereafter and of man's moral accountability. Christianity opposes the thought of suicide and leaves the mortal chances to one's Maker. And the old English law still widely obtained in these colonies, which denied a Christian burial to such as took their own lives.

We read much of enamelled mourning rings, such as were then worn considerably by friends and relatives; also of distributing "scarfs" and gloves. In the dress and decorations for funerals of high personages some incongruous outlays were incurred for friends as well as family. More incongruous still was apt to be the lavish expenditure for refreshments—in punch and hot wine particularly. Families themselves might be very large, reckoning alone the near relatives by blood and marriage; yet open hospitality at funerals went much farther. Agitation arose, in fact, touching the customary funeral expenses, as trouble dawned with the mother country and our colonists felt the pinch of approaching poverty.

The loved one was laid tenderly to rest in the family vault or churchyard lot; or perhaps in some God's acre specially fenced off from one's own farm or plantation, or in some larger parcel of land laid out for general use. Pagan cremation, which sets economy against feeling or sentiment, and ignores the resurrection of the body, if not resurrection altogether, had of course no charm for these simpler Christians; and to all laboratory methods of human disposal is the objection that they blunt the finer sensibilities and may even tempt to murderous experiment upon the dying, whose heirs are impatient. Leave tenderly the remains of our fellow-mortal for nature's own methods of decay to operate, and we trust to God and assume, at least, no personal responsibility to meddle. Perhaps, however, the evangelism of this earlier age invoked too readily the horrors of the grave, as of death itself, to arouse the living to repentance. It was "Hark! from the tombs a doleful sound!" The idea came later to us of large and attractive cemeteries, like Mount Auburn, Forest Hills, Greenwood, Laurel, Oak Hill—reposeful cities of the dead, where art and nature blend their landscape charms with choice marble and granite monuments to foster the hope of a common immortality and teach the living to cherish the memory of the departed. For the churchyard fitly protects its parish dead only while the mute environs linger unchanged through rural generations, as in Stoke-Pogis of our old English home, which inspired the noblest elegy of our tongue that poetic art ever chiselled into expression.

One of the stateliest public funerals of colonial times took place in Virginia in 1770, when Lord Botetourt— a nobleman much beloved and a governor of that province—was buried. At Williamsburg, the little capital of that oldest colony, the bells tolled, and dignitaries, with the military, repaired together to the "palace" or mansion-house in early afternoon. The corpse, enclosed in its leaden coffin, adorned with silver handles and a silver plate, was placed upon a hearse, and the solemn procession marched to the church. Two mutes preceded on each side of the hearse, outward of whom walked the pallbearers, comprising six of his Majesty's council, with the Honorable Speaker and Richard Bland, Esq., of the House of Burgesses; his Excellency's servants, in deep mourning, attended also, with the gentlemen of the clergy, the professors of William and Mary College, the clerk of the church and the organist besides. Immediately after the hearse thus attended (so the newspaper tells us) came the chief mourners, the faculty of the college following, and the mayor, recorder and aldermen of Williamsburg with the mace borne before them; the gentlemen of the law and the clerk of the general court. For the colony, the capital, the college itself, all bore the names of British kings and queens. Students of William and Mary College who had been detailed as ushers wore white hat-bands and gloves; and behind all these a numerous body of citizens brought up the rear of the procession, walking two and two. In the church, which was of the established English faith, a black carpet had been spread for the coffin, which was covered with

crimson velvet, while the burial service was read; altar,
pulpit and his Excellency's pew were hung suitably in
black. Following a sermon, the mournful procession
resumed its march through William and Mary's
grounds to a chapel, where the remains were deposited
in a vault, the militia outside firing three volleys as a
parting salute. The council and House of Burgesses
went into deep mourning for Lord Botetourt, and so,
too, as their spontaneous expression, did many gentlemen of the colony; for this nobleman had made a highly
estimable governor of Virginia, and his loss was deeply
deplored.

The exaggeration of grief witnessed in the funeral
and burial rites of our ancestors may provoke an irreverent age to mirth. For unless one's sympathies go
freely out to the dead or his survivors, the aspect of
mourning brings overstrain, and the tear and the smile
come shamefully close together. Pompous homage
ceases, and with all but the few, worthily illustrious
beyond their times, the torch dies out and mortals, great
or humble, slumber alike forgotten. The casual
rambler of a later age takes somewhat of a sardonic
delight in thinking how little the graven titles or tributes to the departed one can give passports to distinction in another world. But where these old tombstones make most a kindred mourner of casual posterity is in the family group of graves whose inscrip-
tions reveal the universal hope that husband, wife and
little ones, once united, shall yet unite again. From
such a point of view, let us bless forever the old departed of our pioneer age. Though the individual
record of such lives may have perished from human

annals, we surely feel that they have left to the future generations a conjugal and parental example worthy the tenderest commemoration. For these men and women were the breeders and fosterers of a great people; they sowed in our soil the seed that germinated into the grandest democratic experiment the world has yet witnessed. Their life companionship was that of rugged toil, of noble endeavor to lead pious lives and bring up an offspring in that fear of God which the Bible tells us is the beginning of wisdom and understanding. Their households were wholesome; they lived among neighbors without reproach; they died—

> "On resurrection's morn to rise,
> And meet the Lord with sweet surprise."

V

HOUSES AND HOMES

THE land tenure of these colonies, varying as it did under one charter settlement or another, came to affect powerfully the political character of their respective peoples. In one respect, this tenure differed greatly from that in Great Britain: the iron impress of the feudal system was wanting. Instead of being vassals and feudatories, theoretically, under some lord paramount, men owned their land in fee, unincumbered by those onerous tributes which the military despotism of the middle ages had exacted in Europe. Our land tenure on this North Atlantic slope was essentially modern, and the freedom and facility of acquiring a full title in the individual favored here the condition of freehold farmer rather than of a mere tenant, lessee or occupier and tiller of acres owned by a landlord.

In Europe at that day the whole fabric of rank and privilege rested upon the unequal distribution of land. As to these thirteen colonies, the British Crown had given out patents originally to chartered companies, to lord proprietors, to royal favorites; not unfrequently conveying the same lands twice or thrice over, so that titles were conflicting. The primitive grantees in New England, however, laid out their lands as wise founders of a commonwealth. In Plymouth, in Massachusetts

Bay, and in the later settlements planned through such precious example, real estate was run into contiguous tracts ten miles square, called townships, and then granted by the governing authority to forty or fifty proprietors jointly, their heirs and assigns forever, with obligation to build a church and schoolhouse. A settler, unless selling out, would subdivide to his children, and those in turn to theirs; the soil became minutely partitioned for cultivation and improvement, and republics flourished on a basis of equal rights. "Every one in the New England colonies is a freeholder," observed a London press writer in 1767, "and enjoys more liberty than any other people in Europe and America."

But in the middle and southern colonies less of a township system existed, and great inequalities prevailed by comparison. Thus, in New York, the Crown had made to individuals enormous grants of twenty miles square, and much the same held true in New Jersey. Patroons, lords of the manor, built their castles on the Hudson like another Rhine; and one of these, Van Rensselaer, used to bring a New York sheriff with his armed posse to drive off the intruders on his domain. Pennsylvania was one grand domain bestowed by Charles II. upon William Penn; and here millions of acres paid a quit-rent to the family proprietor. Maryland's Lord Baltimore, too, had enjoyed the princely benefaction of a Stuart as proprietor of the colony. In Virginia and the remaining British provinces to the southward a plantation system spread over extensive tracts of fertile land for the raising of great staples for export. Yet in the general competition to induce a settlement, local faults of tenure were somewhat modified in these colonies, and all things

tended, among English-speaking freemen at least, to
political equality.

Our population still clung to the Atlantic coast and
its tributary rivers; nor were the backwoods (with wild
beasts and Indians) far remote as yet, though gradually receding into the interior. Bears in 1766 infested
Hartford considerably, causing great havoc among
sheep and swine; and the inhabitants of the town that
year pursued and shot a large one and roasted it whole.
A "tiger or panther" had been reported at Fishkill,
New York, the year before. Wolves, too, imperilled
various frontier towns of New England and Northern
New York and destroyed sheep by the hundreds. "Informers of deer" were among the town officers still
annually elected in Boston and its vicinity. Bears, as
late as 1750, or even later, were reported shot in the
suburbs of Philadelphia.

Farms were frequently managed on the halves, the
owner thus getting readily his part profit on the
produce in lieu of a rental. Out in the wilderness the
new settler swung his axe, that prime weapon of
progress, more potent even than the rifle. Felling trees
was the first pioneer occupation, that the rich new soil
might open its bosom to the sun and air and fructify
abundantly. Too much wood was cut, however, and
cut ruthlessly; and we are now only just beginning to
learn that forests should be preserved and cultivated
as a permanent investment, by careful choice and selection for harvest, leaving a new growth to come up.
For fuel, for building, too, trees were useful enough to
the neighboring proprietor; but where one could not
transport far to find a market for his lumber, he would
hack and destroy without discrimination, so as to make
room for raising quickly his crop of Indian corn. Yet

the woods of our American wilderness were vast in those days, and spoliation did as yet little, comparatively, of visible damage.[1]

Homes and habitations in every age and country typify the civilized condition of their local dwellers. At the date we are considering, America had advanced to the stage of a fixed and permanent body of inhabitants, many of whom were affluent and of high social influence; while most possessed at least the means of an honest livelihood. Public protection against Indian assaults was no longer needful in our older towns and settlements; and the stockades of heavy logs, once the common resort of inhabitants in time of danger, had disappeared.

English men and women wanted English homes, just as the Dutch, our first settlers of New York, conformed to the quaint patterns of Holland—all alike seeking reminders of their old country. By the latter half of the eighteenth century, then, and before our Revolution, were fine mansion-houses solidly and well built of wood, brick or stone, in which abode persons of quality, many of them staunch Tories and Loyalists. The Craigie house in Cambridge, Washington's headquarters, and later the peaceful abode of our poet, Longfellow; the Hancock house in Boston, which some of us still remember; the brick Chase mansion, and others of a like pattern in old Annapolis; Mount Vernon and

[1]Chastellux, in 1780, deplored this wholesale forest destruction; pioneers, he thought, should disperse their settlements more, so as not simply to clear the land, but to clear while keeping intact the woods as a reservoir to preserve the earth's moisture. While visiting Monticello, he saw distant forest fires, which ravaged until the next heavy rain.

Monticello in Virginia—these may suffice for example
among the many fine specimens of English colonial
homes in one province or another. There was a simple
dignity in such abodes, heightened by the ample acreage
they occupied. For a certain aspect of court life gave
a glory to the social set that was wont to gather in the
capital towns of these provinces about the royal governor; and there did the pride of the wealthy find a
British expression, as also in the maintenance of fine
country seats, with spacious grounds, fit domiciles for
an aspiring gentry.

Yet for generous visiting and merrymaking, these
colonial mansions, with some notable exceptions, were
less roomy and spacious in their internal arrangement
than we are apt to imagine, especially when we consider the immense family of one's own progeny that
might be reared and brought up under a single roof,
to return with their own offspring for the holidays
after being once scattered. Mount Vernon, first among
our historic mansions, was, after all, of but moderate
size and commodiousness in the Revolutionary times,
except for its detached kitchen and servants' quarters;
most of the housekeeping being carried on outside the
main building. And coming down to the less imposing
homes of ancestors less affluent, but more prolific, one
stands in tranquil Lexington at the famous house
whence Hancock and Samuel Adams emerged in flight
near the dawn of that memorable April morning,
and marvels that four small walls should have en-
compassed, besides these illustrious guests, the goodly
family of a country parson, grown folks, children and
servants.

Surely, in those days, and among such Americans
as claimed but a modest competence, young and old

must have doubled up in the halls and chambers at night, and rafters rung by day with merriment and noise on an anniversary occasion. For, after all, the dwelling-houses of our colonial age rarely exceeded two stories in height, with other chambers finished off in the roof; while often enough the final accommodations stopped at the second story. A few of the more stately mansions, however, made a good three stories, exclusive of the roof, and occupied an ample area in square feet besides, with a garden curtilage. Before and after the Revolution some extravagant dwelling-house in town would be put up to bankrupt its proprietor, and neighbors dubbed it his "folly."[1]

For building material, brick was already much used in the middle and southern colonies, being readily made there and well burned; while in and about Philadelphia stone was a common and convenient substitute. New York by 1750 was well up in its building styles, as in everything else. Charleston, after a great fire in 1740, rebuilt in brick, with better taste than before; and in this palmetto region the Spanish concrete came also into use, composed of oyster shells, sand and water; and the soil serving well for brick, lime of the oyster-shell was used for mortar. New England, however, clung long to its lumber materials; and though a choice mansion of stone or imported brick might be visible there thus early, dwelling-houses were commonly of wood, even in the largest towns. Boston was highly inflammable, and as late as 1795 travellers marvelled at its many wooden buildings, which stood endwise toward the street. These wooden houses went largely

---

[1]See mention of one such in Baltimore, in 1754, whose owner presently turned it over to the town as a small-pox hospital, evidently meaning never to live in it again.

unpainted through the distressful days of war, and took on a dingy aspect.

American houses were in those days advertised for sale or rent with two, three and sometimes four rooms on a floor; with a pump and well, outhouses or a woodshed, and a back yard, sometimes paved. A genteel house had its cellar, too; but basement or cellar kitchens scarcely yet existed. It was quite common to carry on one's trade or manual pursuit in his own dwelling. Both sexes grew apt, moreover, in the variety of demands made where skilled labor was not to be readily had and economy was needful. Men built and repaired their own houses; the women folk kept those houses in order inside, and made up clothing for young and old. Almost every small householder could turn his hand to painting, carpentry and petty repairs; and such was the universal reliance placed upon the mutual disposition to mutual help that neighbors would turn out and join in a house or barn raising whenever called upon, asking only the treat of a broached cask of cider or a gallon of rum.

Grand parks and grounds artistically laid out with flower beds were not to be expected among so plain and primitive a people. Nature made her own adornment. Even the rich planter lived in a sort of easy indolence upon his broad acres, among rude laborers who had no tasteful ideas to impart; and our sons of Adam elsewhere were mostly intent upon those products of the soil that yield an essential livelihood. Boston's common, unique in picturesqueness, was something of a public pleasure-ground, and so was the battery in New York; but Philadelphia, our chief metropolis, had not a single promenade or enclosure to give comfort and recreation to its citizens. In many a

little town the village green or common served for
holiday sport or parade; yet, after all, one found the
chief solace of toil, as well as the dainties of life, in
his own private orchard or garden. People raised for
the table their own plums, peaches, pears, apricots,
apples, cherries and currants; and in the kitchen garden
their own potatoes, corn, beans and asparagus; flowers
they cultivated to some extent besides.

The church or meeting-house shared usually with
court-house or town-house the honor of safeguarding
the inhabitants. Williamsburg, of old Virginia, had its
provincial capitol of two stories at one end of the main
street; while the other end was occupied by William
and Mary College. No native city or town of this age
was so cosmopolitan that a stray horse, or a cow with
a bell about her neck, might not be seen wandering on
the highway, to say nothing of domestic goats or swine,
less comely, that long did scavenger work in streets
with a surface drainage. Philadelphia's paving progressed in 1770 under an act of the Pennsylvania
assembly which required preference to be given to such
streets as were most used by country people when
bringing their produce to market. Salutary legislation
of about this same date sent the human scavenger upon
his rounds and checked a former custom of private
pollutions on the highway; at the same time regulating
business signs and cellar steps, that they should not en-
croach upon the sidewalk.

Boston led all the colonial towns of this era
in public cleanliness; and its paving had since 1715
received much attention from the selectmen. Here
economical usage was at first to pave only a strip in

the middle of the street, and in fact there was no side-walk in the town until after the Revolution. Pebbles or cobblestones—smooth, round stones from the beach—long composed the only pavement, and except when carts and carriages compelled them aside the good people walked in the middle of the street. The thoroughfares of Charleston, South Carolina, though narrow, were less crooked than those of Boston, which originated largely in trodden paths and cattle trails; while those of New York, less precise by ruler and compass than in the Quaker City (planned by Penn himself), gave a spontaneous and pleasing effect of breadth and variety. By 1750, New York's streets were well laid out and paved in the more needful parts; and shade trees along the front yielded a grateful screen from the summer's hot sunshine. With only about a quarter mile of cartage anywhere, that city was paved with round pebbles, and showed a Dutch neatness. But Philadelphia seems to have improved quite slowly; and with its rectangular streets, dusty and muddy by turns, as weather varied, people gave it the punning sobriquet of "Filthy-dirty." A man on horseback, as the tale went, having got mired in one of the streets, was thrown from his horse and broke his leg; whereupon arose a public agitation, and pavements were com-pelled.

Increasing dangers by night, with an increasing pop-ulation, had brought about street lighting and a night watch in our leading centres. Good citizens themselves maintained such luxuries at first, while the frugal authorities held back from levying a tax; or perhaps the unpaid duties of watchman and constable were im-posed upon fellow-citizens chosen to the place, who were fined if they failed to serve. Rural towns to this day are reluctant to assume such public burdens. It was general complaint in 1749 that Philadelphia had barely six night watchmen to a population of 15,000, and that even these went their route in company. No watchman's rattles were yet known, but watchmen would cry the time of night and the state of the weather as they went their rounds—a practice derived from old England, it would seem, like the sentinel's cry of "all's well." At night from the earliest times the curfew or nine o'clock bell rang out in New England towns; and Boston selectmen issued strict orders to the inhabitants against walking the streets after ten o'clock or showing lights later in their houses. If there appeared to be dancing or singing later than that hour, the watchman would rap on the door and bid the offenders cease or have their names reported. Philadelphia's regulations were also strict, and the mayor issued his formal instructions to the watchmen somewhat after Dogberry's famous formula. Street bonfires or beacons became the usual night signal in colonial towns among patriots opposed to the Crown; while they whose business or pleasure took them from home after dark must long have carried their own lanterns.[1]

[1]New York City had in its enterprise erected lamps and lampposts at the public cost before the Revolution; so that, as we read, the plan earlier in vogue of hanging lanterns from private windows was definitely abandoned. In 1773 the Massachusetts general court passed an act for regulating lamp-lighting in Boston at the public cost, and imposing penalties for the mischievous offence of breaking street-lamps and emptying the oil. It seems, however, that the selectmen took no action until nearly twenty years later for public lighting. Philadelphia levied its lamp and watch tax in 1772 (if not earlier), discounting the rates to such householders as kept their private pumps in good repair.

No general water-works on an ample scale were found in America until after the Revolution. Pump or well water was good enough for the colonists; and the old well-sweep with its oaken bucket was a familiar adjunct of the primitive home, to which poetry has done justice. But horses fell sometimes into the concealed or covered wells on private premises; while human beings were killed or badly maimed in like manner where owners had failed to keep up proper safeguards. Every New England town had its town pump, upon which public notices and proclamations were affixed. Philadelphia kept many pumps in its public streets. Rain cisterns were also erected. Wells had succeeded the surface springs as local populations grew, and since they had often to be sunk to great depth, and were impregnated besides with impure matter, the demand grew for a pure and abundant supply of water for whole communities.

Fuel for our colonial homes was usually of wood, cut in some neighboring forest and brought by the winter sled to market. In fact, winter's chief occupation in the country consisted in providing the new year's supply, to take its proper turn at seasoning in the woodpile. Measurers and scalers of wood were among the local officers of our provinces; and provincial laws regulated the length or quality of all wood and charcoal exposed for sale. Virginia soft coal was used to some extent; and in 1774 we see pit-coal offered for sale by private owners on the James River, for household or blacksmith use, ready for delivery on their premises at 12 pence a bushel. Anthracite was unknown. Newcastle coal was imported and sold in our chief centres of population. Places of public meeting were hardly warmed in winter, save by the fervid sermons or discussions. About the middle of the eighteenth century appeared the cannon stove—so called from its shape. Franklin's new "fireplace" stove, invented in 1742, while economizing heat, preserved the cheerfulness of an open fire.

In colonial times, keeping one's coach was at the North no essential of respectability; and a one-horse chaise or calash, springless, worth perhaps fifty dollars, and harnessed to a steady family beast, was style enough for any one. Virginians, to be sure, and their neighbors took pride in thoroughbred and well-groomed steeds; such gentry enjoyed horseback riding, fine coaches with livery and the jockey races; but the sleek Pennsylvanian ambled along with an easy pacer and a two-wheeled carriage, disdaining such follies. The householder had his own stable; others, in or near town, placed their beasts with the tavern keeper. Farmers, of course, kept their cattle. Horses that did hard labor on the farm or in the owner's routine business were put into their best harness and shafts for an occasional jaunt, or on the Lord's day to take the family to meeting. Ladies made no pretence in this age to athletics; and yet, besides the routine work of farm or household, that must have called out strong muscular exertion, they took long walks for shopping and social visiting; and if they went out for pleasure and frolic at night, they made nothing of strolling for miles with their swains, even though clad in fine attire. To ride about in town was thought an affectation, nor were livery stables for hire as yet an institution. Hacks were hardly heard of; and when first set up, in fact, their patronage did not pay expenses.

VI

DISTRESSING accidents, such as we find chronicled in the newspapers of our colonial era, bring home vividly to posterity the dangerous personal exposures of that period. How many serious casualties came from trying to do everything for one's own self in this rude state of experience, without expert knowledge or the fair subdivision of industries! Severe sickness or injury was followed more likely by death than nowadays, because less skilfully treated or guarded against. Children, rambling out of doors, and grown persons besides, would pick and eat strange berries, roots and vegetables that turned out poisonous; and in vain did newspapers warn against toadstools resembling mushrooms, against hemlock, ivy and the like, strange growths of luxuriant nature.

Clumsiness at work by the injured or injurer did much mortal mischief. A man dropped from his ladder or scaffolding while repairing a house, or fell into the well he was digging, or got knocked under the frame of the building he was helping to raise, or was scalded to death by an overturned kettle of boiling water, potash or maple sap. One poor fellow was crushed under the wheel of a cart that he or some one else was driving; another was killed by the fall of a tree while awkwardly chopping it down. Not seldom, we may surmise, the victim was under the influence of liquor; for tippling at this date was a vice quite prevalent among Americans. But many an accident was doubtless due to bodily wrenching or straining, while overtaxing one's strength in trying to lift, unload or do a hundred other things for one's self, which in these days would devolve rather upon men specially skilled or seasoned to such labor. We read of a father and three sons who were killed, one after another, while descending, without first making a test, into a pit of noxious vapor. One man was asphyxiated by setting a pot of burning charcoal in his bedchamber at night and then shutting the windows to keep out the cold; another was maimed fatally while prying up a rock; a third was killed by his uplifted axe flying from the handle; a fourth tumbled from the roof and broke his neck while trying to put out a fire which had caught from his kitchen chimney. Pioneer life brings its peculiar casualties, and many accidents of this age were due, undoubtedly, to carrying on one's occupation at home in the presence of his family. So, once more, with a large wood fire left on the ample hearth, a helpless old grandmother or young child would be burned to death in its embers while left unwatched.

People were careless, moreover, in the use of powder and firearms when our Revolutionary era began, as the newspapers show us. Thus in celebrating the repeal of the Stamp Act, injuries were reported in various towns where the charge had been carelessly rammed into the cannon. At Hartford the legislature voted joyfully to the townsfolk two barrels of powder for volleys in honor of the repeal. This powder was kept in the schoolhouse, and the militiamen, when filling their horns with it, left some spilled on the floor. The

school children playing sportively with the black grains,
one boy set them on fire, whereupon, the train leading
to a powder barrel, the latter exploded with tremen-
dous concussion. The schoolhouse was blown up, and
wholesale slaughter of the innocents rounded the
catastrophe. Careless lads in Boston, carelessly looked
after, met a similar fate a few years later while amusing themselves with another stray barrel of this explosive, left loosely about. There were gunpowder
accidents, besides, where grown people used powder
from a horn to start a household fire on the hearth.
Writers in the press of 1770 complained that boys got
hold of gunpowder and firearms, and then fired loaded
pistols out of mischief at a passing carriage, perilling
the lives of wayfarers and frightening their horses.
A stringent police inspection must here have been
wanting.

The individual nature of these accidents, in the main,
forces a comparison with our own more polished and
populous age. Seldom did a fatality of this era in-
volve a general holocaust of lives, as happens so often
in these later days of wholesale risk by tramp or travel.
The canoe or little skiff was overset in summer, the
sleigh broke through the thin ice in winter, yet only
two or three were drowned. From houses and workshops as then built or occupied there was a tolerably
easy escape. Death came, then, or some shocking injury, chiefly as an individual infliction, and strongly
indeed must the heart of the community have responded
to sorrow and suffering. For in these primitive days
all were compassionate toward social equals, at least,
who were bereaved; and to each large household came

in turn the chastening experience of human sorrow. Even in war, they who fought for liberty were fairly identified, far beyond the present conception of our later age; high or low, in each and every community, the brave were mourned and memorized in their deeds. In men's mouths and through press or preacher the moral of the sudden death found expression. "Ye gay and careless on his fate attend," was a frequent comment in the newspapers; nor had the "marvellous dispensations of Providence" passed out of New England study since the days of old Winthrop's Journal. And truly God's hand was recognized in many a strange phenomenon of the times—in earthquakes, lightning, storms, and other commotions of nature, which were faithfully reported, and sometimes a little credulously. There were news of hurricanes from "His Majesty's Caribbean Islands;" and precocious Alexander Hamilton owed his first prodigious lift in life by vividly describing, while a youth, one of those calamities for a local paper. At Amesbury and Salisbury, in Massachusetts, a terrible tornado in 1773 wrecked all houses far and near, while sparing human life. In 1777 earthquakes rumbled at historic Concord and the neighboring towns, as credible witnesses solemnly deponed. Balls of fire, in these eventful years—comets, too, and meteors, were studied by college men in various provinces. Hailstones in Virginia, as big as a pint bowl, whirlwinds and the like, were reported from the South, till our printer himself betrayed scepticism over his information.

Thunder and lightning in particular seem to have been unsparingly destructive in our summer storms, and the variety of accidents therefrom was wonderful. Persons struck by the thunderbolt were senseless for

hours, if left alive; horses, sheep and oxen perished in
large numbers; many a tree was riven sharply asunder.
Fifteen sheep under a tree lost their lives together;
a vessel building on the stocks was wholly ruined. In
or near Philadelphia, in 1772, a house was struck by
lightning one day while the whole family were at
table; some were killed or stunned, others miracu-
lously escaped, while pewter plates, from which they
were eating dinner, had the whole rim melted. Five
years later, at Hartford, on a June Sunday, a violent
downpour of rain began just as Divine service was
over, and, with a sharp detonation like a cannon-shot,
lightning struck the steeple of the meeting-house, shat-
tering the top and carrying away weathercock, spindle
and large timbers. Then the electricity glided, snake-
like, under the roof and prostrated some of the assembly, killing a woman. In terror, the congregation
sought to escape, but the shower hindered them; and
returning to their seats and singing psalms together
they grew calm, and the storm passed on without further injury.

Accidents like these were reported all over America
from year to year by the local press. A Baltimore
sheriff perished in 1767 by lightning. James Otis, the
eloquent seer of revolution, was killed, as posterity
knows, by a thunderbolt. Many a strange fantastic
freak was played by the electric fluid in one rural community or another. Citizens of a scientific turn studied, therefore, how to lessen the danger by appliances
which might treat lightning as a natural agent, rather
than the visible symbol of God's wrath. Hence, by
1770, Franklin's lightning rods came somewhat into
use. Prejudice, however, against lightning rods was
very great, and many insisted that it was better to

trust all to the Divine Will than forefend danger with such impious contrivances. It was to meet a common New England superstition that Professor John Winthrop, of Cambridge, a man of much wisdom, who was the first recipient of an LL.D. from Harvard, commended the new invention, in 1770, in an open letter to the press, arguing that the religious scruples which opposed its introduction were founded in false philosophy and a misapprenhension of those natural laws by which God guides the universe.

The old Puritan idea, that God shapes directly all the details of human life for purposes foreordained toward each individual soul, truly conflicted with the more rational theory of man's responsible existence on this earth and his free choice among the operations of nature's own immutable laws. It failed to apprehend a Divine Will which respects high human endeavor. Hence science must have swung in that century to an opposite side, leaving religion and irreligion in strong antagonism. When the pendulum ceases to react violently to and fro, the real truth as to man's final destiny may reveal itself at equilibrium.

Great suffering must have been caused in this era by the extremes of heat and cold. The temperature of America differed, perhaps, not greatly from what posterity has found it, and weather exceptionally severe may still set in. But the conveniences for resisting storm and stress were far less then than now; though greater, doubtless, than in the previous century, when the winter sufferings of our first New England settlers must have been terrible indeed. Roads scarcely travelled, with dwellers far apart; dense woods and frozen sheets of water; wooden houses built meanly for the most part, and with chinks and crannies through which the winter winds might whistle hoarsely; no furnaces, no large portable stoves or steam radiators to diffuse and equalize warmth; wood fires usually in place of coal, throwing out a fitful and variable heat; imperfect means at hand for alleviating sickness and suffering; no flight for the invalid to a warmer climate, no luxuries,—such were the usual conditions of colonial life for meeting each winter's hardships. Navigation in our Northern ports was hindered much by the winter's ice; small sailing vessels in boisterous weather were tossed furiously about or driven ashore in disaster; great spring floods and high tides, with wind, rain or snow alternate, submerged the piers and streets adjacent in our seaport towns, deluged the cellars, broke up wharves, carried off piles of lumber awaiting export at the water's edge, and damaged such little craft as might be moored at anchor in the vicinity.

Snowstorms which lasted three days in midwinter would pile the drifting snow six or seven feet high in places, thus blocking all travel, preventing the hardy post-riders from making their customary trips, and excluding news for a whole week from the outer world. Then two months later would come great freshets with the first spring thaw, carrying away bridges, impeding the little ferries, and once more detaining travellers and the mails. We read of a severe snowstorm, March, 1761, in Philadelphia, which prevented a quorum of the Pennsylvania assembly from convening; and a merchants' petition, that same year, prayed the authorities to have piers erected in the Delaware, so as to fend vessels from the floating ice. Another intensely cold winter, bringing severe snowstorms, was that of 1765-66. Boston boys skated on the frozen Charles, and sleighs were driven over that river from Cambridge; some fifteen vessels could be counted, locked fast in Boston harbor by the ice, over whose polished surface people walked for miles to visit the castle and various islands. The gales and occasional snowfalls of that winter were terrible to endure; men froze to death while driving, exposed to the keen air; snowshoes were worn out of doors; many chimneys blew down. Hairbreadth escapes were announced, moreover, in course of the voyage between Providence and New York, or where men who went gunning after water-fowl got their boats entangled in the ice about Long Island. It was shown by careful experiment in a closed house in New York City, that, in rooms where there was no fire, a glass of wine froze to the bottom in fourteen minutes, and water in three seconds.

Disastrous fires enhanced the calamity of exposure to severe winter weather like this. Sparks and flame belching from the deep-throated chimneys upon a wooden roof caused many a conflagration. Befouled chimneys were a frequent cause of fire; so was carelessness with a basket of chips; or the foolish custom of keeping hot ashes in wooden barrels and boxes. Other household fires were due to the pursuit of industries upon the family premises, which nowadays would be conducted elsewhere—as where one carried on at home a bakeshop or brewery, tried out tallow, or repaired furniture. Burning brush was another reported cause of such a calamity; or going down cellar with a lighted candle to draw rum or cider for supper.

When weather was icy cold, and the wind blowing
a gale, a spreading fire by night was fearful to delicate
children and the elderly sick and feeble, who had to
be brought out of bed and removed in the cold to such
shelter as might offer. Incendiary fires seem seldom to
have occurred, however. Neighbors turned out
strongly to help on all occasions of calamity, and at
church even, when the shouts of "fire!" from outside
were heard, with the noise of engines in the street, the
males of a congregation would hasten out of doors,
losing the sequence of the sermon. A simple candor
was shown by the press in relating the indiscretion, if
any, which had caused the disaster; as in an Andover
fire of 1770, which burned to the ground an old house
next the meeting-house, its three lonely and aged in-
mates perishing in the flames; though providentially,
as the reporter put it, the church escaped unharmed,
owing to the direction of the wind. Two old maiden
sisters, it seems, were in the habit of smoking their
pipes after they got into bed, whence, probably, the
disaster. "Therefore," adds the chronicler, "it may
not be amiss to caution people against such a practice."

Townspeople in those days kept their own fire-
buckets, made of heavy leather and marked with the
owner's initials or family crest; and the local newspaper, after some important fire, would advertise for
missing buckets. When an alarm was given, by cries
or bell-ringing, each householder rushed with his
bucket toward the scene of danger, and a double line
was formed to the nearest river, pond, or tide-water
dock, as the case might be, whence buckets brimming
with water passed from hand to hand, up one line, and
then dry again down the other, to be refilled or passed

as before. Fire engines of a simple sort had come into use in our chief centres; most were imported before 1765; but after that date, the home-made engines of Boston or Philadelphia pattern were thought even better than those from London. Our fire engines as yet worked simply with a pump and nozzle; hose carriages came much later, while steam fire engines belong to the middle of the nineteenth century. In 1738 Franklin formed at Philadelphia the first of volunteer fire companies in America, and each member at his own cost kept a certain number of leather buckets, with strong bags and baskets besides for packing and rescuing goods from the flames. This example spread to other towns and provinces; and social clubs are still to be found for good fellowship which originated as a local fire company in the eighteenth century.

Fire insurance had made some progress in these colonies before the Revolution, and a few companies, on the mutual plan, took risks in Boston and Philadelphia. Yet there was prejudice against such schemes; and we see the correspondent of a New York paper, as late as 1770, expressing his surprise that no such enterprise had yet been started in that city. "Contributionship," as it was called, against losses from fire, was an idea for another and later generation to appreciate at its true worth. Men took their own risks largely of losses by fire, as in being struck by lightning. All such ordinances were of God, as they expressed it; and the impoverished citizen whose building and contents yielded to the furious flames, had usually to begin life over again, stripped of his hoarded possessions. That situation of life, so unfamiliar to our later age, called specially for sympathy and alleviation from neighbors. Marine risks and marine insurance became

a business in the modern world sooner than fire insurance, just as fire risks and fire insurance preceded
insurance on lives.[1]

Things were lost or stolen in those days, as in ours,
and the loss was advertised in the paper. That trem-
ulous signer of the Declaration, Stephen Hopkins, of
Rhode Island, while returning with fellow-delegates
from Congress, in 1776, lost a large bundle of men's
and women's clothes, made up in a coarse linen wrap-
per. He had sent them specially by a wagon from
Philadelphia to Providence; "the wagon arrived at
Providence," he naïvely announces, "but the cloathes
did not." Another good citizen of New England lost,
in 1769, a bag, whose contents he itemized as one half-
worn beaver hat, a gray cloth jacket, a pair of country-
made speckled stockings, one ruffled shirt, one plain
ditto, and a package of valuable papers. He names in
his card a friend, whom he authorizes to receive the
bag if found, and supposes he lost it in some dram-
shop or tavern while in company with soldiers. The
simple candor of such newspaper statements is sometimes amusing; yet cunning was shown by the loser, as
nowadays, when appealing to the unknown dispos-
sessor. Reward we see offered thus early for restitution, "and no questions asked." In a Boston paper,
one announced his loss of a new beaver hat, which was
taken out of a room in Massachusetts Hall, at Cam-

[1]Drake's "Landmarks" says that the first fire insurance company in Boston dated from 1724; but this seems to have been
a Boston agency of the London "Sun" Insurance Co. Encycl.
Brit. gives the Philadelphia company of 1752 as the earliest
started in America, Benjamin Franklin being one of its earliest
directors.

bridge, on Commencement Day, an old one being left in its stead; and the loser politely surmises that the exchange was made by mistake, though adding that his own name was pasted inside of the missing castor. Another loser, less suave, offered a reward as for articles doubtless stolen from his house, and tried another tack,—he warns the thieves, whoever they may be, that if they escape condign punishment in this world, they will meet it in the next, where they will repent all too late that they had foolishly lost their souls in trying to gain the goods of this world wrongfully.

In English court process of the earliest times and in all formal documents of our common law, the recital of pursuit in station after each patronymic has been so customary as fairly to suggest the origin of various surnames. Thus, probate notices styled the deceased as knight or gentleman, merchant, shipwright, clerk, victualler, smith, brazier, chocolate grinder, and so on. Such was the custom strongly prevalent here and abroad in colonial times. In the colonial press, moreover, one saw the formal notice of executor or administrator followed quite often by a line or two of advertising on his own personal account; for he used the opportunity to do a stroke of business both for the dead one's assets and his own. A husband, for instance, administering on his deceased wife's estate, announces that he has for sale choice Narragansett cheese and Dorchester ale, with other English commodities, cheap for cash. A distiller's widow adds to her probate notice as executrix, that she still carries on the business and customers may send for their rum as before. The relict of a baker or a sugar boiler makes corresponding announcement; and quite commonly the surviving spouse, or widow and children together, advertise a successor to the decedent's business, hoping for the continued patronage of the public. So, again, a family friend, who settled his neighbor's estate, might be seen putting in a good word for himself in connection with the probate advertisement; as where an executor published that he kept good stabling for horses, and that travellers might depend at any time upon his faithful care. Articles to be sold for an estate—such as a horse and shay, for instance—were added, too, to these printed orders of the court; or a request was specially appended that persons who had articles belonging to the estate of the departed would return them forthwith. There seems to have been much neighborly borrowing in those days, as well as a reckoning of small things; for among specific articles thus publicly called for as missing from an estate, we find itemized not books alone, but a blue drab coat, or a pair of boots. One thinks in such connection of that conscientious nicety of the frugal and thrifty Scotch, proclaimed in their own immortal songs; as where the loyal Jacobin tenders his extra bawbee to be ferried over to bonnie Prince Charlie; or boon companions who take together their last "good willie-waught" for "Auld Lang Syne," prearrange that each shall be at his own cost for the extra pint.

VII

THE THREE PUBLIC VOCATIONS

I N no respect does the Revolutionary Age contrast more strongly with our own than in the practical condition of the three public vocations, so termed, of our common law—those of postmaster, innkeeper and common carrier. And the development of those several vocations has immensely affected our national character.

As for the post-office, our Continental establishment at the date of the Revolution was directed by government, as in the mother country. The public post originated centuries ago, in the sovereign transmission of public despatches alone. Thus was it with Persia, with the Roman Empire, with Europe under Charlemagne. In Great Britain, as in these colonies when first setled, common people sent usually their letters by carriers or by private conveyance; but soon after the expulsion of the Stuarts we see the Virginia Burgesses agitating a popular postal system, after the plan already adopted in the mother country, and organized by Parliament during the reign of Charles II. That system was fairly established in these colonies by 1740, so that post-riders exchanged the mails between Virginia and Pennsylvania and eastward also. Henceforth, and through our Revolutionary War, Philadel-

phia, America's chief city, became the great postal and
distributing center of our thirteen colonies or states.
Franklin, when Postmaster-General for the Crown by
1753, took hold of the details deputed to him with
characteristic energy and thrift, and after some private
outlay for improvements, he made it profitable for
government and its agents as never before.   He set
up milestones.   He arranged that the northern mail
from Philadelphia, which had gone to Boston but once
a fortnight, should go once a week all the year round;
so that Boston and Philadelphia letters might be interchanged in three weeks, instead of six, as previously.
So, too, he changed the mail between Philadelphia and
New York, from once a fortnight to twice a week, thus
traversing the distance between those two important
cities in three days.   By the year our independence was
proclaimed, even Bostonians might hear twice a week
from Philadelphia and New York when travelling was
good.   On the outbreak of hostilities in 1775, our Congress took up the general post-office as an independent
system; they established a chain of posts from Fal-
mouth, New England, to Savannah, with riders for
every twenty-five miles and advice-boats besides.
Stagecoaches took gradually the place of the boy on
horseback, or of post chaises or sulkies, for such transportation; and post-riders would sometimes set up a
stagecoach for the common business of mails and passengers.

The conveyance of newspapers in this era was often
the private perquisite of post-riders on their several
routes, since newspapers and magazines did not go
through the public mails at all.   "Post-rider" sometimes meant a sort of private carrier for mail matter,
and many people preferred to send their important let-

ters by private conveyance. During the Revolutionary War, messengers who proposed special trips of peril, to Quebec or Ticonderoga, for instance, would advertise to take private letters with them at a shilling or more each. At times the mail carrier journeyed in peril of his life; but his profession availed him well against casual disturbers of the peace. If assailed by highway robbers, he would say, "I am on His Majesty's service," and they let him ride on. Stress of weather and the bad condition of our roads would keep back the post, particularly in the winter and early spring. Not seldom the latest mails and newspapers from New York arrived in consequence a fortnight old in Boston or Baltimore, for ferries were frozen over with the winter's ice, and bridges swept away by the spring freshets. Few large rivers were in those days bridged over at all, and travellers alternated between boat and wagon. Deep and drifting snow, when it came, cut off communication alike by post or the stage coach.

Postal regulations, issued in 1765, for these colonies proclaimed each postmaster liable who embezzled the postage money paid him in advance; postboys were to be punished who deserted a mail or bag of letters, or loitered on the way, or let any unofficial person ride on their horses or in their wagons. There were no stamps used. The letter postage at that time between London and any port among the British dominions in America was one shilling a single letter, or for letters weighing an ounce, four shillings; and hence, for private correspondence, the advantage of thin single sheets of good size, crossed and recrossed in writing, and folded and refolded, for sealing by wax or wafer.

The foreign mail arrived in our ports by heavy instalments far apart; and news from London two months behind were thought fresh enough in New York port. Tories argued, when our Whigs opposed the Stamp Act, that letter postage was already a Parliamentary exaction in effect, which no one complained of here or thought of opposing; but to this came the fair reply that postage was paid for a special service of the government plainly to the advantage of the individual.

The inn—in this early era commonly styled "tavern" or "coffee-house," or, still earlier, "an ordinary"—made very little pretence of being fit for men of fashion with their families to abide in regularly. Colonists, when they mated, wanted their own household nests for themselves and their expected progeny, and however humble the family home, they secured it. Inns, in other words, lodged travellers, and the strictly transient only, except for single men; and those great organisms of luxury and fashion, such as we know to-day for hotels, were then wholly wanting in America, to attract rich boarders and lodgers of both sexes seeking social ease for a season and escape from the worry of housekeeping. But in default of accommodation elsewhere, the spacious public rooms of an inn came into demand for an occasional concert, ball or assembly, in the larger towns; sleigh-ride parties and excursionists stopped at its open door for a supper and an impromptu dance; while with main office, known to this very day by the suggestive style of "barroom," and with commodious stables, our public house served as passenger station and booking headquarters for the various stages that came and went at fixed hours of the day. And here, furthermore, Americans would meet for jollity or grave conference, with plenty of good liquor at command to stimulate their wits and appetites. Here, as in England, men smoked and drank, taking their ease together in the hours of recreation; here they discussed politics, drank toasts, quarrelled with one another, and even came to blows, since rules of decorum were not rigid. Addison and the *Spectator* familiarize us with the atmosphere of fun and good fellowship which long enlivened the London coffee-house; America, too, had her wags and story tellers, whose local renown mellowed in the genial warmth of a tavern's hospitality. In fine, even before Americans did much travelling, inns were the centre of life and affairs for the men folk; and judges and jurymen, church committees and politicians, idlers and business men, all resorted thither, to discuss and arrange affairs together.

The inn or tavern had usually in those days some fanciful name, with pictured sign or emblem before the door to enhance the effect of publicity. There was the "hat and helmet;" the "ship on launch;" "the golden swan" or "golden eagle," with a gaudy gilding; "the green dragon;" "the orange tree;" "the bunch of grapes;" the "Turk's" or "Saracen's head;" the "crooked billet" or "fagot;" "the pewter plate;" the Indian "King" or "Queen." Atrocious painting might be seen crowded upon the sign-board of a tavern or shop to attract the public by its quaintness. Thus, Philadelphia had "the death of the fox;" "the man loaded with mischief" (who carried his wife on his back); and Sir Walter Raleigh in the act of smoking, while his servant threw water upon him, thinking him

on fire.[1] Boston had, in colonial days, an inn called
"the British Coffee-House," which its proprietors
changed into "the American Coffee-House," with the
sign of a gilded eagle, after that town was redeemed
from British siege. But in colonial times our inns,
like those of the mother country, took often the name
of some British peer, or an officer renowned in the
army or navy; thus, there was the "Marquis of
Granby," the "General Wolfe," the "Admiral Vernon"
—this last, whose nickname was "Old Grog," being
the same officer after whom Washington's elder
brother named Mount Vernon.

Philadelphia taverns were licensed early, but they
did not stand in high favor, and sank readily into tippling and disorderly houses.[2] Of inns in that city, the
"Indian King" was the oldest and most reputable, and
it was here that Franklin's junto used to meet. The
"Crooked Billet" (of wood) was also famous; so, too,
by 1776, the "City Tavern." Philadelphia judges
used once to hold their courts at such houses, but as
this increased hard drinking, the practice ceased. In
New York City, "Bolton's Tavern," with its choice
larder, was a famous resort for feasting, and it was
there that Washington, when the Revolutionary War
ended, took a farewell glass of wine with his chief
officers. Boston had several famous inns with patriotic
associations, and the most famous among them was

---

[1] In the next era, a traveller mentions one of our tavern signs,
under whose picture of a headless female the landlord, during the
heat of the French Revolution, had inscribed the name of "the
beheaded queen of France," and then changed, compliant with
local opinion, to "the silent woman;" but that story dates back
in the mother country to Anne Boleyn and Henry VIII.

[2] They were presented as a nuisance in 1741, at which time they
numbered about a hundred, all retailing liquor.

of two-storied brick, known as the "Green Dragon," whose metal emblem crouched on a rod at the entrance; there the Masons used to meet, with Joseph Warren for Grand Master, and there, too, sedition was hatched by the famous conclave, Warren, Samuel Adams, Otis, and Revere. In the "Raleigh Tavern," at Williamsburg, with a leaden bust of good Sir Walter for a sign, Virginia's Burgesses met to take action, after the Governor had dissolved their House for disloyal expressions to the Crown; they gathered in the "Apollo Room," where many a gay ball and dancing party had been given by the Governor's set in more subservient years. Stabling, we may well conceive, was an important feature of the inn for entertaining travellers of that day; and we find a Lancaster tavern, in Pennsylvania, put up for sale in 1772, which had stalls in its stables for some sixty horses.

When a Boston hatter opened a new tavern in 1770, styled "The Hat and Helmet," he promised, besides the usual entertainment for man and beast, that his house would be "supplied with the newspapers for the amusement of his customers."

Inns in colonial days at our trade centres furnished lodging and meals to men without families who engaged in local business. A Virginia tavern was, in 1772, put up at vendue, where twenty gentlemen had been "constantly boarded at £25 each per annum." City taverns were of such publicity, that at the inn door, auctions used to be held of horses, carriages, or indeed of slaves. It was before the leading inn in one provincial town or another that our forefathers in the years of riotous resistance burned Stamp Act proclamations, or effigies of the royal officials most hateful to them; and when independence was declared, here, too, were bonfires made of the king's arms and emblems, torn promiscuously from the public buildings and borne by the ringleaders of resistance.[1]

For inland conveyance, the great passenger-carrier of this primitive era was the stagecoach; and American ambition and enterprise organized rival extensions of the stagecoach lines, increasing local connections and quickening the time of transportation. On the water, pulling by oar or skimming by sail, propelled both passengers and freight. People travelled much by their own private conveyances and teamed or propelled their own merchandise from place to place. But by land or water, motive power in those days was limited by the speed of horses, or of a vessel impelled by wind or oars; and this for long distances must have been slow enough by comparison with the steam or electric appliances of locomotion with which our present age is familiar. And what was more, the vehicle of carriage on either land or water was made more lasting and durable than swift, in this earlier day, as suited the British temperament.[2]

[1]Chastellux, in 1780, complained of the wretched public houses he encountered in those more remote parts of America where he casually lodged when travelling. "They make nothing in America at an inn," he complains, "of crowding several people into the same room;" and this herding together prevailed, to his surprise, even among the rich and hospitable Virginian planters at their private mansions. The vocation of innkeeper, too, he found often incidental to some other personal pursuit as a householder. Innkeepers were often accosted by a military title of rank or served as Justices of the Peace, maintaining high office and political importance in their local neighborhoods.

[2]For conveying freight long distances, pack-horses were used much in this age; and we are told of their appearance among the defiles of Pennsylvania, fifteen of them in single file, tethered

In Massachusetts, coaches for public conveyance were first established in 1763, or somewhat earlier, when a stage route was made up between Boston and Portsmouth; for when, by 1771, a rival was operating on this route, one Mr. Stavers claimed, in a newspaper notice, that his was the original stagecoach and post-chaise line between these points, and that he, in fact, was the first person who ever set up and regularly maintained a stage in New England.[1] Still earlier, in 1756, was started the first stage between New York and Philadelphia, three days through; and between those choicest termini of traffic were several rival lines and rival routes before the Revolution, involving more or less change by water transfer. A covered Jersey wagon, without springs, offered the first rival line between these two cities, followed (1766) by the so-called "flying machine," namely, an improved wagon on springs; the latter undertook to go through in two days, but in winter took three as before. Shall we ever travel literally by a flying machine? In 1773, came a real stagecoach of improved pattern, by which one might journey in two days between Philadelphia and New York, paying four dollars for an inside seat and somewhat less for a ride on top.

With lines thus steadily extending their facilities, almanacs of the day began to publish full lists of the public post roads with the stages, among other colonial statistics. Proprietors themselves, who combined their modest capital in partnership to consoli-

to one another, one man leading the first horse, while another looked after the rest of the line. The Conestoga wagon was first used in Pennsylvania under another name at the time of Braddock's ill-fated expedition.

[1] M. G., 1771.

date a business, would accost the wayfaring public
with the most conciliatory deference and respect, to
solicit their favors; the stage carrier was "their
very humble servant." But all did not run smoothly.
The Bordentown stage, in 1772, had to raise the fares
of its passengers, owing to the high price of grain.
The coach between Portsmouth and Boston was, in
1768, suspended for two weeks, because of a distemper which affected the horses. Our good-natured
countryman had often to stop his horse when passing,
to help lift the coach out of a quagmire, aiding driver
and passengers. Shocking weather and shocking roads
made spring and winter transportation distressing and
uncertain. Hence we need not wonder that people
travelled in those days rather for business than
pleasure, and took most of their recreation within a
few miles of home.

There were "stage boats," so-called, at this period,
which supplied a water connection in travel for both
passengers and goods; each boat well provided with
the best provisions and liquors, and guaranteed to
make its trip on schedule time, "wind and weather
permitting." The acme of stagecoach travel, on a
single line, consisted in attaching four good horses,
and having four more ready for an exchange on the
way. Much coasting traffic was projected in these
days. By 1771, a sloop sailed regularly once a fortnight between New York and Providence; while brigs
and sloops left Philadelphia at intervals with freight
and passengers for Charleston and other southern
ports along the coast. On that smooth Long Island
Sound, through which glide each night in either
direction those floating palaces of our present day, propelled by steam and brilliantly lighted, the voyage to

New York had its perils in bad weather. From our few chief harbors, packet ships plied regularly with passengers, freight and the mails for London, Liverpool and Londonderry; and the average passage was twenty-seven days between London and Boston. All baggage in such transportation was to be paid for according to weight and size; but each person might take with him "a small bundle." It is of these "bundles" that we read much in the newspaper notices of "lost" or "found." Rival carriers would offer to take the greatest care of all "bundles and packages" —but not a word said of trunks. Baggage was usually left and claimed at some local inn, which served for terminus. Large oaken chests of clothing were chiefly adapted to sea voyages; and where one's effects were charged by weight on an inland journey and shifted so frequently, each one's disposition must have been to travel with as little of a load as possible. In fact, the trunks on our stagecoaches, as remembered long after the Revolutionary period, were small, covered with deer skin, or pigskin, and studded with brass nails. One kept his baggage under his seat and under his own personal supervision as much as possible.

Friendly companionship must have been much promoted by these long journeys, so full of humorous incident, and with frequent shifts, besides, to give variety. The long discussions indulged in on the route, the interchange of stories and of personal experiences for all on board to listen to, the naps and yawns almost in one another's arms as the hours grew tedious, the freshening mug of flip or mulled cider at the tavern, where the horses were pulled up and all got out for a change of posture and refreshment—

all this must have tended greatly to the mutual revelation of character, while for little considerate acts of helpfulness few opportunities could have been better. Such travel, when prolonged, induces life friendships among the congenial thus casually brought together, and it affords, moreover, an admirable opportunity for the study of human nature. The social and the surly alike reveal themselves. People travelled far less, to be sure, in the aggregate, than they do now, but each tour brought them more naturally into acquaintance with one another. They who sought to travel with real seclusion or state, had to go by private conveyance. Public transportation treated the public alike, while staterooms, sumptuous palace cars, and meals served apart,—all these belong to the modern luxury of a republic, in the development of distinctions fostered by modern wealth and training.

Permanent bridges on a costly scale were seldom erected in this age; even turnpikes at the public cost were unpopular, and companies with capital adequate to such undertakings came later. At Gray's ferry, Philadelphia, and other important points of approach to a populous city, a floating bridge might be seen, or perhaps a bridge of boats. For fifteen years or more before the Revolution, Boston debated the project of a bridge across to Cambridge, but not till after the peace, or by 1786, did that debate bear fruit. Small bridges spanned small streams, but ferries served commonly where the water space was considerable, and of these the traveller or post rider made successive use as he journeyed. These ferries, owned and managed by private parties, varied with the importance of the patronage. Some had nothing more for outfit than a simple boat or skiff, propelled by oars or sail. For the ampler accommodation of passengers and their teams, a sort of flat boat came into use; that of Charlestown ferry, in Massachusetts (owned by Harvard College), conveying five horses at a time, besides men and women, which was more than the average. A rope ferry,—such as a foreign tourist may still find upon the Rhine,—took Philadelphians across the Schuylkill. A rope, which stretched over poles the width of the river, was pulled to impel the ferryboat; and if a vessel came by, the rope was lowered to the river bed, so that the vessel might sail over it. At Philadelphia, in 1772, the owner of the "middle ferry" advertised that he employed three sufficient boats, with ropes and a set of ferrymen as good as any; that he had complete sheds, troughs, wagons, horses, and stables, on both sides of the river. In view of such commodious arrangements, he hoped the public would patronize him rather than the ferry higher up, because his was nearer the city, by surveyor's measurement. Ferries were used across arms of the sea, or in traversing lakes, as well as for the narrower creeks and rivers.

VIII

DRESS AND DIET

IN dress and diet, as in other matters of the individual life, great differences prevailed among our colonists, because of the social distinctions they derived from Great Britain. The Virginia Tuckahoe wore fine clothes, drove in a stylish coach with livery, was very fond of horseback riding and of fair women. The planter of South Carolina took his fashions from London or Paris. In our other provinces, north or south, wealthy men, as well as women, of the upper set, dressed richly and even gaudily, following the European fashion. Our Copley portraits—and those, too, of Stuart and Trumbull,—show the richness of dress then prevalent in both sexes among the better colonial families, and suggest differences of style in this respect, even among the eminent. Thus, in the two companion portraits of Hancock and Samuel Adams, which still hang in Fanueil Hall, we may contrast two leaders of affairs whose politics brought them closely together; the one foppish and fashionable, as of a rich and recognized family, the other more closely allied to the common people—Hancock with his gay colors, lace and frogs, and richly embroidered coat and vest; Adams, whose clothes were rather of a plain and sober claret.

Such early paintings recall, moreover, the gorgeous and rustling gowns, the silks, satins and brocades of

our colonial dames of quality and high breeding.
"Silks and satins," Poor Richard used to say in those
days, "put out the kitchen fire." Such women dressed
in imported brocades, lute-strings, taffeties, sarsenet,
poplin, serges, shalloons, silks and satins; they adorned
themselves with garnet or pearl necklaces, breast-
flowers, aigrets, ruffles, Brussels lace, and handkerchiefs superfine; silk gloves and mitts, satin shoes and
silk hose gave delicate protection; muffs, furs and tippets were donned in the winter. They sported jaunty
riding hats of white and black beaver, with feathers,
or warded off rough weather with quilted bonnets
from London. Cambrics, lawns and muslins served
for summer wear. Dress and undress caps with becoming ribbons were in demand in those days; their
lawns were spotted or flowered; their handkerchiefs
flower-bordered or checked. This was the era, withal,
of stiff stays and buckram—of hoops, besides, which
the fair freighted one would manage with consummate art and decorum when steering in or out of a
room.

Picta vestimenta were, in short, in that age, the
style for ladies or gentlemen of fashion. Gold or silver
lace on dress occasions adorned the cocked hats and
smallclothes of men well born and well placed. Their
coats for cold weather had ample cuffs, and were made
with skirts reaching to the knees and stiffened with
buckram, while tightly fitting inexpressibles were
lined to make them warmer. No cotton fabrics were
worn in those days, and scarcely underwear at all.
Hose were of thread or silk in summer, and fine
worsted in winter; men wore no suspenders, and tradition asserts that it required no little skill to keep
one's buckskin breeches well above the hip. Young

bloods, the gay and the gallant, wore swords, withal, and so did military men; but elderly civilians carried gold-headed canes in preference, and would sit in public places holding the knob close to the chin; the gold snuff-box, too, was used and offered with exquisite grace. For the general idea with men of rank was to look imposing, and impress upon others their superior claims to distinction. The three-cornered or cocked beaver hat and dressed wig aided in such effect, though adding not a little to the discomfort of the wearer, when under full sail, particularly when the sun's rays were hot. Even the boys of good family wore plain or laced hats for their best in those days.[1]

For protection against rude weather, we hear much of the camlet cloak, blue, brown or red, which vied for favor with the great or top coat. During the Revolution, our continental officers brought Dutch blankets into temporary use, in place of cloak or overcoat. Boots came into fashion with the Revolution— having rarely been worn before, save by mounted army officers. Pumps for company, adorned with gem or paste silver buckles, and shoes of various patterns, leather or morocco, had been the footwear, imported or native made;[2] "spit-blacking" balls serving for a shine. Ladies wore dainty high-heeled shoes, often of satin, while clogs and galoshes or pattens served them on the streets for rain and the wintry exposure. India rubber protection against the weather was unknown in those early days. Cloaks, with sometimes an oiled linen cape, after the pattern we still

[1]Beaver was in the best style, but castor or raccoon skin was inferior.

[2]Lynn, Massachusetts, had already a reputation for shoes; and "slave shoes" were largely retailed in America for the lower classes of menials and mechanics.

observe in the sailor's tarpaulin, guarded either sex against the elements; but umbrellas (called "imbrillos," and imported from India) came somewhat into fashion before the Revolution, though ridiculed as an effeminacy. As first imported, the umbrella was of varnished linen, but silk became the stylish substitute; made of colored stuff, green, blue, or crimson, this mechanism was borne aloft upon a rattan cane.[1]

Ceremonious dress and ceremonious manners go together; and if men of fashion set the pace for a stiff and artificial style of adornment, woman, in her imitative zeal to please and conform, was sure to stretch farther in the same direction. The full toilets of women of fashion were elaborate, especially as to the hair, which was arranged on crape cushions so as to stand high and upright. Sometimes, as we are told, ladies had their heads dressed the day before a ball or party, and slept in easy chairs to keep their hair in condition. In fact, the fashionable of both sexes gave, in this age, at home or abroad, absurd attention to the minutiæ of wigs, perukes, and hairdressing generally. Women endured great torture in this respect, not to add in others, and sat for hours at a stretch to get the proper crisp to their curls.[2]   In our

[1] A New York hatter of this period offered a superior cocked hat of home manufacture which had a device of his own for shedding the rain. Franklin, when visiting Paris in 1767, saw, to his surprise, men as well as women carrying umbrellas in their hands, which they extended in case of rain or too much sun; and he computed the lesser space thus occupied on the street, than where rich people used coaches for bad weather, as in London. 4. B. F. Works, 38.

[2] Of the rollers or cushions, stuffed with wool, which thus fluffed out the natural hair, a Philadelphia paper of 1771 mentions one

chief towns and cities were barbers and hairdressers
for both men and women, ready to wait upon customers at their own houses; and at Philadelphia, an expert from Paris proclaimed his special skill in making
for the ladies handsome frissets, "which imitate nature,
and may be set on with very little trouble." He would
arrange brilliants and flowers to advantage, dressing each patroness in a style suitable to her complexion and natural hair.

Men went in our colonial era smooth-shaven, and, if
of the upper set, sent their wigs periodically to the
barber to be dressed. After Braddock's defeat, however, King George is said to have discarded his wig,
and, at all events, wigs from that date began to go
gradually out of fashion both at home and in these
colonies. Next succeeded the mode of dressing one's
natural hair by queuing or clubbing it, and wearing
the tail with a ribbon or in a black silk bag.[1] The
passion grew among our yeomanry to have a long
whip of hair, such as the sailor or rude plough boy
would tie with an eel skin. Hair powder was used
plentifully.[2] Pomatum, too, our barbers kept on hand,
with ribbons and silk bags of styles to suit the personal
taste. Hair dyes were used to some extent, and for

which fell from the head of a lady who got injured in the street,
and which the boys, after she was borne away, kicked about as
a football. Toilet arrangements like these, however, were not
mere mysteries of a lady's boudoir, for a local wig-maker of that
same year is seen advertising a hair roll of his own contrivance
which weighed but three ounces, in place of the former eight.

[1] "Imagine me," wrote Franklin in 1769, of the new French
fashion, "with a little bag wig, showing my naked ears." 4 B. F.,
39.

[2] Barbers of the Stamp-Act period sold it both for wigs and the
natural hair; one in Philadelphia, at the sign of the bleeding
lady and barber's pole, made it himself, and of a superior quality.

a lady's full outfit in her toilet lavender water and
sal volatile were indispensable.

"Cloathes" (the usual spelling of those days) must
thus have taken up much of a provincial man's thoughts,
if he claimed to belong to the aristocracy. Yet we hear
of these splendid suits—men's as well as the women's
—sent with economy to be dyed and turned and then
worn again. With menials and mechanics, of course,
and our simple yeomanry, there was no such elegance,
save, perchance, in the wear of faded finery at second
hand or in livery. The prevailing dress of poor
laborers and the working class I have indicated elsewhere. Mechanics wore the coarse apron of their
craft: caps, and plush or plain leather breeches were
the common garb of the humble; and these, too, wore
largely their natural hair, cropped closely.

In provincial times the farmer and his sons raised
wool and flax, which the wife and daughters of the
household spun into thread and yarn and knit into
stockings and mittens. The next and later step, when
patriotism preached self-dependence, was the cloth of
homespun woolen fabric, for coats and garments.
Such was the old-time process which gave to humble
women one of those industrial employments all the
better for being conducted in the home and family.

There were a few public or meeting-house clocks in
those days. The plain clock on the staircase might
be consulted at home—that faithful monitor, clicking
"never! forever!" as the poet says; but watches,
whether of gold or silver, were not as yet in common
use, being bulky in make as well as expensive; and,
dispensing with fine chains, one fortunate enough to

own a portable timepiece would carry it in a fish skin
or a case of imitation tortoise shell and use a plain ribbon, from which dangled its key, with perchance a gold
seal and cornelian stone for a companion ornament.[1]
Spectacles, moreover, were rare, except for old folks,
for the young kept and gloried in their normal eyesight; but temple ·and bridge spectacles (the latter
mounted on the nose without side supporters) were
on sale for need, though clumsy for ornament. Den-
tistry was rude enough, as compared with the present
age; but surgeon-dentists in the larger towns fixed
false teeth singly or in sets, and offered to do such
work with the greatest ease, safety, and secrecy—yet
not guaranteeing their patrons against incidental pain.
"Essence of pearl" was a common dentifrice of the
day. But if the truth must be told, our people as a
whole took no great pains with their mouths, so far as
appearance went; and long after Revolution, our
typical young woman, as described by travellers from
abroad, was chiefly disfigured by her poor teeth—a
criticism which must long since have spent itself.

As for diet, plenty and variety awaited all in this
new world who chose to avail themselves amply of
nature's free abundance. Deer, wild turkies, pigeons,
partridges, were readily hunted; wild hares and squir-
rels were so many that people looked upon them as
pests for devouring grain; a host of marine fowl, can-
vas-back ducks and other delicious game flocked about
the shores of the Chesapeake in the autumn months.

---

[1] In the *Virginia Gazette* one advertises as lost in 1775 his gold
watch; it is described as having a neat china dial-plate, an imitation tortoise-shell as its outer case, and a riband showing a key.

Wild honey gathered from the hollow tree-trunks, or the sap of the sugar maple, made a welcome sweetener for such as found the West Indies brown sugar or the white sugar loaf high-priced.

Fish of the greatest variety came here to hook or net. The seas, the rivers, the lakes of this North Atlantic area yielded wealth to our English tourists greater than any gold mine, such as many of the King's charters had prospected in vain; while the colonial fisheries of New England proved an enterprise that won Burke's eloquent encomium. Lobsters, in that era plentiful, were found of length about equal to that of the men who caught them; crabs, too, of a size much larger than we see in our day; and oysters actually a foot long. The gigantic breed of fish lessened much in American waters as human captors increased, with their intrusion, yet the rivers and bays were still amply stocked for human sustenance. In 1766, at New York City, when meat and butter were costly, and provisions scarce, the common people were saved from distress by living upon fish and oysters.

Codfish was already New England's peculiar emblem and a leading staple of her commerce. It consisted of three sorts: "merchantable, middling, and refuse;" the first grade being sold to Europe, the second consumed mostly at home, and the third exported to negroes of the West Indies. Dunfish—so called, we may presume, from their dun color, though constantly advertised as "dumb-fish,"—were the best of the three in quality. Disdaining to observe the Popish churchman's Fridays, the New Englander chose Saturday for his fish dinners, and no Yankee dinner on that day of the week was complete, while the eighteenth century lasted, without boiled codfish on the table, served with

pork scraps or sauce of drawn butter. Fried codfish
balls followed for the Sunday breakfast. Codfish with
cream pleased the palate in our middle provinces; and
all these native dishes were from a single variety of
fish, when salted down for general use. Smelts, hali-
but, perch, mackerel, trout, Potomac herring were
among the many other kinds of fish held in esteem,
especially when freshly caught; terrapin was a luscious
product of the middle and southern states, since rare
and costly enough. But of the sturgeon, Indians partook rather than the white man; while, strange to say,
salmon and shad, best esteemed of all fish to most
epicures of the present day, were in that earlier age
despised.

Barnyard fowls,—hens, geese, ducks and chickens,
—were raised by farmers for the family table, with
the domestic quadrupeds besides. Beef, veal, pork and
poultry thus supplied the table from one's own live
stock. Hams, cured in the smoke-house, hung in the
cellar for winter's use. Pork, pickled in brine, and
corned beef helped out a family provender for the
winter season. Good housewives soused and salted,
besides, many kinds of fish and game; for there were
no good means of keeping meat fresh in mild weather
long after it had been killed.

Rice went northward, as well as abroad, from South
Carolina. Wheat in America was widely cultivated;
and New England imported most of her ground flour
from Maryland or Philadelphia, her own soil being
given largely to grazing or the other grains. Rye
grew better than wheat when our colonies were first
settled, and Indian corn better still. Indian corn, in-

deed, should rank in history as the great indigenous
cereal of America, which red aborigines cultivated before the landing of the white man, and prepared intelligently for their own simple food. Its abundance
and variety of wholesome nutriment saved our Pil-
grim fathers from starvation during their first intense
tribulation, and instilled into the British-born, under
Indian precept, new tastes and theories in cooking.
At the foot of the old Senate staircase, in our capitol
building at Washington, as first constructed, may be
seen columns patterned upon stalks of the Indian corn;
and surely no emblem more unique or appropriate
could be designed for a temple of this new world's
development.

Indian corn (or maize) and potatoes, let us bear in
mind, are the two great indigenous food products
which the soil of this new continent gave first to civilized Europe; and when one speaks of Irish potatoes,
he should recall that Ireland first gained that essential
plant from Virginia. Beans, once more, typical of
mental culture and nourishment from the days of
Socrates and old Athens, were Boston's peculiar gift
from the uncultured savage; for they were baked by
the Indians three centuries ago, in earthen pots, just
as we bake them to-day.

Settlers in all these British provinces raised kitchen
vegetables largely for their private tables; and they
planted their own orchards, too, which blossomed and
bore fruit in abundance—the cheery apple, chief of
them all in juicy adaptiveness for the sons and daughters of Adam, and still consumed by the people more
than any other fruit. Berries and grapes grew wild
here before our colonists transplanted them for garden
cultivation. An asparagus bed yielded in those times

the first table delicacy of the season among native vegetables; and sweet corn came last—not with tomatoes, however, as nowadays, for, as yet, the tomato was commonly thought poisonous.

Nutmegs, cinnamon, pepper, and the other spices still favored were thus early in use, though much of the grinding of them, as well as of coffee, was done at home; salt in America was largely an imported article, from Lisbon or Liverpool, or from one of the British Bahamas, known as Turk's Island. Molasses, brown sugar, and London refined sugar were used for sweetening, while a sugar loaf was cut by shears into lumps for company occasions. Lemons and China oranges were imported as an ingredient for punch. For this was a tippling age among men, and of America's early settlers of the sterner sex it used to be said, that they drank water only when they could get nothing else. Sobriety, to be sure, was favored by the religious and those of strong principle. But total abstinence men seldom preached, either here or abroad.

Excessive liquor-drinking was, in truth, America's great social vice, until far down into the nineteenth century, when temperance crusades first began. A rude climate, hard labor and exposure, with but little light recreation, increased the indulgence among our common people; while convivial habits, after the coarse fashion of the mother country, might debauch the upper circles. Idleness and ease gave to one class occasion for using stimulants; while another drank to relieve thirst or to vary the tedium of life. The sale of liquors was licensed in our several provinces, so as to produce a revenue; and one seldom saw a respected city merchant or a country grocer, who did not make liquors of one sort or another a very important part of his stock in trade, as well as an inducement for individual customers to purchase. Bakers and apothecaries retailed ardent spirits. Distilleries, too, were quite a respectable industry. Stern Samuel Adams at one time ran such an establishment next his Boston dwelling-house, though he did not succeed well in the business; and scores of such factories were maintained near the chief seats of commerce.

Our native gentry, when they took wine, preferred Maderia, Oporto or Malaga, to French wines, true to English prejudices; London ale and porter were imported, with brandy, gin (or "Geneva"), and wine bitters besides. Philadelphians brewed hop beer; ginger was worked up into pop or other compounds, but America's great alcoholic beverage was the New England or Jamaica rum, distilled from molasses. Even cider—that delicious crush from a prime orchard product—could not stand on its own more innocent merit, but brandy was vaunted as its fit preservative.

Rum was widely commended for medicinal use— as a summer corrective after drinking too much cold water, or as an ingredient with nauseous physic, in treating the bloody purge. Rum punch was in choice esteem, flavored with shrub, lemon, or orange juice; and so was grog, or plain rum and water; a mixture known as toddy when sugar was added to it. Often and often does the report of a fatal accident in those days indicate that the injurer or his victim was drunk, or that one who rode alone, half-mellow, fell into the snares of the vicious, to be robbed or murdered.[1]

[1] In rural towns of New York, so Chastellux tells us, somewhat later, much intoxication prevailed on New Year's Day; and

Punch was dealt from the flowing bowl at weddings, funerals, college commencements, and on public occasions generally; at elections, too, where, in Virginia, candidates of the gentry were expected to spend money, not to bribe but to "treat" their constituents. Travellers by stagecoach freshened the nip together when dismounting at the change of horses to stretch their legs, and the egg flip, heated by the plunge of the red-hot loggerhead or poker, was a favorite mixture for cold weather. Liquors were kept on the side-table of many a stately mansion for guests and callers. They were served at auctions to make bidders fast and furious in their competition.[1]

Hard drinking prevailed among our colonial gentry, much as in the mother country; and in the bibulous feasting after a hard day's sport, men of fashion thought it good fun to get friends into that state of booziness where they would slide under the table and fall asleep. Most convivial songs of the day induced the whole company to drink repeated bumpers. Formal toasts with the clinking of glasses were the common accompaniment of a public dinner; while the custom of drinking healths even at private meals caused many

boisterous youths made midnight rounds, as the old year expired, with uproar and the firing of pistols, calling at each tavern to get the guests who were abed to send money downstairs and treat them to a drink.

[1]A Boston gazette of 1771 recites eighty English phrases then current in the vernacular to denote a good fellow who is more or less under alcoholic influence. While Dutch colonists liked beer, most of British stock preferred the distilled liquors. We see Philadelphia Quakers complaining in the press of the too frequent drams then habitual, and of early temptation in giving young children a taste from the tumbler or letting them get at the sugar leavings of their elders. In the New York *Prices Current* of 1770 the price of rum is quoted next after bread.

to drink imprudently, lest personal offence should be given. That fashion seemed all the more absurd, when people sat at long, cornered tables instead of round ones, and hence could not well see the fellow-guest who saluted. At decorous dinner parties, such as Washington himself gave when commander-in-chief or President, there was often more of ceremony than compliment in such interruption of the meal; and strangers seated far apart would mournfully fill glasses and drink in unison, unable to exchange a word with one another.

Tobacco and snuff were in this era a common stimulant or sedative, according to the temperament of the taker. Tobacco was not seldom a portable standard, at the south, as a substitute for money—just as it became there during our Civil War; and we read that, in 1723, Maryland imposed fines payable in tobacco, for selling strong liquors or brandy. The clergy of Virginia were long paid their salaries in this convenient commodity. Tobacco in a pipe, or smoking, was a great solace; but our people chewed tobacco besides, while cigars came in a later era. For a long time, Virginia tobacco was imported to England, to be made up there and reimported for colonial consumption; but Philadelphia makers offered their "Kite-foot tobacco" and snuff, by 1772, as equal to any imported. Tobacco was one of the red man's chief indigenous plants, raised for the old world's renovation—to some a detestable weed, to others the herb of supreme pleasure.

Americans inherited largely the British tastes and appetite,—with abundance of meat and hearty dishes plainly cooked; but they ate too fast, and the hot bread and biscuits of which they partook brought on dyspepsia. In a somewhat later era, when Jefferson brought back from Paris, after serving there as minister, a fastidious taste for French wines and cookery, Patrick Henry denounced him on the stump in a political canvass, as a recreant to roast beef, and one who "abjured his native victuals." One of Poor Richard's maxims reflects upon the uncurbed native appetites of this earlier age: "I saw," he says, "a few die of starvation, but hundreds of eating and drinking." Sermons were published and discourses printed in colonial almanacs on such excesses. But our people were hard workers, commonly in a hurry to get through the meal hour, intent upon the cares and routine of life, and little given to table relaxation.

There were, of course, the lighter beverages, such as tea, coffee and chocolate, of which the two sexes partook together, or women apart. Bohea came much into use among the fair sex, by way of stimulant; though nervous disorders, it was claimed, increased in consequence. Taxed tea, we all know, was emptied overboard; and in those throbbing years when families denied themselves of spring lamb for the sake of encouraging wool breeding, and when seniors at Harvard unanimously resolved to wear home-made broadcloth on the day of graduation, the women of America were not behind in noble self-denial. In place of the Chinese decoction, a native berry substitute called "Labrador tea" came widely into use about 1768— "that naseous weed," one writes of it; and the spinning-wheel was put to rapid revolution. Spinning-wheel parties were given by New England "daughters of liberty," who would rival one another in turning out so many skeins of yarn in an hour. The product of parish contests of this kind, in labor and materials, was usually bestowed upon the pastor; and when Labrador tea was served up at the parsonage afterwards, with other refreshments, the young men came upon the scene to praise the busy virgins and close the occasion in singing liberty songs. While the pleasurable excitement was on, women dressed in homespun when visiting, even to handkerchiefs and gloves. "Save your money and you save your country," was the maxim of the day. But by 1772, the spinning fad had subsided, and ladies of the higher circle went back to Bohea and their London fineries. History shows that the non-importation league worked hard for our luxurious consumers of British goods, who at heart were fond as ever of them; and that the middle provinces, New York in particular, broke down badly under so strenuous a test, causing an abandonment for the time of home-made wearing apparel, and of home-made substitutes for the Chinese beverage.

Franklin sent home to Philadelphia, in 1758, some breakfast cloths, which he picked up in London, where nobody (as he found) breakfasted upon the "naked table;" also some carpeting for the guest-room floor, and some printed calicoes (a new invention) to make bed and window curtains; and he looked up, besides, for his daughter Sally a London harpsichord. Some China bowls and coffee cups he bought, in addition, and their interesting little figures he wished his wife to look at with her spectacles, for they would well bear examining. As he travelled about in the course of his long mission as colonial agent, he could not forbear making comparisons between resident Britons and the people of his own land in point of average comfort. While the spinners and weavers of England, as he noted, wore rags that they might make cloths and stuffs for all parts of the world—while in Scotland men went barefoot to export their shoes and stockings —while in Ireland the peasantry lived all the year round on potatoes and buttermilk, shirtless, so as to send to other countries beef, butter, and linen—America was well clad and well fed. In England, civil society depressed multitudes to the savage plane that a few might be raised in rank and fortune. On the other hand, "every man in New England is a freeholder, has a voice in public affairs, lives in a tidy, warm house, has plenty of good food and fuel, with whole clothes from head to foot, the manufacture perhaps of his own family."[1]

[1] 4 B. F., 440 (1772).

IX

Wrote ITH the rich and luxurious of a community work consists in devising means of amusement; while scholars and brain workers seek a vacation wherein the mind may relax its energies. But toilers with the hands—the great mass of humanity—find most of their real recreation in life by turning its needful work into pleasure; and going through the vale of misery or dulness, they use its pools for wells of water. Farmers have their husking or logging bees, their barn-raisings, their harvest homes, and Nature herself relieves the monotony of an agricultural life by the varying tasks of the seasons. The mind need never be wholly torpid in a new country.

To social recreations and amusements in the colonial period our common people did not strongly incline. On the whole, they were soberly set; they worked hard for a living, and when not working they stayed at home and found ease with their friends and families. To most of our native born, withal, the local horizon of life was not ample; and from one's dwelling house as a central point, a radius of twenty miles might have described the whole circumference, in those days, of average observation. When Americans of that century went out to see the world they travelled by horse and carriage, and such meagre vacations as they might allow themselves were passed not far from home. Sunday

recurred one day in seven, and on rare occasion came
a secular holiday besides. There was, of course, no
pleasure travel on the Sabbath, but a sort of surprise
party for a weekday was made up by harnessing the
family carryall and making an unexpected descent, with
young and old, for a dinner and a day's outing at some
of the folks, resident ten or fifteen miles away; for a
corresponding absence from home or preoccupation was
never to be presumed. Long rides at all times gave
opportunity for breaking the journey and dropping in
upon friends unawares, that a call might haply merge
into the acceptance of an ampler hospitality. Surprise
parties made thus a pleasurable excitement on either
side, to which any household was liable.

All this, of course, involved making one's self at
home, and the character of the entertainment was meant
to be homelike, though putting the good housewife to
her best. Americans of this age, as a whole, were
neither vivacious nor given to the lighter dissipations
of life. Chastellux, whom I so often quote, could not,
as a lively Frenchman, get great enjoyment, even from
those of rank and fortune whom he visited here. In
bad winter weather, as he relates, when snow and stress
kept our country gentlemen in doors, the hearty eating
and drinking went on earnestly enough; the men enjoyed some good conversation among themselves while
the women were absent. But not a word would he hear
of light games with playing cards while thus confined to the house; and as to music, drawing or reading aloud, he found very little.

It must not be supposed, however, that table games
indoors were unknown here thus early, or that the fair

sex took no part in them. Among those strict in religious tenets playing cards were widely denounced as frivolous and a device of Satan; yet packs were certainly imported into America to a considerable extent before our Revolution, and in genteel society many of the lighter games were indulged in by both sexes. Among Philadelphia's upper ten one might at parties play promiscuously, though "commerce" was the only game of which the proper approved. It was in Boston, as late as 1782, that Chastellux played his first game of whist after coming to America; and there, by the way, he observed that social leaders were much disposed to cultivate foreigners of distinction who brought from abroad good letters of introduction. For a well-bred tête-à-tête in our higher circles, chess, checkers or backgammon might serve to beguile the long winter evenings.

While the Continental Congress sat at Philadelphia, in Revolutionary times, that city became the centre of social gayety for all America, despite its sedate atmosphere; and thither flocked a motley and mutable society, which comprised not only statesmen and civilians from all the thirteen States or colonies, but military officers, besides, of the Continental Army, and French compatriots on war and pleasure bent. During the winter months of those years a subscription ball or assembly was given, with dances and partners arranged by billet and signature; whereby, as French beaux complained, men and women bound themselves as by precontract for an entire evening. Neither waltz nor polka appeared on the list in those days; but programme dances, such as they were, bore such names as "Burgoyne's surrender," "the Campaign success" or "Clinton's retreat." Distinguished patriots and their wives figured on the list of managers, and the affair came off, after the London fashion, at some public hall. About midnight, dancing was suspended for a supper, after which the ball went on until two in the morning, the final time for dispersing.

The select dancing assembly had been something of a social function among the colonial gentry at our chief provincial capitals long before the Revolution; and Jefferson, one of those Virginia youths who were fond of dancing, used to recall with delight winter balls at the Raleigh tavern in Williamsburg, which he used to attend while a college student at William and Mary's. As far back as 1765 and the Stamp Act we read of a ball given at Boston, in which the British army and navy officers were prominent—a brilliant social affair. In 1774 Virginia's tide-water gentry honored by a public dance the anniversary of St. Tammany, and the ball was opened by men dressed in Indian costume. But from all such gatherings mechanics and the tradespeople were excluded, for social lines were carefully drawn, as in England.

Dancing schools were set up already in Philadelphia, Boston, New York and other large colonial towns, and the agile dancing-master invaded at intervals the more quiet communities, to instruct people in the graces of fashion. Many such instructors were French immigrants, versatile in the polite accomplishments. It was not uncommon for one to teach French or music besides, to give lessons in fencing with the small sword or in playing upon the violin or guitar. The sprightly foreigner might be seen mincing the steps with violin or bow in hand, and showing our sexes apart how to behave in fine company. A dancing-master from Paris was the French instructor at Harvard College. French women, too, helped fill the conjugal purse in such pursuits; and one fencing-master's wife, fresh from Paris, advertised to take in fine washing, starched lawns, muslins and laces, and proffered, moreover, to teach young ladies either the French tongue or elegant embroidery.

"Concert hall" was the usual name of the building at our American centres where dances or musical performances came off. For besides subscription balls were subscription concerts for people of means and fashion. A series, vocal and instrumental, would be announced in Boston, New York or Philadelphia, lasting perhaps for six or eight weeks, with one concert a week, and drawing "a very polite company." Such evening amusements came off rather early, 6.30 being a favorite hour. Gentlemen or their liveried servants purchased for both sexes; and as these concerts were select affairs, one who inclined to subscribe could learn the terms by applying at the hall, all season tickets being sent to the several subscribers. The usual price of tickets for a single concert was half a dollar. Airs and duets were sung, and some skilful solo vocalist or performer upon the violin, French horn, hautboy or harpsichord gave special zest to the programme. Occasionally a chorus or two was added from some standard composition. Sometimes a royal regimental band would aid the performance, especially if the occasion were a public one. Handel was decidedly the favorite composer, as programmes were then made up, and selections were given from his "Acis and Galatea," or his Coronation anthem, or finally from the "Messiah."

Many of the occasional concerts of those times were

benefit concerts, in fact, for some local organist or music teacher, who arranged and conducted the performance for his own emolument.[1]   At a Boston concert of 1771, Mr. Propert between the acts performed some select pieces on the guitar and "forte-piano"— the latter instrument quite a novelty then in these colonies, and named with the compound words in that order.   Sometimes, where the audience was select and composed of subscribers, the hall was cleared at the end of a concert and the young and frolicsome remained for a dance.   On rare occasion the full concert programme was published by the press;[2] but it was not in good form to announce publicly the names of the performers, since most of them were amateurs who moved in good society.

Then, as in all eras of mankind when polished people gathered as an audience, were to be seen the elderly and sedate, who came to be edified by the performance, and the young and giddy, whose chief enjoyment was in one another.   Bostonians were always wont to carry their complaints to the press; and an anonymous citizen of the former description is seen airing his grievances in the local newspaper in a tone of well-bred sarcasm. "Should not these young lovers," he inquires, "either

[1] See in Boston, 1772-73, the eager rivalry in this respect between two church organists of that day, Propert and Selby, as recorded by the local press.

[2] The programme of a benefit concert given in 1771 by a British regimental band may be worth quoting here.   Act 1st comprised Handel's overture to Ptolemy; a song, "From the East Breaks the Morn;" a concerto by Stanley and a symphony by Bach. Act 2d began with a duet, "Turn, Fair Clora," followed by an organ concerto and a symphony by Stamily.   For Act 3d came an overture by Abel, a duet, "When Phœbus the Tops of the Hills," a violin solo, a new hunting song, and a symphony by Ricci.

sit quiet and languish while the music goes on, or, if wishing to give a vocal accompaniment, mount the stage? Would not the thoughtless young lady with greater propriety defer her animadversions upon fiddlers, mantuamakers, milliners, high-frizzed heads and sword knots, until she retires home to supper with her friends? Might not the two sexes, when under the irresistible impulse to converse, content themselves, while a piece is being performed, with the usual eloquence of the eyes, assisted by certain languishing attitudes of the body and half a dozen melting sighs?"

Music, "heavenly maid," gave the motive for many a social gathering in our private colonial houses, each guest who could play or sing tolerably bearing part in the general entertainment. One young lady would play the spinet or harpsichord, another sing with a harp accompaniment. In the less serious efforts there were pretty love songs, some of them quite sentimental. The manly vocalist went hunting, roamed the sea as pirate, did deeds of imaginary prowess, or even in mixed company avowed himself an unrestrained votary of Bacchus. Church music, with anthems, plain psalmody or fugue-like phrasing, was often heard in the houses, and adjusting one's voice to the four-part meander of harmony through hymns of many verses, friends made a Sabbath evening happy when the tuneful of both sexes came together. Americans in a cultured or uncultured way were fond of music, and the rural singing-school was a memorable delight. Young men and women made harmony together of bass, treble, alto and tenor in the rural choir loft Sundays, looking down upon the congregation below, who turned during the last hymn to face them.

Other entertainments were recognized in those days as worthy of the people's patronage. Lectures were advertised at our larger towns with philosophical experiments "for the entertainment of the curious." Such exhibitors pursued Franklin's tests with electricity, or produced suction by the air pump, or showed how iron could be heated in cold water. While the King's accredited agent was negotiating with the Indian tribes, a Seneca chief, taken by his white entertainers to one of these shows at Philadelphia, was strongly impressed by the artificial thunder and lightning of the lecturer's creation. Other courses were given in 1772 in our Quaker city upon "pleasant and useful geography," where the figure and motion of the earth were explained, with the moon's phases as affecting wind and tide. One favorite lecturer in these colonies, less serious, made "Heads" his subject in a so-called "moral and satirical" exhibition. Wigs and ladies' headdresses he would put on or off in turn, with grimace and mimicry appropriate to each wearer; songs were interspersed, and the performance usually wound up with some comic or dramatic recitation. Nor even thus early was the roving magician of two hemispheres wanting, who had had the honor of appearing before sundry crowned monarchs of Europe, at their palaces, and yet was not too proud to perform privately in any plain citizen's house for a special remuneration.[1]

[1] One of these "masters of sleight of hand and magic," who exhibited his "surpassing performances" at a shilling a head, thus epitomizes his feats in the *Pennsylvania Chronicle* of 1769: (1) He produced fruit on a table as natural as though grown on trees. (2) He showed an infallible method of curing all scolding wives. (3) He devoured iron and steel as ladies would eat a bit of bread and butter, and washed down the food with liquor which streamed from several parts of his body, "to the

The ingenious Mrs. Wright was another caterer to public recreation in those days. Wonderful imitations of nature were comprised in her wax-work collection; and various personages of distinction in the Old and New World had condescended to sit to her for their "effigies" while she was abroad, his Majesty himself among the number. Dr. Franklin, Garrick, the actor, and Mrs. Catherine McCauley, "the celebrated female historian,"[1] were among the life-like specimens to be seen in her show; while imaginary figures presented Cain's murder of Abel and the treachery of Delilah to Samson.[2]

Feats of horsemanship were displayed on pleasant afternoons for several weeks during the autumn of 1773, at the bottom of the mall in Boston Common, by a Mr. Bates, another protégé of the sovereigns of Europe, who condescended to a tour of these colonies. He would mount and manage one, two or three horses, and his performance ended with an equestrian burlesque entitled "The Tailor Riding to Brentford." Seats were arranged secure from danger at his exhibitions,

amaze of the spectators." (4) He dissolved silver and other metal without the help of fire. (5) He showed how a Prussian spy vanished in the French camp and then reappeared in Prussia with his report. Besides all this, he performed various tricks with eggs, money and cards; he showed the shape and form of the person designed for one's future spark or mistress, and foretold what lady in the audience would be first married; "with fifty or more other imposing things too tedious to be inserted."

[1]This learned lady, whose name anticipates the greater historian of the next century, presented in 1772 a set of her works, in six volumes, to the Redwood Library of Newport.

[2]While these wax-works were in New York City for exhibition, children at their careless play set her house on fire, and, most unfortunately, the whole collection perished, with the exception of Whitefield and John Dickinson, both of whose figures were rescued from the flames.

but the spectator was kindly requested to bring no dogs with him. It appears that this new courtier of the public attempted the exorbitant price of a dollar for the best seats at his performance; but jealous opinion compelled him to lower his rates. For in an angry pamphlet which came out in Boston, styled "Bates Weighed in the Balance," it was proven that his exhibitions at such a price were impoverishing, disgraceful to human nature and a downright breach of the Eighth Commandment.

Exhibitions in those early days involved, we may infer, no such lavish outlay as is now customary; and claims upon the public were put forward tentatively and with much deference. A maiden dwarf, fifty-three years old and only 22 inches high, who had come to pay a visit in America "at the advice of some gentlemen," offered to exhibit herself as a show to such ladies and gentlemen as were desirous of gratifying their curiosity, at a shilling, lawful money, for each person. But the mountebank drew to his free show a gaping and impecunious crowd; and in 1771 a fearful catastrophe was nearly the result of such a gathering near New York City. An imposingly dressed quack doctor, who sold his nostrums from a movable stage in Brooklyn and diverted bystanders with his harangues, aided by the tricks of a merry andrew, drew hundreds across the East River daily. Once at sunset, when the day's business was over, a crowd of returning spectators swarmed upon the Brooklyn ferryboat to return, 110 of them in all. The overcrowded vessel struck a rock, and the loss of life would have been immense had not those in danger been rescued at the last moment by other boats, which struck out boldly from the shore to save them. The New York press sermonized upon the lasting impression to be made by this incident upon all concerned—first by the imminent prospect of immediate death, and next by so Providential a deliverance.

But theatricals in that age fared hard in most provinces, so strongly was the prejudice of our people set against them, whatever might be said for other public amusements. Virginia and her rulers, however, showed much tolerance in that respect; and the first dramatic performance ever given on our American mainland by a regular company of actors, sheltered in a suitable auditorium, was seen at Williamsburg, the capital of that province, on the 5th of September, 1752. Shakespeare most fitly introduced the British drama to our new world; and the curtain rose to his "Merchant of Venice," a farce entitled "Lethe" closing the performance. It was Lewis Hallam who organized these players under the style of the "American Company;" they were brought over from London in May, and performed in Annapolis and the Maryland colony, so some assert, as early as July, and, hence, previous to the Williamsburg performance.[1] But the theatre at Williamsburg, fitted up and opened by direct permission from Governor Dinwiddie, had the full equipment of pit, box, gallery and stage.   Both Maryland and Virginia gave encouragement to Hallam's company in those years, and furnished good audiences at Annapolis and Williamsburg until the Revolution broke out, when amusements in the colonies were mostly prohibited by local law, and the company sailed for the British West Indies, having meanwhile performed occasionally in Charles-

[1] See Scharf's Baltimore.

ton, South Carolina, and in the great middle provinces.

Garrick led in the British theatricals of that era, and here, as in London, his taste and style as actor and purveyor for the stage predominated. Players alternated between the grave and gay; "The Beggar's Opera" was the favorite among comic musical dramas, and an evening performance which began with solemn tragedy would close with a roaring farce. This "American Company" was heralded as from London; and affection or disaffection toward the mother country had much to do with determining the public attitude toward it. Provincial governors gave generally a readier license than the local legislatures, and citizens of the court and Tory party favored the drama under such auspices, while the rebellious Whigs opposed it.

In New York City a regular theatre was opened in 1761, under the patronage of Governor Delancy, whom the Assembly and its Presbyterian leaders violently opposed on that issue, claiming that all theatricals tended to debauch the public morals. There, in May, 1766, while distress extensively prevailed, religious opposition pleaded specially the temptation to which the poor were exposed at such a time to squander their money foolishly. The wrath of the inhabitants was accordingly kindled. A mob broke through the doors of the little theatre with noise and tumult just as the drama began; the play was interrupted, and actor and audience—those before and those behind the footlights—fled for their lives. Some were dangerously hurt; the theatre, no solid structure, was quickly demolished, and a bonfire was made of the remnants.[1] Yet reaction came; and a few years later New Yorkers

[1] M. G., 1766.

enjoyed the play phlegmatically at a new theatre on John Street. There, the American Company, by permission of his Excellency the Governor, opened in April, 1772, with comedy and farce, continuing its season for six weeks. Milton's "Comus," one of the plays, gave scope for fairy scenes, transparencies and a rude sort of ballet; while another play of less lofty poetic merit concluded with a country dance by all the characters. The band of his Majesty's regiment of royal Welsh fusileers was detailed at these performances by way of orchestra. The doors opened at 5.30 in the afternoon, and the performance began an hour later.

Both in New York and Philadelphia performances in those days were commonly set for once or twice in the week. At Philadelphia by 1772 we see a new American theatre in the suburb of Southwark, where performances went on "by authority," as the play bill announced. Sometimes the programme was "Romeo and Juliet," followed by the "Old Maid;" sometimes the comic opera "Love in a Village" was afterpiece to the "Mourning Bride." A new play which had quite a good run was styled "The Shipwreck of the Brothers," and the local press vouched for the sentiments of this highly attractive drama as "of the utmost propriety." The doors of this theatre were opened at 4 and the play began at 6 o'clock sharp. Places in the boxes might be reserved by ladies and gentlemen who sent their servants at the former hour. Tickets, "without which no persons could be admitted," were sold at the bar of the coffee house. The boxes were priced at 7s. 6d.; the pit at 5s.; the gallery at 3s. Malicious rogues broke into the gallery one day and carried off the iron spikes which divided the gallery seats from the

upper boxes; a reward was offered for their apprehension.[1]

Elocution, or the so-called "lecture," was a substitute, or rather subterfuge, for the play in some American centres, while laws or the local magistrates placed
theatricals under the ban. Thus in 1769, at Philadelphia, began a series of readings, which soon merged
into the recitation of a play or of a whole opera, such
as "Love in a Village," with all the music and parts. So,
too, in Boston, that same year, at a large room in
Brattle Street, were sung all the songs and personated
all the characters of the popular "Beggar's Opera;" an
experienced actor and singer proposing in his printed
card "to enter into the different humors or passions as
they change throughout." In this Puritan town raged
through the following year a tempest of controversy
between the strait-laced and the scoffers. One pamphlet in which a polemic divine arraigned the stage as
"the highroad to hell" called forth a response, dated
from London, applying a like epithet to the pulpits.
Such blasphemy boded little good to the cause of the
drama. The laws of the Massachusetts province still
sternly forbade play-acting, and Boston's selectmen
suppressed theatricals with a firm hand.

[1]This Southwark theatre, the only one in or about Philadelphia
until after our Revolution, appears to have been first erected in
1766 to accommodate the Hallam Company, which played after
1759 in that city to fairly good houses. But theatricals in Philadelphia had fared hardly at first. According to Mr. Watson,
the "Tragedy of Cato" was enacted there as early as 1749. The
Quakers expressed their disgust, and the magistrates drove the
players from the city. In 1754, once more, under a permission
carefully restricted in terms, theatrical performances were resumed at Philadelphia, while those opposed to the stage sent
broadcast their pamphlets of denunciation.—*Watson's Philadelphia.*

In vain did our Royalists contend that an act of Parliament had the effect of superseding a provincial prohibition so as to make dramatic entertainments lawful in fact throughout all America. The trend of native politics certainly was not to sustain a constitutional theory of that color; and the more theatricals appealed to the public as a political issue, upheld with the Tory cause, the more intense became the hostility of patriots. During the bloody strife of independence, British officers, while in forcible control of Boston, New York or Philadelphia, might give scope to dramatic performances; but as a rule, in all these thirteen colonies the Revolutionary War swept plays and play-actors aside, with all other frivolous amusements, and their reinstatement was at least postponed to a new era of independence and union.

Besides the indoor recreations I have described were many borrowed or adapted from the mother country, both romping and sedate. Blind man's buff—or perhaps "still palm," its less boisterous substitute—befitted a rustic frolic; and so, still better, those various games which mate off partners—girls and fellows—to the amusing confusion of the bashful. Forfeits in the games of both sexes together induced kissing and other familiarities; while bundling, the coarsest of all promiscuous frolics of the embracing sort, seems to have been known in the middle provinces and New England, if not brought over from the mother country. In dances, however, the sexes maintained their distance better than in modern times.

From Strutt and other English writers of that day we gain insight into the out-of-door sports and pastimes

of the people of Merry England, and these came naturally enough to our English colonies also. Cricket
was never popular in this country; it was a slow game,
and required, besides a holiday, some costly preparation
on chosen grounds. But games rapidly played, easily
improvised on any open lot, and inexpensive to arrange,
such as football, marbles, kite-flying, baseball and
hockey, were much in favor here. In climbing, jump-
ing, leaping and wrestling, amateurs measured themselves against one another. Bowling, too, and pitching
quoits found their votaries. But the gymnasium had
scarce an existence, for people trained their muscles
over daily tasks which yielded something in return.
During our cold northern winters, the steel-shod
skater skimmed the frozen pond or river; while swimming in the summer time was a pastime everywhere to
which nature freely invited. So good a swimmer was
Franklin in his youth as to astonish even Englishmen
by his feats in the Thames while serving his brief
apprenticeship abroad; and in fact he nearly
missed the high destiny in store for him in the land
of his birth, for he once thought of becoming a London athlete and opening in that city a swimming
school.

They who kept a horse and carriage were not at a
loss for riding parties in summer or winter; nor for
going sparking with a single sleigh or sulky. Punch
or a mug of flip warmed the inner extremities when
the merry sleighers alighted at some country tavern,
perchance to tread a measure on its polished parlor floor
before betaking themselves once more to the buffalo
robes and jangle of bells on the homeward trip, while
the stars twinkled in the dark canopy overhead. Of
summer recreations, chiefly among the leisure set or

those who found a holiday, tradition preserves a record. New Yorkers made excursions up the Hudson or East River to enjoy a turtle or fishing frolic, or took a day's picnic in the woods together. Rhode Islanders had even thus early their clambake or chowder parties. Thirty or forty ladies and gentlemen would drive a few miles out of town to meet and dine, amuse themselves among nature's surroundings, and return in their chaises suitably paired. We see foreign caterers contending for patronage of this character.[1]

An exhibition of fireworks gave emphasis already to a public or private celebration. From China we derive the pyrotechnic art, in adapting a deadly explosive for harmless sport and display, which nations more civilized employ rather for the destruction of their fellowmen. Our ancestors here could use gunpowder for serious effect, as the course of that century showed; the wild beast, the savage, the redcoat, dropped before their steady aim; but beyond flashing off the black grains or firing a salute, they seldom wasted those destroying compounds upon mere effect. London, however, sent over its pyrotechnist to minister to colonial allegiance and enhance the pomp of royal birthdays. Thus in 1772, on an occasion when Philadelphia's State House was to be illuminated and a grand concert given "by permission," the day's celebration was arranged to conclude with "a superb firework, such as the performers

---

[1] In the suburbs of Philadelphia, a Frenchman opened a place called "Labanon," and offered to his patrons of the two sexes choice tea, coffee, bottled mead, cakes, fruits and comfits. He praised his place as well adapted to those who came to visit the bettering place or hospital near by; and none, he assured his patrons, would be admitted on his premises but orderly, genteel and reputable people.

humbly suppose has never before been seen in America."
The tickets for concert or fireworks were to be sold
separately. *"Vivant rex et regina"* was the loyal
ejaculation with which the advertisement of this exhibition ended.

X

OUR Revolutionary ancestors were surely no great readers of books or newspapers. To the great majority among them came the necessity of daily toil, while idlers devoted their chief time to their families or to out-of-door life and social pleasure. Our people seldom wore spectacles before they had passed their prime; their eyesight was well preserved, and they learned to master what befitted the immediate pursuit in life and little more. An appetite for reading and self-improvement was here and there strong among the lowly born; the comparatively few bred to leisure might add literary culture to their other accomplishments; but this was an age for developing rather the rudiments of civilization on a new soil and under new conditions, leaving the ripe fruitage to posterity.

Yet books had here their friends, and a moderate amount of reading might be mastered from year to year. Circulating libraries—well-assorted volumes which neighbors might pass from hand to hand—scarcely existed thus early in rural towns. The resident clergy or gentry might make themselves local benefactors by lending from their fairly stocked shelves; and since the homes of our yeomanry had each its little cupboard pile of books, which gained accessions from time to time, like other family furniture, one's thirst for reading

went not wholly unquenched. And a fact now quite
noticeable was the healthiness of our individual culture—the vigorous digestive power that enabled the
mind of this pioneer generation to stomach and assimilate the dull and didactic in huge quantities, like their
copious draughts of medicine. We read of learned men
in these thirteen colonies; of apt classical scholars in
Greek and Latin, especially among the clergy; but in
modern belles-lettres the mental acquisition was not
great, while the lighter mental range was neglected.
Life was serious in these colonies. Reading and culture sought immediate utility, the plodding needs of a
present existence, or the pious concerns of the soul for
a better life to come.

Except for the rare newspaper or rarer magazine,
the indigenous almanac, so indispensable, and occasional sermons or political addresses of immediate interest in pamphlet form, most reading matter for our
colonists was shipped direct from London like other
British manufactures. From the announcements of
American booksellers like Henry Knox of Boston—a
militia magnate soon to become famous in the Revolutionary fight and still later as Washington's first Secretary of War—or like John Mein, his Tory predecessor
in the trade, who got hooted out of town for his politics,
we see that at our so-called "London bookstore" were
to be had imported books in divinity, history, law,
physic and surgery, with "sea books" besides, and
school books and Bibles of every variety. Ledgers,
account books and all sorts of stationery were sold at
these stores besides.

The choice books of 1772-75, as listed, were Jonathan Edwards's Sermons, Witherspoon on the Gospels, Whitefield's Letters, "Domestic Medicine or the Family Physician," dissertations on the gout, essays on comets, treatises on the keeping of bees, Bishop Burnet's History, Pope's "Essay on Man," Dr. Priestley's "Experimental Philosophy," Dean Swift, and Clarendon's "History of the English Rebellion." The patron with plethoric purse invested, not in fiction or humor so much as in Duhamel's Husbandry, Bailey's or Johnson's Standard Dictionary, or the Dictionary of Arts and Sciences; he chose from among the various handy compends of the day in mathematics, grammar, classics and geography.[1]

A book in great demand among the women was "The Frugal Housewife and Complete Woman Cook," a London importation of 1772. Watts's psalms and hymns sold largely in America, as also did psalters and books of psalmody, spelling books and primers. Perennial among the last—in Eastern households at least— was the famous "New England Primer," a native product, whose Scriptural doggerel upon the alphabet is perhaps at this day the best remembered poetry of colonial times.

Our common folk in those days were deeply concerned in religious problems. The great revival had swept the land not long before. A keen zest for theological disputation and polemic pamphlets prevailed,

---

[1] How useful to the young were some of these little compends—not all of them imported—Washington's example reminds us; for the "Young Man's Companion," his *vade mecum* of early years, not only taught him writing, the drafting of deeds and the rudiments of his surveyor's profession, but instilled, besides, those precepts of good behavior which he transcribed for the regulation of his conduct in life.—*P. L. Ford's "True George Washington."*

and sermons of the native clergy seem to have paid for the printing, and were read as well as listened to. The parade of some Scriptural text or Latin quotation upon its title-page gave piquancy to the contents of such a production. One clergyman announces "Sermons upon doctrinal subjects with practical improvements;" another "Sermons to the unregenerated;" a third records "A surprising instance of Divine Grace in the conversion of a revenue officer." Among pamphlets well advertised were "Heaven upon Earth," "A Penitential Crisis," "Considerations Against Visiting on the Sabbath," "The Whole Duty of Women," "The Religious Education of Daughters," "Serial Sermons for the Days of the Week," and twin discourses, one preached before and one after a noted execution. Controversial tracts on theology increased during the last years of our colonial era. Popery was freely assailed by our Protestant settlers as a foe who could not strike back; and over the issue of establishing an English Episcopacy in America arose a more equal discussion. "Palæmon's Creed Examined" was a Boston pamphlet in 1765, which maintained "the Protestant doctrines of covenant of works, covenant of grace and justification." Over the book counter were sold special expositions of 2 Corinthians, chapter 3, and of "the rational explication of St. John's vision of the two beasts." One favorite book of the day was "Contemplations" on four subjects—the ocean, the harvest, sickness and the last judgment. "Death Realized" was the caption of a native poem in the form of a dying soliloquy, inspired, perhaps, by the ambitious verses of Pope.

This was an age when literature, here as in the

mother country, partook considerably of the pompous and artificial in expression, like life and manners in good society. "English poetry," it has been said, "lost her eyes when Milton lost his;" nor had even the gentle Goldsmith, who preached rustic simplicity and the homely virtues, restored our Muse's vision. Pope, with his splendid diction, and a host of impecunious imitators, read Nature in her external aspects, as though from some back window in London's crowded dwellings. They guessed at landscape as garreteers who saw not. For prose dissertation, the learned Dr. Johnson had lately superadded ornament to the graces of Addison; so that the balancing of phrases and the search for the stately and sonorous harmed correspondingly the essence of sincere expression. With the growth of Oriental commerce had come, too, into passing literary vogue the pseudo-Eastern allegory, in which our concrete English mind indulged in fanciful speculation, as Cassim, Ahmed, Mirza or Abbas Carascan—a familiar personage, ill disguised with turban, robe and light slippers. The age of morbid or romantic fiction, of voracious novel reading, was for America still remote, though sentimental studies of British social life and manners were not wanting. A popular book among those imported in the era of the Stamp Act was "The Vicar of Wakefield"—"supposed," as the bookseller explained it, "to have been written by himself;" and besides Goldsmith's immortal tale, our people read to some extent Richardson's "Clarissa Harlowe" or "Sir Charles Grandison," and with reservation the more humorous but coarser novels of Fielding and Smollett. Serious and sentimental stories were preferred at all events in our colonies to those of irreverent and immoral strain, and Milton, with his sublimity of religious inspi-

ration, was a poet more acceptable to our colonists than
Shakespeare, the player.

Moralists, like the poets and writers of fiction, seem
hardly to have been separable from their creeds in religion or politics; and hence, while Burke was justly
admired as the friend of America, Johnson repelled us
by his dogmatic Toryism and his faithful devotion to
the Church of England. Among solid historians,
Josephus, Rollin, Robertson and Hume found American readers. The works of all such writers were on
sale at colonial bookstores.

Native literature could not have flourished thus early
under a colonial and dependent establishment. Yet the
American mind, whithersoever its energies had been
directed, was found ingenious, logical and acute. In
personal religion, theology, interpretation of the Bible,
the probable conditions of a future life, were grand
themes of cogitation for our ancestors while politics
were dull; and among native preachers who were shep-
herds of the people in those times, Jonathan Edwards,
whose eyes closed on the world while Wolfe was contending for Canada, stands unrivalled. Defender of the
doctrine of original sin, profound in fathoming the de-
pravity of the human heart, to him the horrors of hell
were as real as the joys of heaven, and sinners trembled
at his utterances. Other New England clergymen
there were, like the Mathers, who had earlier worked
Biblical theology into schemes of temporal government;
who, while the mother country was preoccupied in civil
war, devised the Mosaic dispensation of a commonwealth of God's own elect—Jewish as to the outside
unconverted, but with remarkable assertion of indi-

vidual liberty and equal rights among the predestinated.

And now came civil oppression by the parent government; and resistance, revolution and political destiny became in men's minds the paramount theme of discussion and meditation. The truths which underlie all human government were now explored—doctrines of civil liberty as against the divine right of kings, the individual as safeguarded from his rulers, man's inherent right of expatriation, and the possible adaptation of institutions by new dwellers upon a new soil for their own welfare as against perpetual allegiance to Europe by the accident of human birth. What abler defence of the people's cause as opposed to blind monarchy than those addresses of Boston and the Massachusetts General Court which Samuel Adams chiefly drafted? What nobler or more forcible eloquence, by patriot orators who differed in style and manner, than that of James Otis, John Adams and Patrick Henry, each of whom stirred deeply his special audience? What better or more convincing masters of the pen for lucid expression of a coming establishment for this continent than the sagacious Franklin, earliest among Americans born to stand before kings and to impress Europe by his writings and personal efforts in science, diplomacy and constructive politics? Or than Jefferson, the idealist, who addressed his sovereign as one fellow-mortal does another, and whose statement in the Declaration, of truths self-evident, has brought this Union back to first principles at more than one crisis of national peril? Of him, with that admirable measure of enthusiasm which moves without leading astray, wrote James Russell

Lowell in 1858[1]: "Jefferson was the first American
man; and I doubt if we have produced a better thinker
or writer."

But of æsthetic interpretation or of tranquil literary
themes in song or story, America had little indeed to
boast thus early. And when men rushed to mortal
strife in battle, there could be little scope for poetry,
unless lyrical in strain; nor of that was there much
worth preserving. Native literati, such as had thus
far deserved that title at all, were but imitators of their
British contemporaries for the most part. Yet, as the
late Professor Tyler has recorded, a large mass of
native literature of one sort or another was produced
here during the twenty eventful years which preceded
the peace of 1783.[2] Much of it was trite and commonplace, most of it was argumentative or dealt with simple
facts. There were travels into the wilderness, studies
of the Indians, ponderous local histories of the colonies,
among which Thomas Hutchinson's "History of Massachusetts," in two volumes, deserves, perhaps, the pre-
eminence—handicapped in fame though the author
found himself by loyalty to the King. Even in æsthetic
literature Yale and Princeton were fountains of inspiration. Princeton's bard was Philip Freneau, whose misfortune it became in later life to offend Washington, as
a political press writer. John Trumbull and Timothy
Dwight were the earliest bards of the Yale set. Trumbull, Dwight and Freneau were all American born, and
the two former were of Protestant ancestry. Trumbull's distinction was that of political satirist; and his
"McFingal," immensely popular at the outbreak of our
Revolution, was full freighted with the logic and humor

[1]Scudder's Lowell, 218.
[2]1 Moses Coit Tyler's "Literary History of America," Vol. I.,
1-6.

of this great uprising of the king's subjects. Of Freneau it should be said that if rebellious America had truly a lyrical interpreter, it was he. Though most of the poetry of our Revolution was too roughly wrought for permanency, Freneau's bears at times the stamp of real genius. Scott commended him to a later generation of Britons; while both Scott and Campbell borrowed images from his verse for their own more famous poems.

Among contemporary letter-writers and pamphleteers of this period indigenous to our soil, Washington and John Dickinson deserve mention; so, too, does Francis Hopkinson, a nimble poet and wit of the middle section, and a signer, withal, of our Declaration. Of aliens born, Hamilton impressed himself upon New York when Revolution opened. But the most famous pamphleteer of the times was Thomas Paine, who arrived from England in 1774; and his "Common Sense," which, more than any other appeal to public opinion through the press, brought these colonies to decide for independence, won conviction by sheer force of words and argument, for his tract was published anonymously.

To go back, however, to more general symptoms of the age we are considering, American literature, while colonial conditions lasted, imitated with subservience the style then prevalent in the mother country, which was sentimental and stilted. Elegance of phrase was affected for trivial thoughts, jewels not worth the setting; fine description, fine writing, was all the fashion. The pose and affectation of virtue, sentimental and vapid reflections, supposed to be suggested by scenes of nature viewed commonly at second-

hand—these characterized the literary effusions of
London magazines, which our colonial printer transferred to his own columns to fill up vacant space and
render homage to culture. Hence, in the years just
preceding the wrath of solemn conflict, we see printed a
variety of fugitive effusions, some originating abroad,
others indigenous. Many of our votaries affected the
lounger's dawdling essay to be gallant or satirical. One
sends airily to the editor some ambling verse, with
Horatian couplets for a text—"the result," he styles it,
"of an idle hour." Another, as "Theodosius" or "Cory-
don," dedicates an amorous sonnet full of compliment
to some fair lady whose name is veiled in the vowels
and yet discerned through the consonants. A fireside
ode is addressed to "Dear Chloe." One fair poetaster
composed verses which began "Genteel is my Damon;"
and a provincial newspaper, printing them in 1765 as
the production of "a great lady," assured its readers
that the poem "not only convinces of her extraordinary
language, but also the greatness of her natural genius."

Contributions of this cast, I imagine, were chiefly
of the sect which adhered to King George after the
struggle began and disappeared from America with the
Loyalists. More earnest and passionate was the strain,
though rude and robustious, of our Revolutionary versi-
fiers. One poem of 1775 described the military aspect
after Bunker Hill. An Old-World ruin, whose unhappy picture was once familiar in American houses,
supplied the parallel:

"Palmyra's prospect with her tumbling walls.
       *   *   *   *
Yet far more dismal to the patriot's eye
The drear remains of Charlestown's former show,
Behind whose wall did hundred warriors die,
And Britain's centre felt the fatal blow."

Our patriot press of those years printed various fugitive poems in which passionate feeling for human rights struggles for adequate expression; not to add the mechanism of acrostics on the names of George Washington, John Hancock and other favorite sons of liberty.[1]

Before the surge of political passion began thus with the Stamp Act, the theme for poetry which most stirred men's hearts here was religion, or, one might say, the moral and didactic. Among the imported books offered to the public in 1765 was "The Messiah," a poem whose author was held in esteem as "the Milton of Germany." And again we find "Providence," an allegorical epic in three books, by a clergyman, Mr. Ogilvie. "All the proofs of revealed religion are here epitomized," says the advertiser; "scenes of misery and distress incident to human life, drawn by the pen of so feeling a writer and heightened by the color of genius, will wring the throbbing breast with pangs of commiseration, will awaken all the finer movements of the soul, and improve the reader in the virtues of humanity."

Of corresponding merit were those scattering prose productions which only the press of our colonial era preserves from oblivion. Besides effusive sentiments such as I have described, literary taste indulged in elegant rhapsodies over the phenomena of nature—a storm, a whirlwind, a waterfall, the reflection of the moon upon the tranquil lake, and so on. The vapid essayist was of the same mould as the vapid poet

---

[1] As the British captors of our cities would get up dramas which ridiculed the American cause, so, in 1776, soon after the siege of Boston was raised, a patriot play described the various scenes that the town had witnessed; "alternately diverting, shocking or affecting." This was a tragi-comedy in five acts entitled "The Fall of British Tyranny, or American Liberty Triumphant."

of those days, appealing to the happy few of culture and leisure. Lucy, Lycidas, Philomath, were among the favorite pseudonyms of this fraternity. They touched upon gallantry, the education of women, and fashion's foibles; they described visits to Virginia's natural bridge, Niagara being scarcely yet accessible; they praised patronizingly the efforts of mechanics to found a debating society; they criticised fastidiously the use of certain words or phrases in popular composition. One produced a brace of sentimental essays—"City Night Reflections" and "Country Night Reflections." "How sweet it is to be virtuous" was the theme of a pastoral paper of this sort in one of the magazines. I speak of times ten years before the fight at Lexington.[1]

This we should remember: that Americans in those years had little capital, owned or borrowed, to bestow upon literary ventures such as sought remuneration. Hence, open proposals were made and subscriptions taken in advance as a prerequisite to almost any native publication which involved pecuniary risk or outlay. Even in London, during that early period, the book trade pursued such a course to a considerable extent. Literature fawned upon the rich and powerful, as its needs compelled it to do, and sought out patrons. In colonies whose inhabitants most inclined to reading and culture, booksellers would tempt the public with their proposals through the press for mere printing or reprinting; and thus was it with acceptable books of all

[1] A panegyric appeared in the press to the memory of a highly respected professor at Harvard College; "it evinces in the writer," remarks the printer admiringly, "a promising genius, laudable requirements in literature and the respect he had for the deceased."

kinds from Josephus down to the latest controversial tract upon civil or religious liberty. A clergyman sought subscribers for his own occasional discourses. Publishers tickled artfully the vanity of desired patrons.[1] In 1776—that year when men's minds were set rather upon earthly conquest—proposals issued for young Timothy Dwight's "Conquest of Canaan," a native epic, to comprise nine books and 350 printed pages. Subscription agents were announced to solicit names in all the leading towns of New England and the Middle States, and all who subscribed for twelve copies would receive a thirteenth gratis.

If the poet, the preacher or the controversialist sought thus the wherewithal for bringing his production to the light, readers, on their part, expected to pay for literary wares of every description. In politics as in religion, men bought the tracts that might enlighten them, and the pamphlet, sold broadcast, did more in those days to direct and mould men's thoughts than even the newspaper. Thus, of Paine's "Common Sense"—that famous tract to which I have alluded— not less than 120,000 copies were sold among the people within three months from the date of its issue. For political funds were not used in those days for sending out free documents to constituents; campaign committees had not the public printer at their behest; nor did colleges, learned societies or even the bureaus of government dump their loads of printed erudition upon the public, that men might read and be influenced. That golden age when calendars, picture cards, time

[1] In 1772, at Philadelphia, the miscellaneous poems of a deceased missionary were to be gathered into a volume, beautifully printed on fine American paper from elegant type; the names of all advance subscribers to appear in type among the contents, while later purchasers would be added to the list in a second edition.

tables and blotting pads might be had gratis from the managers of a business enterprise was still far in the future.

While emulous bards and prose writers, Americans by birth and breeding, appealed with meagre result to the pride of a native literature, the "infant manufacture," as our publishers styled it, of cheaply reprinting standard English books of one kind or another was better appreciated. The public liked good reading matter, good standard works, when obtainable at a reduced cost, even though type and paper were poorer. Press proposals appeared in 1770 for "the first English Bible ever printed in America"—a long two-column announcement, phenomenal for those days of economy in advertising. And from the Stamp-Act year onward, the public disposition to foster home industries rather than pay tribute to the mother country was a patriotic symptom to which book publishers, like others who made or sold in these colonies, catered for profit. And since lawyers in every age are the most liberal patrons of literature among men of moderate means—good readers and good political leaders alike—it would seem that the culmination of our colonial zeal in publishing was reached about 1773, by a reprint of the most famous of English law text-books. "Blackstone's splendid Commentaries," as the advertiser termed it, came out in an American edition, the prime venture of a daring Philadelphia publisher, backed by brethren of the craft in Boston and elsewhere. The British edition, which comprised four volumes, cost four dollars a volume; but for half that price, with a fifth volume added by way of index, for two dollars, our votary of the profession might stock his shelves to good purpose and at the same time save money. "Sons of science in America"—for science in those days meant rarely the study of physical nature—were eloquently invoked to sustain this republication, whose promoter styled himself in his prospectus as "an humble provider to the sentimentalist and handservant to the friends of literature." "Those," he glowingly added, "who buy and thus economize will greatly contribute toward the elevation and enlivening of literary manufactures in America."

Thus, with England's great commentator—peerless still among sound expounders in the language who have striven to make our common law readable, but whom Jefferson disliked with all his honeyed phrasing, as an apologist of monarchy and the whole status quo of British institutions; unlike the sturdy Coke, whom he superseded—America may be said to have started, just before the Revolution, upon that high career of cheap and instructive reprinting and reproduction which under later conditions of an independent national sovereignty has had immense influence upon the literary education of our common people and the diffusion of popular knowledge, though doubtless in disregard of the just rights of authors.

Not to speak yet of the magazines and newspapers of our colonial period, I may add that in this era, and, indeed, far beyond our Revolutionary age into the nineteenth century, literary aspirants found place for their fugitive efforts in the published annuals of the times. Those morocco-bound volumes of contemporary taste and elegance which in succession long adorned, as gift books from friends, the shrine of the darkened parlor, as some of us still remember—the "Token," the "Amaranth" or the "Wreath" of a designated year—brought out in print for the first time the verse, the sketch or short story of many a native author whose fame survives his early poverty. The varied literary contents of such annuals were enhanced in attractiveness by all the pretentious embellishment of steel engraving, typography, presswork and fine binding that progress in the art of bookmaking could then permit. Perhaps, however, at the date of our Revolution, that art, like American literature itself, was more truly embodied in the plain and worldly-wise almanac, sage and homely of aspect, whose circulation was very great among our people as compared with most other books.

As humble purveyor to the prevalent taste and culture, the useful service performed among the people by America's old-fashioned almanac should not be ignored or forgotten. What trustier vehicle for carrying to the home and fireside choice thoughts, choice maxims, sententious information, alike in household management and the higher philosophy of life? Even at our own day the almanac method of instilling ideas is employed, not for trade's reiteration alone, but so as to inculcate choice precepts from the world's best writers and thinkers in prose and poetry and from texts of Holy Writ. Since the art of printing was invented, no compend can have been more universal in circulation and use for recurring reference among grown-up folk who could read at all than the calendar—that annual chronicle of days and months set to appropriate figures, whereby we know at a glance the tides, the changes of sun and moon, the approach of birthdays and anniversaries, sacred or secular, which concern us, that one may arrange his programme of personal life intelligently. If civilized man at the present day needs a watch or clock to regulate his daily routine, not less does he find some calendar indispensable for ready reference, to post himself upon the relation that one day bears to another, and adjust for the coming weeks and months his broader arrangements.

But the popular almanac of our Revolutionary age and earlier printers was not like that of to-day, though quite as useful and popular in its generation, and far better adapted to lodging sound precepts in the mind. The ample card calendar, with figures arranged by squares, which shows the whole chart of the new year at a glance, and hangs before us in the living room at home, in the office, the workshop or the counting-house—donated by some advertiser who wishes his name kept constantly in sight, or purchased in the store at a nominal cost—this seems not to have been specially in vogue in colonial or Revolutionary times; but the almanac came out rather as a pamphlet or bound book— each month with its own page—and the farmer, the merchant, the mechanic—men and women generally at their homes—consulted the silent sybil by turning the monthly leaves in succession from January to December; and they used blank pages for a diary.

How easy, how natural, then, for so familiar a guide to embody sagacious hints for the house or farm along with his dry chronicle; to make vague forecasts of the weather for special weeks and seasons; or, if more strenuous still in pleasing and improving the reader, to speak with sententious wisdom of the higher things of life; or in his lighter moods to make jests, tell anecdotes or drop into verse, and make himself entertaining. Franklin, as the world knows, gained literary renown with the pen for himself and his fellow-countrymen as an almanac-maker, and his success here was a solid one in pounds, shillings and pence, and not in fame alone. "Poor Richard" was the earliest character in the fiction of this New World to really attract the attention of the Old. While Shakespeare before him, and Scott much later, peopled the realm of literature with new creations of the brain, it was our colonial Benjamin who first made of the imaginary sage of the calendar a living personage, as it seemed, in flesh and blood; and those pithy and admirable sayings which taught our colonists thrift, economy and the curbing of their baser appetites are still the seed-corn of homily and dissertation wherever the English tongue is spoken. Not, to be sure, the only personified chronicler of his times, he was beyond comparison the best and the broadest of them all in philanthropy and sound philosophy, for his almanac man was himself. The success of his "Poor Richard" bred many an imitator in the years just preceding our Revolution.[1]

One surely observes, when exploring the remnants of that age, an increasing literary character in the almanac, but with literary assumption no greater than the constituency of those times could bear. Of all the literary output of the press in any age, few works, after all, prove less ephemeral than those which delight or amuse the public for a whole calendar year. But as readers turn naturally to the almanac for casual purpose, and

[1]Nathaniel Ames was before Franklin in the field as an almanac-maker who set forth wit and wisdom. Franklin originated neither the newspaper nor the readable almanac, but he improved upon former methods.

chiefly to ascertain or verify a simple fact, the man of
genius who would fascinate and detain like the ancient
mariner must take his chance among the vulgar and
commonplace in such a world; he has not that genteel
introduction to culture and good society which in later
years the choice annuals conferred, to which I have
alluded. Of American almanacs in colonial years, lay-
ing more or less claim to literary merit, there was a fair
variety; for besides "Poor Richard's" might be found
"Poor Will's" or "Father Abraham's;" while the
Boston Almanac had already a good footing among
rivals which it long survived. Annuals like these
asserted their claims as literary vehicles, whose jog was
midway between the shifting newspaper or magazine
and those books, more expectant of fame, which keep
up the procession indefinitely. To increase their circulation, country traders and shopkeepers bought large
quantities, receiving a liberal discount; so that the jobbing of popular books in a department store, which
to-day makes such trouble for our retail booksellers,
began before the Revolution, and with the rural general
store.

Of the choice and varied contents of these colonial
chronicles we gather some conception by sampling the
literary contents of those once popular publications as
advertised in the colonial press. The Boston Almanac
for 1772, besides its calendar record and "judgment of
the weather," set forth stage distances of the chief
towns on this continent, the civil list of the Massachusetts province, and the dates when the several courts
held their sessions. Assuming, moreover, the easy
function of household adviser, it set forth the correct
treatment of gout, bruises and bunions, and showed
how to build chimneys that would not smoke, and how

to dress the soil in order to get good crops. Among
the anecdotes, veracious or otherwise, listed in its table
of contents, was an account of Mahomet's extraordinary journey to heaven, and the tale of a bloody fight
between a sailor and a large shark. For poetry or exhortation, it contained an ode to washing day, an
epigram upon an old maid, and a warning to immoder-
ate drinkers. A rival almanac of that year advertised
an original epigram on the miseries of Job, the verse
dialogue of a young spendthrift and an old miser, and
an ode commemorating a lady whose death had been
hastened by her anxiety over a lawsuit which involved
the whole of her husband's fortune. Still another
almanac in New England vaunted in 1773 among its
miscellaneous contents "Timoclia, or the Power of
Virtue," an heroic tale for ladies; and for poetry "an
excellent new song" entitled "Bo-Peep."

Many were the sailor yarns in such publications
wherein figured the shark or the mermaid. In Philadelphia "Poor Will's Almanac" of 1769 set off its more prosaic information by a short tale, "The Way of Happiness,
or the Affecting Story of Constantine and Lysander."
This ambitious annual for 1773 stole a march upon its
more famous competitor for public favor by coming
out as early as September 30, 1772, "Poor Richard" following in October. And besides the usual chronicle
of dates, the calculation of eclipses and tides, and other
scientific matter, "Poor Will" brought together "various useful and entertaining essays"—such as a pre-
scription for using asses' milk to cure consumption, a
poem on the universe, together with receipts for making
quince wine, and for the cure of worms in sheep, or of
the swollen head in young turkeys. For nothing was
too trivial to be set down in the printed menu of our

annuals. Another and later almanac preached to its readers a lay sermon from the text, "If thy right eye offend thee, pluck it out." "Father Abraham's Almanac" for 1770 mingled essays on toleration, prejudice and affection among recipes for raising turkeys and curing horses of the spavin. In short, the incongruous contents of these almanacs, designed for the appetite of the general, was recognized by both seller and buyer with the utmost frankness.

When the call to arms rang through these colonies, our almanac publishers, with the rest, showed the mettle of Whig politics. Portraits of John Hancock, George Washington and other patriot leaders, original in the block or adapted, would appear in the annual issues, with appropriate lyrics or acrostics. One New England almanac for 1777 printed the prayer of Oliver Cromwell among its contents; nor was this thought stirring enough to suit the age without a reprint of "the celebrated speech of Galgacus to the North Britons," exhorting his army to fight for their liberties. "This speech alone," argues the bookseller in a local press,[1] "breathes such a spirit of heroism and liberty that it ought to be read by every friend of his country, and is alone worth treble the price of the almanac."

[1] I. C.

XI

THE COLONIAL PRESS

BEFORE considering what we call newspapers, or the journalism proper, of our Revolutionary era, let us touch briefly upon the subject of magazines or periodicals of that date. I have already considered colonial literature in its general aspects, and one may readily infer that in any æsthetic sense the magazine product of our native press at that era was of very little worth. There were, to speak candidly, neither literary writers of merit and culture, on the one hand, nor patrons of means and leisure, on the other, to foster that sort of enterprise. The burden of printing must have been heavy enough for a publisher, without adding that of paying for the contributions sent in to him. In fact, the popular magazine of the present day, affording its wide variety of contents for readers of various taste, with sketch, short story, discourse, poem, and continuous novel thrown in together; whose editors are accustomed to pay generously for writers well known to fame, and whose publishers seek, by the costly embellishment of art and a rich array of appetizing contributions on one theme or another of immediate interest, to attract a suitable constituency of subscribers at a suitable scale of prices—all this developed only after the nineteenth century had well advanced and lavish outlay replaced a niggardly parsimony and economy.

Nor do purchasers and subscribers alone in our day reimburse the immense cost to which conductors of periodicals are put in the inflated and extravagant years which open up this twentieth century; for advertising patronage and the co-operation of those who make newspapers and magazines alike subservient to building up their own business fortunes figure largely in the income estimates of a magazine of the present age. Advertising was meagre enough by comparison a century or more ago, and the newspaper proper absorbed all there was of it. To any publication, indeed, that pretended to dignity and literary taste, such means of livelihood were abhorrent.

Magazines and newspapers were clearly distinguishable in those earlier times; but they grow more and more to resemble each other. For if some newspapers are issued weekly, so, too, are some magazines. Each sort of publication tends to absorb into its pages the literary output of the age by subsidizing popular writers and seeking to monopolize, as to readers, the whole time which our average man can fairly bestow. This was not so in colonial times. Yet culture was even then recognized as a duty by the fastidious, and sporadic efforts were made to foster in the community by means of periodicals the native love of letters.

Literary magazines were brought forth in one or another of our chief towns in ambitious succession. They were mostly of the monthly order, and each gave up the ghost after a few full moons of feeble existence.[1] America took her cue from the mother country; and in England the *Gentleman's Magazine* had been reared

[1] Isaiah Thomas, himself a pioneer in that line of publication, gives some interesting statistics under this head in his "History of Printing," Vol. 2.

and confirmed in health while yet the colonies were
loyal to their king. Conceived after such a type, six
serials were set up in Philadelphia, one after another,
and the same consecutive number in Boston; but all fell
immature, to perish by the wayside. In New Jersey
a magazine of hardier endurance issued in 1758, under
the auspices of a British provincial judge of versatile
tastes and acquirements, who appears to have had not
only a tenacious purpose, but, what was of equal consequence, a long purse besides. This periodical lived
for twenty-seven months—much longer than the average—and then paid the debt of nature with the rest,
unable to meet its other claims. "American Magazine"
was a title so much in favor in literary ventures of this
kind that were it not for Thomas's History the genealogy of those early productions would be difficult to
trace.[1]

For journalism proper, however, or the newspaper
press, with its more attractive mirror of passing life
and its reiterated impulse to immediate conduct, the
prospect of successful circulation and influence in our
society was stronger. And yet the colonial press was

[1]That one which seems to have lived longest in our colonial
era was Boston's *American Magazine and Historical Chronicle,*
its publication lasting for the full and remarkable space of three
years and four months. Perhaps, in a historical sense, the two
most notable periodicals of this epoch were the two latest of the
list, the *Pennsylvania Magazine or American Monthly Museum,*
of 1775 (for which Thomas Paine wrote), and Isaiah Thomas's
own ill-fated issue of 1774, the *Royal American Magazine or
Universal Repository,* whose chief serial (in monthly instalments) was Governor Hutchinson's "History of New England."
Double titles were at this time quite the fashion, and, like an
ox or a dilemma, each literary bantling of the day bore two
horns.

not thus early a strong force in America; and where it seemed impressive at all, that impressiveness was mostly confined to the constituency of a single province or of a provincial neighborhood. We may safely confirm what others have already asserted,[1] that the pamphlet in this primitive age had more powerful effect upon the popular mind than the newspaper. Perhaps the very fact that pamphlets sought their constituencies far and wide, free from local trammel, or from that recurring official presence whose familiarity may breed contempt, contributed to such a result. The immense continental circulation and influence of the pamphlet "Common Sense" is in point. For our people in those days read and spent money in purchasing whatever might interest them deeply at the moment and instigate immediate conduct, whether books or pamphlets; while to weekly instructors, bearing this name or that, they were less susceptible and gave less heed. The newspaper, moreover, came to hand too infrequently in that age to be to British subjects either a constant mentor or a constant purveyor of tidings. Men took the printed news of the day much in the retrospect; they interchanged old numbers of the *Gazette* or the *Chronicle* to read over at leisure; and very many depended upon the chance of a stale perusal of journals which they cared not to purchase individually. The most stirring announcement of Revolutionary incidents—of a battle, of a measure passed in Congress or the British Parliament, of a public proclamation—came not so often by the newspaper as by some public messenger, speeding on horseback, by some special post or courier, or by some vessel just arrived from abroad, whose captain or passengers arrived primed with intelligence

[1] Tyler's "History of American Literature."

well stored during the tedious voyage. It was the private letter-sheet upon which a careful collector of news would rely, more than upon information direct from the press as then conducted. Neighbors picked up local information apart and then interchanged their intelligence.

We at the present day, who take as matter of course the huge expenditure to which the chief newspaper conductors are daily put, in vigorous competition, so as to place before millions of readers in the aggregate the happenings of each day and hour in places near or remote—and this not by an army of wandering spies and reporters alone, with every possible facility to speed from point to point in person, but by local agents, posted all over the world, at whose instant service is placed the inland and ocean telegraph, with lightning speed for despatches—we, I say, cannot readily realize the far inferior and really humble facilities which the presses of our Revolutionary age possessed for disseminating their meagre information. With bulletin boards exposed daily before our eyes, whose headlines change from hour to hour, to give the epitome of each day's happenings; with newsboys hastening to and fro, forenoon and afternoon, eager to supply to each one who walks our streets the world's fresh tidings, in successive editions, for the smallest possible outlay in coin; everyone, in our cities at least, tends to become the reader and sole owner of a sheet made up to please his particular palate, and ascertains for himself almost at a glance the latest news and the lesson to deduct from them. The very appetite thus created must be regularly gratified; so that newspaper reading and getting the latest intelligence become a sort of daily dissipation, a craving at recurring hours, like the alcohol or morphine habit.

Instantaneous photographs of what is passing here and at a distance merge into one another confusedly, like the successive scenes of a street camera or rapidly moving pictures on the retina of the eyeball. But from all such stimulants, such rush of impressions, our forefathers were remarkably free, as they must needs have been at that imperfect stage of the world's inventive progress; they might muddle their brains with rum or brandy, as many do even nowadays, but the delirium of the world's stereopticon sights did not afflict them. When news came, except those of their own immediate vicinity, they came in a huge mass, and time was needful to digest and assimilate or to cast up the consequences.

Thus do we realize and appreciate why the pamphlet was the potent factor of our colonial age rather than the newspaper; a condition which has since been notably reversed. Yet native journalism found its sphere of usefulness even then. Such business brought together no vast capital in brains or money for developing influence and gaining a circulation; but humble, impecunious men were its creators and conductors. It was carried on usually as a convenient adjunct to the book and job-printing trade; hence the proprietor of a newspaper was commonly styled the "printer," and in the mechanical plant of his publication consisted the main outlay. This "printer," though he might rise by personal merit above his rank as a craftsman, was a sort of impersonal potentate with the public; and with rare exceptions the editorial skill bestowed upon these colonial newspapers was of the slightest. Editors, men of real intellect and capacity, who, using the "we," gave, nevertheless, a personal spice and flavor to the journals under their control, belong to the later epoch of

America's independence and union. Still less was fore-shadowed thus early the co-operative intellect and energy which nowadays and still later in point of time contrive to vaunt with business push the particular sheet—the *Sun*, the *Herald* and the like—as of itself, with its own ideal name and abstraction, a fit object for popular admiration, the editor ceasing once more to pose as a personality.

In short, in those earlier times the printer of the newspaper made his profit, if he might, upon his me-chanical work, through the patronage of the public; while intellectual matter for his columns had to be made up after a scrambling fashion and gratuitously. In a literary sense, the press was fed by crumbs from the tables of its patrons and by fostering the ambition or vanity of such as might like to see themselves in print as contributors. Yet our deity of the machine was a public benefactor, in a sense, and deserved all such amateur assistance. When religious or political excitement was high, local leaders gifted with the pen would discuss in such columns the burning question of the day and harangue their fellow-citizens as from a rostrum. These were the real conductors of a press in colonial and Revolutionary times—a splendid, unpaid staff, moved by patriotic fervor or the ambition to gain substantial reward elsewhere. Their pseudonyms were various and chiefly classical—"Lucius," "Brutus," and the like, for they were largely collegians, bred to the bar. This condition prevailed as well with the press of the mother country, where, too, in that era the printer could little afford to engage talent for his news-paper at his individual cost. For the English-born statesman here or at home gave such influential service as a gift to his fellow-countrymen; while the printer ran his own sufficient risk of the suppression of his sheet or a criminal prosecution should government deem the matter seditious and apply the screws of the law.

It was between 1766 and 1772 that the famous "Junius" letters appeared by pseudonym in a London press, and startled British society by their pungency, vehemence and intrepidity, not to add by the scathing ferocity with which they attacked men high in official station. And, with a like vindication of the public liberties as their motive, did John Adams, John Dickinson and other colonists of America remonstrate somewhat later against Parliament and the British ministry through the colonial press, with an authorship similarly veiled. Whether, indeed, it were by letters in the local press or by pamphlet, the anonymous character of the appeal was quite commonly preserved, for prudence or modesty's sake, or so as to follow the fashion, or, once more, in the belief that one's effectiveness would be greater if the reader had to guess who was addressing him. And this custom lasted in contributions to our press long after the Revolution, the younger school of statesmen, like Hamilton, Madison and John Quincy Adams, using freely the columns of a newspaper to impart under one fictitious name or another their personal views upon passing politics.[1] Though a few—a very few—newspaper printers and editors of those early times dropped their own seedcorn to fructify for Revolution in the public mind, like their anonymous con-

---

[1] Recall, e.g., the *Federalist* newspaper letters of 1788. We know the names of the authors of that series; but who asks the name of the newspaper in which they appeared?

tributors, posterity has found little occasion to recall or
honor them in the silent oratory of our human race.
And this, too, while the printer's personal name was
advertised at the head of the page and widely known,
while these writers could be discovered in their true
identity only through those who took pains to inquire.
Even Benjamin Franklin—an exception to this as he
was to most other conventional rules of his day—
gained power and renown not so much by the press into
which as owner he infused his own liberal ideas and
methods as by his almanac, and still more from the
public posts to which a prosperous and successful printing career transferred him.

So, once again, in matters of social comment, in ani-
madversion upon follies then fashionable, in censure or
applause, it was the contributor who chiefly supplied
matter for readers to ruminate upon. News came
to the printer by the oral report of unpaid callers or
through extracts submitted him for publication from
their private correspondence; while such local intelligence as he might otherwise gain he collected in person
without special assistance. While authenticity was con-
scientiously sought, qualifying words would appear in
the printed paragraph in case of doubt; and informed,
as the conductor often was, by those of the highest
social standing, or by public men most qualified to know
the inner trend of politics, the shield of impersonality
was to all concerned the constant tegument of safety.
Beyond this it should be said that our colonial newspapers made up their matter to a large extent by using
the scissors and paste-pot. The latest London budget
and extracts from London newspapers served to fill
many a column of the week's issue; while with so many
presses of different provinces whose specialty was local

information, our newspapers, like some species of fish, may be said to have lived upon one another.

As with books, so with magazines and newspapers in that colonial age, we were prone to be imitators or purloiners from the mother country. And not to speak of English news matter, our native presses would transfer to their own vacant pages from the latest English newspaper a poem or sentimental essay whenever native happenings failed and the village versifier or Addisonians, or the choice champions of political discussion with classical masks suspended their free effusion.

Printed newspapers, so far as these thirteen colonies were concerned, came in with the eighteenth century; and the *Boston News Letter* of 1704 was the first real press of the kind that ever lived here actually after being born.[1] "Every one is well born," says Dr. Johnson, "who is born at all." Both in our own undeveloped colonies and in the mother country the immediate precursor of the printed newspaper was the "News Letter" itself in its primitive sense: in other words, a manuscript which was issued in form of a letter, multiplied in copies by the pen and posted in coffee houses or taverns where men were wont to resort for discourse and discussion. This manuscript, originally for shipping intelligence alone, added presently the items of leading local news and miscellaneous matter. The *Boston News Letter* had, in fact, been thus issued in a written form before its publisher sought to create a wider circulation by printing the sheet. Features of

[1]Hudson's Journalism makes mention of *Public Occurrences,* a sheet which appeared in Boston in 1690, but was suppressed by authority as soon as it issued.

social gossip and criticism bloomed early in the
eighteenth century into that series of printed essays—
half pamphlet and half periodical—whose coffee-house
fragrance diffused its most perfect aroma in the still
famous *Spectator*. Manuscript newspapers were still
put forth prior to and during the Revolution in parts
of this country where the inducement for a printing
outfit was wanting.[1]

Our Anglo-Saxon or Anglo-American newspaper,
then, was not ushered into existence as a social or political organ, a formulator of public opinion, but rather—
and so the word itself imports—as a disseminator of
news; though its potential influence as a corrector of
politics or of social fashions soon followed. Hence we
should not think it strange that in the earlier years of
newspaper circulation men preferred for guidance in
affairs their pulpit preachers, their orators, or those
who in printed book or pamphlet put themselves frankly
forward to discuss a pending problem without pro-
fessing to be the general purveyor of information.
Hence, too, the primitive posture of a newspaper printer
in lending his columns occasionally to local readers and
men of education who sought to influence opinion,
rather than obtrude himself upon his own readers as a
competent shepherd of the people.

While in the age I am describing presses bore such
names as the *Spy*, the *Mercury*, the *Journal*, the *Post*
and the *Chronicle*, decidedly the favorite title was the
Gazette. The *Boston Gazette*, dating from 1755, was
a famous organ of the king's rebellious subjects in that
town; Ben Edes, its conductor, being a fearless patriot

---

[1] See *New Jersey Plain Dealer*, whose manuscript was printed
later as a literary curiosity. Of this volume the Boston
Athenæum has a copy, which I have consulted.

during the palmy days of his influence. The *Pennsyl-vania Gazette,* Franklin's more even-paced and prosperous sheet, spread its widening influence through our middle colonies in the earlier days of peace and tranquillity; and its sagacious founder infused into it a wise progressiveness, studying how to make it useful and attractive in every direction.

When the grand issue stirred native hearts, our patriotic presses put forward some memorable devices. There was the famous wood-cut of the severed snake, with "join or die" for its prophetic motto. One Philadelphia paper announced its own epitaph in 1765, when the Stamp Act was about to operate—"Died of a stamp in the vitals;" but that act failing of operation, it rose to life again. When in 1776 the liberty bell rang out its proclamation in Philadelphia, the *New England Chronicle* of Boston changed promptly its name to the *Independent Chronicle;* its title-heading was embellished with the words "appeal to Heaven;" while the figure of a continental officer with drawn sword appeared on one side of the first page and a scroll "Independence" on the other.

In colonial days the premises of the printer, whence issued his sheet, served as a sort of intelligence office and headquarters for such as might advertise in his paper or come to answer the wants. Servants and laborers in search of a situation, the respondent for things lost or found, met often here promiscuously; and "apply to the printer" was the tail phrase of many a paid insertion in his columns, with more than a formal meaning. We read in one paper of 1772 that a lady had lost her "black double satin cardinal, almost new," which she suspects was "stolen by one of the various nurses wanting a situation whom she found at the house

of the printer when she called there to engage one for
herself."

Among the general news which our press afforded
in those days were those relating to politics, announcements of local marriages or deaths, with a passing compliment or obituary tribute; the weather phenomena,
shipping or business intelligence, gained chiefly from
posters at the custom-house, and items of accident and
sudden death, or of the conviction or punishment for
crime. The *Pennsylvania Gazette* gave little, comparatively, of local information, except for shipping
news and the leading prices-current, though promoting
various local reforms. Most items furnished to the
public were set forth by the editor in sober earnest; and
the general tone of our press in colonial days was that
of honest and downright sincerity, as from a publisher
who honored the powers ordained of God and meant to
keep clear of prosecution. London clippings yielded
most of the jokes or rumors afloat in high society; a
well-prepared pun, or perhaps some original poem,
essay or private letter would enliven the more prosaic
contents of the printed sheet. Contributors were commonly in earnest themselves, save where they affected
to be of learning superior to the mass and hit off social
follies with conceit. Among the favorite names of
the social or political contributor were Chronus, Tullius,
Junius, Americanus, Civis, Fervidus, Lenitas, Can-
didus, Probus and Publius; and certainly it was not in
good taste to publish a contribution over the writer's
own signature. Most Latin names, phrases and quo-
tations were printed quite accurately, indicating, perhaps, that the writer revised his own proof; but where

one of these classical contributors had started out in his essay with a Greek verse by way of text, the deferential conductor apologized publicly in his paper for omitting it, assigning the excellent excuse that he had no type on hand in that language.

To the style of advertisement in the press of this early era I have alluded elsewhere.[1] Advertising patronage even thus early constituted an important item in the printer's reckoning, whenever his balance sheet was made up. But advertising was not so very great or profitable, so far as the people were concerned; and jobs from government were much sought after. For our merchants and business men were rather niggardly in expenditures of such a kind. Mixed advertisements might often be seen; and where a person had needful occasion to pay for newspaper space on one account, he used it on another. Thus one would insert an item of "lost" or "found," and within the space so occupied he managed to give the public a hint of his trade. A surveyor who offered for sale a manual on that special branch of practical knowledge solicited employment. A disconsolate widow, or even the personal friend who gave the usual probate notice as executor (of which most probably the estate bore the cost), announced a personal business conducted at the old stand or elsewhere. One offers his horse for sale, and adds in a postscript that some excellent snuff may be bought on his premises. For if printing space is paid for by the inch, the full area may as well be occupied profitably. In disputes matrimonial, I have alluded to a prevalent disposition, among New Englanders at least, to take their quarrels to the press, and try to enlist public opinion by way of a leverage. And so was it in many of

[1]See pp. 20, 70-72.

the other disputes of ordinary life. In short, people tenacious of their own rights, and disposed to argument, made through the press in those days a sort of referendum of their disputes, as though in town meeting; seeking to hurt an opponent, if nothing more, by processes which might take the place of litigation, on the one hand, or the lawlessness, on the other, of a knock-down blow.

As photographing primitive manners and customs, the press of this period affords, perhaps, in its advertisements, matter quite as apt and entertaining for historical use as the so-called news which it more consciously supplied. And the same may be said of most other epochs in journalism; for the advertiser is one of our common people soliciting his own contemporaries and thinking how to make cleverly an immediate impression for his own profit. Hence he reveals the hum and hurry, the business intent and ingenuity, the working-day habit of his times with all the fidelity of a snap-shot from the camera. How houses and lands were sold or rented in the days of our Revolutionary ancestors; what chattels, goods and merchandise were chiefly in demand; how the posts or the stages went and came; how people dressed or looked, what they ate, drank or were disposed to seek for their domestic wants; what sort of things, lost and found, had been carried about the person—all this we discover in detail by the press advertisements of that age still preserved to us. We see, moreover, from the printed cards of those who furnished amusement or instruction, how programmes were made up, how deferentially the teacher or purveyor accosted his patrons, and how rarely, moreover, the great majority of our progenitors indulged in public sports or public indoor amusements.

To attract wide attention by expensive advertising was not cultivated, other modes for gaining popular notice being in vogue. Hucksters with leathern lungs called out in the street the wares or provender they had to offer, while the town crier, with bell or horn to attract a crowd, went his daily rounds to make petty proclamation. Mercantile advertisements in our papers stood not seldom as cards from week to week, but the space of a single advertisement would rarely exceed three inches, and was usually much shorter. Patrons like these were often postponed for the sake of the general reader; and where the occasional load of European news bore with heavy pressure upon his four pages, the printer would omit standing advertisements from week to week, with a public apology for want of room, publicly assuring such customers that when news were dull and his columns became clear again they should have the most conspicuous part of the paper. A few conductors at our larger provincial centres, more worldly wise, met a crowded situation like this by issuing a half-sheet supplement, so as to afford more room for news and advertisements together; but such extravagance was rare.

As to the adaptation of newspaper space to an exigency in colonial times, I may remark more generally that the postponement of local and domestic matter by reason of some important intelligence from Europe was by no means uncommon. For such a reason the printer would ask specially the indulgence of his readers for deferring to the next weekly issue an appeal for building a fort, or some contributor's letter, or, more accommodating, he would cut the one or the other, printing half in the present issue and postponing the residue to another week. One Philadelphia paper of 1769 divided

thus a poem on liberty, "to be concluded in our next."
Newspaper readers of the day bore all such shifts with
complacency, learning "to labor and to wait." On the
other hand, whenever his usual supply of matter ran
short, the printer felt no compunction at filling his
vacant space with selected poems, essays and other literary compost transferred boldly from the London
periodicals. As elsewhere, the prosaic or matter-of-
fact predominated in our press, aside from preaching.
In a *Pennsylvania Gazette* of 1771 may be seen an ex-
tract from Smollett's "Humphry Clinker," which,
newly issued, was then creating quite a sensation in
London circles; but the products of imagination found
seldom such recognition at that date.[1]

We may recall that the model provincial newspaper
of Stamp Act times was in size only a folio, or four
pages quarto, with two or possibly three columns to a
page; that twelve inches by six was the average
measurement; that half of such space was the maximum
for advertisements, and that the gift to subscribers of
an extra supplement, printed as a single page or perhaps on both sides of an added sheet, was an outlay
very rarely permissible. "Blanket sheets," enlarged
so as to make the most of four pages, came much later
into vogue, and that fashion has disappeared with our
later disposition for less area and an increased number
of pages. With the average limit of four modest-sized
pages, then, the exact occupation of space must sometimes have been perplexing, though fortunately for him-

[1]Solid books, such as Robertson's "History of America," made
the preferable padding when times were dull and the space
unoccupied.

self the printer or conductor of those early times had what in our day would be thought an ample leisure for putting his matter together. For newspapers in those times were issued only weekly, or, in rare and unprosperous instances, semi-weekly. Not a single daily press had as yet been established in all America, and one experiment of a tri-weekly issue had been a notable failure.[1]

As for the price of our colonial newspapers at the dawn of Revolution, this, exclusive of postage or of the carrier's expressage, which might amount to considerable, was commonly reckoned at about 8s. a year ($2) for weekly numbers. Of that subscription price, half was nominally payable in advance and the balance at the end of six months. In 1777, when the American currency was inflated, the cost of printing materials forced up the price of the newspaper considerably. Paper was to some extent a home industry, and native paper mills were started early, both in the Massachusetts and Pennsylvania colonies. But the scarcity of rags became a serious hindrance to such manufacture in this country, and many were the expedients devised for procuring such household remnants by a house-to-house collection. Naturally enough, the journals of our remote and sparsely settled regions acquired a peculiarly dingy look when paper rated high in the market; and the straits in this respect became dire in all America whenever and wherever the pressure of Revolution was sorely felt. Our presses and metal type were largely imported from Great Britain; and on the whole, colonial

[1]It is related, however, that while New York was occupied by the British troops the several newspapers so arranged their respective days of publication that one or another would come out each day; and this was the acme of American journalistic enterprise in those times.—*Hudson's Journalism.*

newspapers presented, from a mechanical point of view, a neat and creditable appearance. The proof-reading was careful; and so punctilious were some establishments in this respect—for the printer as proprietor appeared ubiquitous—that we see sometimes the newspaper's latest issue stating the slight correction of some misprinted word contained in that of the previous week.

Post-riders in those days carried newspapers to out-of-town subscribers, and such special delivery yielded to that class of public servants an important perquisite. Local newsboys seem to have been unknown, nor could the cash sales of single numbers on the street or over the counter have been greatly provided for. There was no shouting or hawking about of such weekly wares. It was regular subscribers, special donors and advertisers upon whom the paper really depended for support; and the credit system of subscription, pursued in that day by printer and carrier alike, kept each anxious and impecunious. We see a newspaper printing its meek but urgent request that customers send their subscription money by the carrier "where they have owed for more than a year." Most humbly and pathetically does one of these printers set forth special reasons why the arrears due him ought to be settled—that he has many accounts of his own which are not yet discharged; that he has been confined many months by sickness and by the death of his late partner, and hence has been prevented from collecting his dues.[1] One Boston press in 1776 urges all indebted to the printer to pay up, inasmuch as he has suffered great loss by the blockade. Other excuses were piteously alleged for dunning the delinquent—that the printer has bought new types or a press, or that he plans improvements in his business.

[1] M. G., 1767.

To such appeals the post-rider—who not seldom travelled with a special power of attorney from the printer,
duly signed and acknowledged—would dolefully add a
dun of his own. "I cannot afford to serve customers
longer unless they pay up arrears," complains one of
these. Such appeals, appearing in the journal's own
columns by way of advertising card, were couched, of
course, in general and impersonal terms, giving no
names to identify the parties delinquent. In the town
or city of publication the printer himself, or the printer's
devil, often made delivery of papers in person to the
local subscribers.

Subscribers, on their own part, we may opine, were
many of them heedless of their own petty obligations in
this respect. It is one thing for a man whose subscription
is asked for a publication upon the deferred payment
plan to put down his name with pomp or effusive compliment, but it is quite another to produce the cash promised when the canvasser comes round. Influential men
of that period, and, indeed, of times much later, were
wont to look down contemptuously upon printers and
editors and all of that plebeian craft who lived or sought
to live by journalism. But the day for editors and
moneyless or scurrilous press writers had hardly
dawned upon America when Revolution broke out; for
hitherto the printer had done most of his own editing,
such as it was. The press, however, as thus owned and
conducted, was of undoubted service to the cause of
independence. Printers in the several provinces or
States were frequently urged by the Continental Congress to circulate its public appeals; and the patriotic
among them did so with hearty sympathy.

It was a familiar Delphic saying as far back as 1767
that "the liberty of the press, when not abused, is of

inestimable benefit." Yet the old common law of libel was quite severe; and the only British safeguard of an outspoken and imprudent expression, however honest, against men in power lay in the submission of the case and its facts to a jury. The truth of the alleged libel could not be shown in mitigation or avoidance of damages, for "the greater the truth, the greater the libel;" and the point on which a verdict was to turn—could only a jury of twelve commoners divest themselves of their individual sympathies, which they did not—was whether the words themselves were of libellous import.

Newspapers of every era aim to please their constituency of readers and pecuniary supporters; hence the prevalent taste of journalism during colonial times was to avoid criticism and bitter personalities and pay formal compliments. Certain set phrases were much employed in type when reporting local occasions of interest; and many such reports were doubtless contributed from the headquarters of those who took part in the event. The sermon at an ordination was likely to be "elegant and spirited;" a paragraph which announced a wedding usually paid a passing tribute to the bride as "a lady of superior accomplishments;" while funerals and obituaries gave a peculiar opportunity for stock phrases of the elegiac kind, with pious application of the sad event for the good of the living. For the printer, like the preacher of those times, was prone to moralize upon the providential course of events which it became his duty to describe.

To some of the small, rude wood cuts of our provincial press I have made allusion.[1] These went

[1] *Ante*, p. 20.

usually with advertisements, and served in a sense to classify or identify them for the reader's convenience. Thus a runaway servant was pictured with a bag on a staff, which he carried over his shoulder; the horse thief was seen riding his stolen steed under a gallows tree, whose rope and noose dangled ominously above his head. A brig or schooner under full sail accompanied the shipping items of arrival or departure. The generic house "to let" or "for sale" stood between two sturdy trees of equal height with the roof. And this brings me to consider the general subject of fine art in America during our Revolutionary age, which may properly be postponed to another chapter.

XII

THE FINE ARTS

THE fine arts do not flourish well on a pioneer soil, and America's advance in respect of painting and sculpture was not great in the days of our Revolutionary forefathers. Native talent sought all such instruction abroad, and much of the patronage, besides, that might afford the artist a living. Even for wood or copper-plate engraving we depended chiefly upon the mother country whenever choice specimens were sought.

But Americans showed talent and ingenuity wherever their practical efforts were earnestly directed. The versatile Franklin shows us in his Autobiography that, after serving abroad in a London printing-office, he mastered the art of working in copper-plate sufficiently to strike off colonial bills of credit after a tolerable fashion. And Paul Revere produced geographical charts and rude pictures of Boston which to-day have an historical value.

The ambition for illustration appeared in some of America's magazine projects, to which I have alluded; and coarser efforts bore fruit in the almanacs, their attractions in this respect being specially advertised, as well as the literary contents. Thus the Boston Almanac for 1774 announced, as specimens of art within its covers, besides its reading matter, "curious engravings," so styled; "the head of the son of a New Zealand chief," with that of the chief himself, "tattooed after their custom;" to which were added the heads of George II. and George III. Other pictures which gave luscious temptation to the book were a war canoe of New Zealand engraved on copper and the anatomy of a man's body as governed by the twelve signs of the zodiac. Another almanac, two years earlier, boasted "the elegant head of the Right Honorable William Pitt, Earl of Chatham," together with the figure of "a wonderful man fish." A third almanac of the same period offered its readers, by way of appetizing illustration, "the famous wild beast in France which in the year 1765 destroyed upward of eighty persons." Still earlier, Boston's Almanac for 1768 displayed an "elegant cut" of the giants called Patagonians, lately discovered.

Anthropology seems to have much occupied the learned men of Europe in those days, a new world with strange aborigines having opened its portals for .discovery and development. The North American Indian, by this time tame, comparatively, and disposed to treaty negotiation, was taken about our leading towns of the pale-faced, to see the sights and incidentally place himself on exhibition. We are told of some copper-colored chiefs in New York City during our later colonial days, who visited the theatre and were much edified by the play of "Richard III.;" and who, taken to one of the scientific lectures then popular, where artificial lightning was produced from an electrical machine, were moved to astonishment. In 1766 four Indian warriors with three squaws were conveyed across the seas to make a London tour. After an official call upon William Pitt, the premier, they attended an Assembly ball, which was opened by an English duke, and in the

course of the evening entertained their courtly hosts
by performing one of their own tribal dances upon the
floor, with accompaniment of the war whoop and wild
gesticulation.

Most of our book engravings of this period were
of very moderate merit; and wood cuts in particular
were rude and coarse both in design and execution.
Some eighteenth-century edition of the old New England primer, or an old copy of "Mother Goose," or the
"Nursery Rhymes," once familiar to our young children and their caretakers, may serve to recall the style
in vogue. The pictures were usually small; and blocks
once prepared underwent strange vicissitudes in the
hands of penurious printers and publishers. When the
fervor of Whig patriotism brought forward new candidates for continental fame and favor, it was not found
difficult to reproduce some former likeness of the
British monarch or his minister, with its indistinct,
blurred and blotchy features, as that of a veritable
Washington or "the Honorable John Hancock, Es-
quire." I can myself recall an instance of the commercial shifts to which cheap wood-engraving blocks
were formerly put in this country as late as 1850 or
thereabouts in my native State. The Almanac had
somewhat earlier printed in one of its annual issues
little engravings designed to illustrate consecutive
months of the calendar year, from January to December; and these pictures reappeared in random numbers
of a new temperance magazine, with a story or suggestive sketch written up for each one, to inculcate the
lesson of total abstinence.

More ambitious engravings were sometimes exposed

for native sale in our Revolutionary age, nor were they always imported from Europe, though such was usually the case. Besides plain steel or copper, the mezzotint process was at this time in much demand; and we see a native publisher issuing in 1775 his proposals for a mezzotint portrait of the great John Hancock, and testing the probable profit by canvassing subscriptions in advance. There were, of course, colonists of taste, affluence and social position who ordered costly paintings direct from London; but for the general public, the dealer in mezzotint prints and engravings sold and advertised them for household adornment, in company with maps, looking-glasses and picture-frames. A list advertised in 1772 by a fashionable importer and dealer in Philadelphia may suggest to us the style and subjects most favored at that date by prosperous commoners, in our middle colonies at least, for furnishing one's private house. Allegorical pictures figured largely in this list, such as "The Seasons," original after Rosalba; "Peace and Plenty," "finely colored and beautifully ornamented;" "Flora." Scripture and heathen mythology contributed some erotic scenes: there was Joseph and Potiphar's wife, Venus attired by the Graces, the blinding of Cupid. This catalogue included also the letter woman, the oyster woman, the bathing beauty, Miss Yates (a famous actress of the day) in the character of Electra, and a lady's maid soaping linen. Among pictures of more general mention were landscapes, views of capital cities in the Old World, Scriptural pieces, sea pieces, sporting pieces, whale fisheries, floral sets of the twelve monthly flowers in beautiful frames, sets of nosegays, sets of baskets of flowers, and, finally, a series of engravings designed to exhibit the various passions of the human soul as expressed in the countenance. All of these, together with a variety lately imported of the most elegant engravings and mezzotints "by the greatest artists in Rome or London," were offered for sale at the dealer's new exhibition room in our Quaker city, besides numerous maps.

Works of sculpture adorned to some extent, in late colonial times, the homes and gardens of the great and opulent; and these in like manner were mostly imported. George Washington, soon after his wedding to the rich widow Custis, sent to London for some busts, through his business agent who resided there, and his personal taste inclined to images of conquerors and men of action in preference to all others. Those he selected were Alexander the Great, Julius Cæsar, Frederick of Prussia, Marlborough, the Prince Eugene and Charles XII. of Sweden; and his letter to the agent specified the size wanted, which was to be after a certain precise measurement. "There *is* no busts" (sic) wrote the London dealer in reply; none at all of Charles XII., and as to the others, none of the size ordered. To make special models of the measurement sent would cost at least 4 guineas each. But he offered to supply images of the desired size from a long list of the world's great celebrities in philosophy and literature: from Homer, Virgil, Cicero, Plato or Aristotle among the ancients, or, among modern men of thought, such worthies as Spenser, Ben Jonson, Shakespeare, Milton, Pope, Addison, Dryden, Locke and Newton. Washington seemed averse, however, to substituting such models for the heroes of his own fancy, and the business was dropped.[1]

On the whole, Americans of that age were utilitarian in their pursuits, displayed little real culture or taste

[1] 2 Wash. Writings (Ford ed.), 175.

in art, and appeared averse to spending a surplus upon delicate creations of the brush or chisel. The bald Protestantism of their religion, withal, kept them out of sympathy with those great masters of Continental Europe whose inspiration had come to them as submissive children of the Roman Catholic faith. For saints and Madonnas the Puritan of the eighteenth century, whether here or abroad, cherished an infinite contempt; and, in point of fact, Bostonians only a few years ago became casually aware of the coincidence that the battle of Bunker's Hill, whose recurring anniversary they had been celebrating for more than a century, was fought on the day of St. Botolph (the 17th of June), as specified in the old church calendar—that patron saint from whom English and the Massachusetts Boston had successively been named.[1] Even the heathen deities of Greece and Rome had then a far better show for adornment than the saints and martyrs whom Romanism had canonized; for scholarship, at all events, revelled in the classics, and paganism gave us no offence.

Now and here, as in all ages and areas of art, the chief interest of a patron was in having his own likeness taken, and well-to-do Americans employed such artists as pleased them upon the portraits of their prolific families. Miniature painters came over from Europe and did good work on canvas or in ivory, which sons and daughters of the Revolution have preserved among heirlooms to this day. "Limner" was a favorite word among persons of fashion and affectation to

[1] The new St. Botolph Club of that city undertook to make anniversary celebration of the day of its patron saint, and thus the coincidence was discovered.

denote an artist who took people's likenesses; and we see a "limner" advertising himself in the local press as drawing faces in crayons for two guineas each, glass and frame included.

But America had already given birth to two real artists of the brush, whose fame became broadly European before they died. John Singleton Copley and Benjamin West belonged, the one to the Massachusetts province and Boston, the other to Pennsylvania and the suburbs of Philadelphia. West, though somewhat the younger of the two in years, was the earlier to achieve a reputation; and when established in London, he aided his fellow-countrymen, Copley, to find a footing there. Each forsook America to gain a European training for his art; and Revolution, instead of enlisting him for its cause, served to confirm him in residing abroad as a loyal British subject for the rest of his life. West rose to high influence among the English of his profession, and became president of the Royal Academy as successor to the great Sir Joshua Reynolds; while Copley reared upon British soil a family which gained lineal distinction in law and politics after his own death. West brought elevation of mind to his profession and sought for his brush grand subjects, Scriptural and historical, requiring a wide breadth of canvas. Him Byron lampooned as

". . . West,
Europe's worst daub and England's best."

But such detraction must have been due to the antipathy which that errant poet felt toward one who was his opposite in morals and conventional attitude. West's lofty style of treatment is rarely emulated at the present day; but his "Death of Lord Chatham" and "Christ healing the Sick" were long admired. A replica of the latter picture, which he gave to the Pennsylvania Hospital in 1817, to be placed upon exhibition, long yielded that institution a handsome income. Copley's fame, on the other hand, was that essentially of a portrait painter, and the native press used often to refer to him as "our American limner." His portraits of the great personages of colonial and Revolutionary times, men and women in and about Massachusetts Bay, endeared him closely to the land he had left behind and kept posterity familiar with him. None of the choice minutiæ of dress or feature escaped his artistic eye, and the rich rustling of silks and brocades seemed almost literally transferred to his canvas.

There were other American painters of younger renown in this and the succeeding era of American independence and union, and some of them studied abroad as pupils of West. For Europe afforded the field for study and patronage to artists. The ingenious and versatile Charles W. Peale, a native of Maryland, painted at Mount Vernon, in 1772, that early portrait of Washington which shows him at three-fourths length in the colonial uniform of a regimental colonel. Gilbert Stuart of Rhode Island, after studying abroad, returned home to gain fame as a portrait painter long after the Revolution was over, and the favorite portrait of Washington's latest prime was by him. Washington Allston of South Carolina, who in the choice of subjects resembled West once more and lived abroad, was but a babe when the British invaded his native soil; while John Trumbull of Connecticut served as a young military officer of the Revolution before he went to London to study. Trumbull (who, by the way, must not be confused with the political poet, John Trumbull, his contemporary, also of good Connecticut stock[1]) was ambitious to shine as a painter of historical subjects; and he alone of those I have mentioned seems to have followed the advice of Chastellux, to let the love of America's great worthies and the commemoration of the great battles and scenes in which American heroes had participated attract them to subjects worthy the gratitude of their countrymen.

American sculptors belong to times still later; and of these, Greenough and Crawford, perhaps the earliest in genuine repute among them, found their instruction in Continental Europe. Houdon, the French sculptor, visited the United States under the patronage of Franklin, and made the famous marble Washington which still adorns Virginia's State House at Richmond. In William Rush of Pennsylvania, a native-born of the eighteenth century, America had an excellent ship carver, but no more.

Architecture, practical, prosaic and yet comprehensive among the fine arts, must in some rude form or another have engaged Americans thus early. Yet the best artistic talent of this profession, no less than the more finished products for building material, came from Europe; and there, at all events, was the place for an architect's liberal training. Many of our finer dwelling houses belong to the last years of the colonial period.

So, too, in music, instructors or performers who made this art a source of livelihood in America were mostly of foreign importation during our colonial epoch. But of native amateur musicians there were some; and Jefferson, to an extent that few readers of history

[1] *Ante*, p. 128.

realize, partook when young of such diversions from his dry professional work in law and politics. The new "forte piano," so called, charmed him as a melodious invention; and having ordered a clavichord from Philadelphia as a gift, he wrote in June, 1771, to the dealer to send this other instrument in its place.[1] "Music," avows, in 1778, this author of the Declaration, "is the favorite passion of my soul; but fortune has cast my lot in a country where the art is in a state of deplorable barbarism." Some of his servants were detailed as musicians while he was governor of Virginia, but his means, to his great regret, did not admit of a band for performances. Singular is it that men, the most illustrious in achieving for their own age and posterity, have cherished dreams of indolence and fond seclusion in the midst of their immortal task, solacing their immediate labors by visions of the future illusory as a rainbow. Two things were in Jefferson's private thoughts in 1775, soon after Bunker's Hill was fought: first, he wished a restitution from Great Britain of our just rights; next, to retire from the public stage and pass the rest of his days in domestic ease and tranquillity, banishing every desire of hearing what went on in the world.[2]

[1] I Jefferson's Writings, 395. In this same letter he orders "a large umbrella with brass ribs, covered with green silk and neatly finished."
[2] I Jefferson's Writings, 482.

XIII

PHILANTHROPY AND DISEASE

PHILANTHROPY—a love of our fellow-men conjoined with the fervent wish to do them good—finds its most perfect fruition in this life under the benign influence of the Christian religion and the teachings of a Divine Master. The best-ordered schemes, moreover, of Christian benevolence and endeavor spring up in the hearts of a community who recognize the brotherhood of the whole human race and tend in their institutions to equality of condition, discouraging among themselves all arrogance of class privilege and distinction founded in pedigree or wealth, and, still more, that oppression of weaker races which feeds the pride and avarice of the stronger.

Private munificence has worked out far more splendid results in the United States during the last hundred years, under a voluntary system for relieving want and suffering, than ever rulers or the governing power alone could have accomplished through systems of tithe or taxation. Yet organized charity had not far advanced by the Revolutionary age, whether in public or private means of relief. The imperfect systems of the mother country were ours, but with a far narrower range of application; and progress was very slow toward combining States or colonies into united continental action. Charity for local or provincial objects seems to have been fitful and spasmodic rather than systematic. But when Boston was harassed by the port bill, in token of the king's displeasure, other towns in Massachusetts and the sister colonies hastened with spontaneous relief. It was less in money, however, that relief was furnished than in native produce. Contributions in July, 1774, and thereabouts came in coastwise sailing vessels by way of Marblehead. Maryland set a good example; from Baltimore came 3000 bushels of Indian corn, 20 barrels of rye and 21 barrels of bread; and from Annapolis, 1000 bushels of corn. Boston in town meeting gratefully acknowledged the noble sacrifice thus made of a remote sister colony's staple commodity. Among the local Massachusetts donations for Boston's sufferers was a yoke of oxen.

Hospitals for the treatment of the sick and wounded appear to have been established in India, through the influence of Buddhist priests, even before the birth of Christ; and it is alleged that ancient Greece and Rome supported like establishments. But such institutions the world over are mainly the offspring of Christianity, and in Christian countries seeking to apply to mankind the golden rule they take their amplest range. Such hospitals as European countries maintained in the eighteenth century gave general clinical treatment; while special establishments for the eye and ear, for children, for women, for the insane, and the like, had as yet no distinctive footing. Nor were there hospitals of the dispensary order, where convalescents, or those not wholly confined to their beds, might expect relief and attention. And again, the hospital, like its counterpart, the almshouse, bestowed most of its work thus early upon the poor and needy, or upon those, at least, who presented some distinctive claim for public support. At the present day we see a far greater and more compassionate extension of such privileges; so that even the sick and suffering who are possessed of means seek lodgings upon such premises, for which they pay during the extremity of medical treatment or a surgical operation; finding in the ample organization of a hospital staff—surgeons, physicians, nurses, attendants, with fit nourishment and due and constant vigilance—comforts and an appliance of skill far beyond what would be possible in their own homes at such a crisis.

Two hospitals only, so far as I can discover, were fairly and fully established in these colonies prior to the Revolution. They were of the general character I have described; one of them was in Philadelphia and the other in New York. It was fit that the earliest of such institutions should have been founded by Quaker benevolence and located in the city of brotherly love, foremost at that time in population. The Pennsylvania Hospital was organized just about the middle of the eighteenth century, though earlier efforts had been made to separate such work from the city almshouse, where medical treatment was bestowed upon the sick and injured. The name of Franklin appeared as clerk among this hospital's earliest list of officers; he drew up its rules, and served later for a brief space as president; but men locally eminent in the medical profession gave to that enterprise its strongest direction. The Pennsylvania Assembly granted in 1750-51 its first £2000, on condition that a like sum should be raised by private contribution. Hence this important foundation was the joint product of public and private charity, and, as stated in 1755, when its foundation stone was laid, it owed its existence to "the bounty of government and of many private persons."

The second of our native hospitals was founded in New York much later,[1] and known as the "New York Hospital." Its site, just "out of town" and on high ground, was judiciously chosen, and hence a good money endowment was secured. Comprehensive treatment was afforded at both the Philadelphia and New York hospitals before the Revolution; each ward had many beds; insanity was not yet specialized, and besides medical treatment in general diseases, contagious or otherwise, surgery was applied with such skill as the knowledge of the times permitted.[2]

Efforts—not very successful—were made in other American centres shortly before the Revolution to establish good hospitals. In 1772 a public hospital for idiots and insane was founded by the General Assembly of Virginia at Williamsburg. At Boston, in 1765 or thereabouts, a town meeting publicly accepted a liberal donation of £600 under the will of that generous benefactor, Thomas Hancock, toward erecting a hospital for the insane; but no such institution appears to have been in successful operation until after the war.

[1] In 1771.

[2] The Pennsylvania Hospital, up to the outbreak of Revolution, was partially supported from charity boxes; there were also irregular contributors, besides specific endowments by gift and legacy. Some revenue was derived from an exhibition of anatomical paintings and casts donated to the hospital. From the much later gift of Benjamin West (*ante*, p. 171) it is said that nearly $20,000 were realized in the aggregate, this picture being likewise placed on exhibition. A report for the year 1772 shows that 492 poor and diseased persons were treated here—among them 70 insane—and that 242, or nearly half, were discharged as cured.

In dealing with the infirm, shiftless and indigent of
provincial inhabitants, such as require not hospital
treatment so much as victuals and lodging, colonial
methods copied those of the mother country, which
were rude and repulsive enough. The lessening of
pauperism, on the one hand, and judicious relief, on the
other, of those who, from one cause or another, are
found unable to support themselves or to gain assistance from relatives, becomes a burdensome problem
for every age and community to consider and apply.
The county poorhouse is not an inspiring theme for
description, and they who come upon the public for
support may always expect coarse fare and only the
barest comforts in furniture and surroundings.

Such, perhaps, is, on the whole, the better policy;
discouraging beggary or public dependence, as a rule,
by keeping it, in a sense, humiliating and comfortless.
But the Pennsylvania colony set a notable example thus
early in respect of her own paupers; and in Philadelphia
might be seen Quaker almshouses of a cosy cottage
pattern, both unique and attractive, where the poor and
dependent folk were lodged somewhat as in their own
private homes. A home for every family was the ideal
which this city, and Baltimore, too, strove to encourage,
so that domestic privacy might be the boon of the poor-
est and humblest of the community, and the noisome
pest of the promiscuous tenement-house reduced as
much as possible.

Pauperism proves, however, a difficult problem to
deal with practically; and out-of-door relief, such as
specifically encourages the maintenance of family life
among the miserable, has never yet worked safely clear
of that other method, the public institution, where the
dependent poor are congregated for systematic atten-

tion to their wants. The best authorities of our own day argue that both methods should be applied together, according to the local conditions, especially in large communities; and furthermore, that the charity dispensed by public and private benevolence should be of an associated and co-operative kind. While secret and partial relief may in various and deserving instances enable our struggling fellow-creatures to maintain themselves in life, nature inclines mankind so readily to eat the bread of idleness when the way is smooth in that direction that the dread of public segregation and a public poorhouse proves a needful stimulant to family and individual exertion. Private charities were not greatly organized in America in our Revolutionary age; nor had vagrancy and beggary any such strong footing among our people as in the Old World. The whole trend of our busy colonial life and independent civilization notably opposed such conditions.

The English law in respect of private support applied largely to these thirteen colonies. Wherever a husband was capable of providing the necessaries of his wife and young children he was bound to do so, and his credit might be pledged for such support if he proved personally remiss in his duty as head of the house. The statute of Elizabeth, moreover, compelled adult children to support their dependent parents, and competent parents to support adult dependent children; it even required capable brothers and sisters to provide for each other in distress—to the extent, at all events, of keeping such a family from becoming a public charge. And thus were the English ties of family and consanguinity set toward the abhorrence of pauperism and public dependence, even where the safeguard of family pride or affection might be wanting. Among our primitive

colonists, although organized charities were yet wanting, townspeople combined for the special relief of some
neighbor in distress, while the church congregation and
its ministers aided the sick and suffering of the little
flock. In Boston, quarterly charity meetings were held
in Faneuil Hall, and the sermon was followed by a collection for the poor. There were regular overseers,
chosen by the voters, and winter contributions of wood
were distributed among the industrious poor. In Philadelphia, in 1772, following a charity sermon which
was preached for the benefit of the prisoners and other
distressed poor, the sum of £27 7s. 5d. was collected,
and large contributions were added of victuals, bedding,
wearing apparel, fuel and other supplies; all of which
were sent to prisoners in the jails, many of whom were
imprisoned debtors.

While in Philadelphia the Friends early maintained
almshouses for Quakers only, a public almshouse was
established about 1730. The Philadelphia Almshouse
of 1732 was probably the first one in this country,
though others followed in Boston and other chief seats
of population. Such houses developed, according to
the public need, new or additional buildings and specific
objects. The great increase of foreigners and penniless
strangers with their families who were stranded by
immigration, to linger where they arrived, made all this
quite needful at our chief Atlantic seaports. In Philadelphia, before 1740, sick emigrants arriving in Philadelphia were placed in empty houses about the city,
and medical treatment was provided for them at the
city's expense. Sometimes diseases spread into the
neighborhood in this way; hence the erection of a pest-
house in 1742 on a neighboring island. Philadelphia's
poor rates were high; there were many vagrants in

those days who lived by begging and stealing; and
tramps were lodged in the "house of employment" and
made to work, whose expense of maintenance was large,
besides the sums paid to out-pensioners. In Boston, as
in other of our large towns or cities, schemes were
devised for employing the poor, young or old of both
sexes, rather than leaving them entirely dependent.

It is interesting to note in every age the influence of
heredity as inducing habits of shiftlessness and public
dependence. In the workhouse of Marblehead, Massachusetts, in 1770, might be seen one great-grandmother,
two grandmothers, three mothers, three daughters, two
grandchildren and one great-grandchild—in all only
four persons.

How rough was the penal discipline of this age may
be readily inferred from what I have said of runaway
slaves and servants.[1]   His Majesty's jails and prisons,
whether at home or in distant dominions, were houses
of torment rather than of correction, for the aim of
society was not to reform so much as to inflict punishment and retribution. Look at Hogarth's pictures of
contemporary London life, where imprisoned women
were set to work under the uplifted rod of the brutal
taskmaster; where the vilest of men malefactors were
herded with young transgressors; where the gallows-
tree showed over the Thames its hanging skeleton;
where the ride to Tyburn to be executed was in the
presence of an unseemly mob; and where, too, the insane, failing of discriminating treatment, whether in
the criminal or the innocent pauper class, raged about
in bedlam like wild animals, the raving, the elated, the

[1] *Ante*, p. ——

harmless and the besotted ranging about together in adjacent rooms as though abandoned by the wholesale to a hopeless hell.

The sanitary arrangements of British prisons in those days, at home or in the colonies, were vile, the cells unfit for decent habitation, and abuses were constantly invited in the abominable system of fees and perquisites to the jailers, whereby a prisoner's treatment and accommodation must have largely depended upon the money he might be able to command and bestow upon his keepers. It was not, in fact, until 1773 that John Howard, as high sheriff of Bedfordshire, began his systematic studies of prison reform, and entered upon that "circumnavigation of charity" which endeared him to after generations as the prisoners' friend. His first great work on the reformation of prisons was published in 1777, while these distant colonies were in desperate fight for their liberties. "He has visited all Europe," said Burke eloquently in 1780, "not to survey the sumptuousness of palaces or the stateliness of temples, . . . not to collect medals or to collate manuscripts, but to dive into the depths of dungeons, to plunge into the infection of hospitals, to survey the mansions of sorrow and pain, to take the gauge and dimensions of misery, depression and contempt, to remember the forgotten, to attend to the neglected, to visit the forsaken, and to compare and collate the distresses of all men in all countries."

Repression and retribution were the penal objects proposed in those days; not reformation. Some have observed further that the jail or prison-house down nearly to the nineteenth century was largely for detention in those days, preparatory to one's trial or the inflic-

[1] 2 Burke's Works, 387.

tion of some more positive punishment; that imprisonment for a specific term, as such, was not customary. And indeed, when we reflect how many of the lesser crimes, such as burglary, horse stealing, forgery and counterfeiting, were punished by the death infliction— and not murder, manslaughter, treason or highway robbery alone—a prison must have been to many of the law's victims but the half-way house to extreme torture. Then for a minor summary discipline stood the stocks, the pillory and the whipping-post. Banishment to these and other British colonies was still another final expiation for crimes in the mother country. Yet punishment by a long and lingering confinement within prison walls, as in itself a means of wreaking arbitrary vengeance or of putting a victim conveniently out of one's way, has well been understood in all ages of mankind; as France's bastille, the Tower of London and the dungeons of mediæval castles testify. Prisoners of war and of state might thus be held for ransom, or for some other ulterior advantage to those who held them in stealthy confinement. Even imprisonment for debt had largely for its object a private creditor's revenge, in expectation that the friends and family of the unfortunate one might be rallied in distress to get him released at their own impoverishment.

Our British colonists, especially in their sparser settlements, treated public wards after a promiscuous fashion, as the limited means and knowledge of the times suggested; and public institutions, such as they were, gave little opportunity for the public to separate criminals from the pauper objects of charity—the sick and the simply dependent. Almshouses and prisons in so primitive a condition were of local necessity combined or contiguous dwellings. In our more populous

towns might be seen a Bridewell for the detention and
confinement of the disorderly; a workhouse where the
shiftless and vagrant, when able-bodied, were set to
doing something to earn a support; while the almshouse, near by or under the same roof, received confirmed and helpless paupers, with only a reluctant separation of the insane after such public quarters became
overcrowded. Filth or bad ventilation was a frequent
complaint; but until a later age reform came slowly
enough; for the better class of society, avoiding such
purlieus, confided in the selectmen or overseers, and
desired to be somewhat in ignorance of what went on
there. The pound for stray animals was a place of convenient detention for the brute creation; and so, too,
his Majesty's jails themselves were largely in demand
for the apprehension and detention of slaves and indentured servants of whatever color, those human chattels and runaways with a price set upon them.

The Quaker spirit, observes our historian Fiske, was
admirable in dealing with pauperism and crime in this
colonial age, though the ideal of Pennsylvania could not
yet be realized for confining the death penalty to murder
and treason.[1] This commonwealth, I may add, after
freedom and continental union had become secure, led
America, and one might say the world, in new schemes
for making the prison a place not of punishment only,
but of reformation.

It has been remarked—and truthfully, too—that the
diseases of a people are modified from generation to
generation by their changing habits of life. To-day the
extreme tension of living produces brain and nervous

[1] Dutch and Quaker Colonies, 326.

disorders; but it was not so in our Revolutionary era, when out-of-door pursuits modified of necessity the monotony of intellectual labor, and few found the mental strain incessant, whether in business or social occupation. Life in the free open air brings cheerfulness, and where families are large one seldom gets lonely. The chief casualties in colonial America were those of undue physical exposure or imprudent regimen; added to which were such epidemics as smallpox or yellow fever, which failed of skilful personal treatment or spread their germs of contagion for want of sanitary measures of general precaution. Large families were gathered in a home; but the home life itself was chiefly in the country, or, at least, where dwelling houses were built quite apart. Such farmer's chores, as plowing, reaping and woodcutting, may well supply a bodily substitute for the gymnasium; distant vacation trips, inland or over the seas, are not needful to those who walk, ride, row or sail about their wild domains in the ordinary discipline of life; nor are costly out-of-door sports needful, like polo, golf or tennis, where the constant daily routine is that of physical exertion.

In this earlier age, however, people who dwelt remote from large towns suffered for want of skilled surgeons or physicians in a sudden emergency. Their wholesome life in the open air, with its robust pursuit of industry, did much to keep them in normal good health; and these ancestors of ours were indeed a tough and hardy race of men and women. But when casualty came, or a severe illness, death followed all too surely, because of ignorant treatment in such a case, or of no treatment at all. It was not until 1760, writes the learned Dr. Ramsay,[1] that the Carolinas undertook to

[1] Ramsay's South Carolina.

settle doctors of medicine in their midst, or even to raise
them; but by that time a medical school was set up at
Philadelphia, such had become the stress of the situation, and young men of our colonies began going there
to learn the rudiments of the healing art.

Impudent quackery imposed, meanwhile, upon the
simple and credulous of our common people, as it doubtless will to the end of time. One travelling aurist and
oculist is seen puffing through the colonial press his
arrival in a Northern town; and his manifesto parades
a learned quotation from Cicero, a rhapsody upon the
blessings of sight and hearing vouchsafed mankind by
Almighty God, and a pompous list of the various disorders he comes prepared to cure. It was common for
these self-trumpeted itinerants to proclaim "no cure,
no pay;" or, in proof of moderation and philanthropy,
to offer treatment gratis to the poor at certain hours
of each day. Mr. Watson,[1] the annalist of Philadelphia,
mentions an empiric in that city who advertised in those
days as a bleeder, tooth drawer and horse doctor; and he
further relates that in 1732 there arose much excitement among the fashionable of that city over a self-
styled M.D. who professed to cure toothache by ex-
tracting a worm from the tooth.

Surgery in our colonies fared even harder than the
art of medicine, and mechanics were seen applying the
rude implements of their humble craft to relieve the
bodily agony of some neighbor. American ingenuity,
however, rose often to such occasions where no professional skill could be had. Dr. Ramsay himself saw
in his day a South Carolinian whose leg, when badly

[1] Watson's Philadelphia.

crushed, had been amputated some ten years before by
an uneducated friend with a common knife, a carpen-
ter's hand-saw, and tongs heated red hot to staunch the
bleeding; for no surgeon dwelt at that time within sixty
miles of the sufferer. At continental centres like
Boston, New York and Philadelphia lived good surgeons and even specialists in surgery, some of whom
performed operations of a delicate and difficult nature
with high success. Such men, like the best of our
physicians in America down to the Revolution, had for
the most part studied their profession abroad. But how
could the skilled operator deal with distant patients,
dangerously disabled, when travelling was so slow and
difficult? Nor in these days was there ether or other
anæsthetic application for assuaging pain. No wonder,
then, that in so many of the individual accidents of
which we read in the colonial papers speedy death or .
a horrible maiming for life was the victim's accepted
fate. The present worth, too, of a particular life had
closely to be considered; and the young children of a
prolific family who swallowed pins or ate poisonous
berries were pretty sure to die in consequence, while the
superannuated bore his fate as a martyr.

Medical practice, furthermore, in this early age erred
much against nature, even when applied with all the
skill that experience and the schools could muster.
Upon a medical theory, since discarded, that morborific
matter should be expelled from the blood as the primal
cause of disease, the sick patient was closely confined
to his room to sweat out his disorder, with the windows
and doors closed tight and all fresh air excluded.
Medicines, too, were administered in excessive quantities with that same end in view. There were purges,
vomits and other sweating medicines; and besides such

remedies, cupping, bleeding and blistering were externally applied with little sense of discrimination. For
chills, pleurisy and rheumatism, the lancet was freely
used; and Washington himself, there is good reason to
believe, perished as the century closed rather from this
weapon in the hands of his indiscreet physicians at
Mount Vernon than from the cold he had caught, which
brought them to his bedside.

Among favorite medicines of our Revolutionary age
were ipecac, mercury, opium, bark and wine. People
dosed themselves freely for their own ailments, and
among favorite specifics of the day were pills, drops
and balsams with appropriate trademarks. Pokeweed
was used as a cure for the cancer. Apothecaries sold
both native and imported compounds, and rhubarb was
so much in popular demand for medicine that grocers
as well as druggists supplied it over their counters.
Currents of cold air under the door and through chinks
and window-sashes in the wintry weather, before the
days of air-tight stoves, furnaces and steam pipes to
take off the chill of our sleeping rooms, may have considerably offset the stifling effect of those pent-up
chambers and curtained beds wherein our ancestors
sought repose, strongly prejudiced as they were against
fresh air and ventilation as a safeguard of health. And
a more plentiful use of pure water, externally and in-
ternally, might doubtless have checked or prevented
many diseases which gained headway among them, had
aids to health so simple been popular in those days.
The hygiene of clothing, with frequent change of
apparel, we understand much better to-day than did
the average colonist, who usually dressed for the day
when he dressed for breakfast. Flannel is now the appropriate underwear, as it was not in those days; the

fair sex have discarded whalebone stays and tight lacing, while swaddling bands for infants have ceased to be in vogue.

Among diseases familiarly recited in those days were the king's evil, running evil, dropsy, bilious cholic, cramps, rheumatism, bleeding of the nose and sore eyes.[1] Some eye disorders came from the flying grains of wheat where farming was carried on after the usual plain and toilsome fashion. A distemper once afflicted the eastern shore of Maryland known as "jail fever," which was said to have been brought over by prisoners on board a convict ship; but under a strict quarantine it presently disappeared. Yellow fever did deadly havoc in Philadelphia in 1749, as it did in years much later. Malignant fevers in our towns and cities, where the population lived comparatively close together, might often have been traceable to imperfect sanitation.

Smallpox was a scourge of our thirteen provinces, perhaps the most fearful of all in contagious spread, and frequent allusion was made to its ravages in the press of these late colonial times. Slaves and bond-servants, in fact, were held at a stated premium who had safely gone through that distemper; while many a runaway was published for identification by its disfiguring scars. Philadelphia had a smallpox epidemic in 1731; Harvard omitted its commencement exercises some thirty years later because of a like disorder which spread at Cambridge. We were as yet far from Dr. Jenner and the precaution of modern vaccination; but some preventives of the malady were in special vogue.

[1]In one of Franklin's letters, in 1773, will be found some useful hints about taking cold. This disorder, he writes, which is expressed in English and no other language, prevails probably only among the civilized.

Inoculators in those days loaded their patients with
mercury, tortured them with cruel incisions for forcing
in extraneous matter, and finally nailed blankets over
the fast-closed windows to exclude fresh air from them
altogether.[1] About the time of Boston's troubles with
the king, smallpox hospitals were set up in Massachusetts, and the selectmen of various towns sought
to treat the disease more intelligently than before. At
one of these establishments bedding was so scarce in
1776 that patients were asked to bring with them their
own supply and claim a corresponding reduction from
their board. So greatly, indeed, had our patriot army
in that vicinity suffered from the scourge when revolt
became Revolution that British officers were charged
with spreading it purposely—a false report, we may
well presume. So when Boston was at last relieved
from siege and the redcoats sailed away, its selectmen
dispatched all smallpox patients into the country, as
the provincial legislature had directed; and in the programme arranged for Washington's triumphant entry
into the town only councillors "who had had the smallpox" were allowed to appear in the procession.[2]

Travelling in colonial times was too costly, too slow
and too difficult for one to really gain the change and
variety of scene and climate that at the present day is
prescribed so largely to induce convalescence. One
might, to be sure, tramp into the backwoods, camp out,
fish, shoot and inhale the balsams of the pine forests;
but such trips were rather for the hardy and vigorous,
and they had their attendant dangers. The youth in

[1] 2 Ramsay's South Carolina.
[2] M. G., 1777.

feeble health took, sometimes, his special voyage in a merchant vessel to the Barbadoes or some other tropical port; but little comfort could be had in such water craft, and unless nature supplied a new tonic, one might be worse for the long, listless and tedious exposure. As our inland settlements progressed, however, "mineral springs" were occasionally found, whose medicinal waters were sought by the fashionable after British precedent, for health, and, haply, some dawdling social delights. Chalybeate waters were already sold to some extent in the suburbs of our Quaker metropolis; and Philadelphians, it is said, were greatly stirred in 1773 over the accidental discovery of a so-called mineral spring, whose bitter virtues, hailed readily as medicinal, proved owing to the nauseous remnants of a sunken pit.

New Englanders about 1767 took eager interest in proclaiming their new mineral spring, opened in Stafford, Connecticut; while almost simultaneously was announced from the New York province another healing fountain whose waters gushed somewhere between Kinderhook and Albany. The more remote New York spa of famous Balston, and its still more famous rival, Saratoga, had yet a renown to gain; but for two or three years preceding 1770 Stafford Springs were perhaps the most renowned for their healing properties in all our northern colonies. The same potency was claimed for those waters as at Tunbridge and the other famous resorts of the mother country; they had an astringent taste, and upon analysis were found impregnated with iron and sulphur in fit proportions. All bodily disorders to which flesh was heir might be cured or alleviated by copious draughts at this healing source. Eminent physicians journeyed specially to Stafford in consequence to taste, analyze and pronounce expert

opinion. In May, 1767, a stage-coach and wagon set
out from Boston for this halcyon resort, its passengers
paying five dollars each to be carried through. Doctors
gave grave caution through the press that the waters
should be judiciously imbibed under strictly professional direction. While public excitement was at its
height, a shrewd citizen, it is related, who had been
hired to fetch some of this God-given water for the
relief of his sick townspeople in Connecticut, retailed
the transparent fluid at a dollar a gallon to such travellers as he chanced to meet on his journey, and then
refilled his cask at a babbling wayside brook, whose
water was eagerly drunk by his patrons at home, who
knew nothing of the substitution; and it did them a
great deal of good.

In 1769, at Bristol, near Philadelphia, was built a
large bath-house over a local chalybeate spring, whose
waters had been duly recommended for invalids by the
Philosophical Society of Pennsylvania. And in 1772
we see a sort of sanitarium advertised, situate at the
end of a pier in Perth Amboy, New Jersey, whose
aggregation of luxuries combined to invigorate the
weak and weary. These consisted, as its manager
specifically explained, in a room for dress and undress
and a staircase which led down into a bathing room
accessible to the ocean, so that those who wished might
run off into deep water; while, furthermore, only two
miles away was a mineral spring on the pattern of the
German spa, whither one might walk for a healing
drink after taking (and of course paying for) his re-
freshing bath.

The warm springs of Virginia were not unknown at
this early period. Washington visited one of them for
his health in August, 1761, and found there a gathering

of about two hundred people, full of all manner of diseases and complaints. The journey thither was a hard one, through a rugged mountainous country, with trees fallen across the road, which for the final twenty miles was almost impassable for carriages. The place was well supplied at that time with meat and provisions; but visitors had to provide their own rude lodgings, and Washington's party lived in a tent procured at Winchester. The gain he received from the healing waters was largely neutralized by the fatigue of his journey and the weather. Located on the east declivity of a steep mountain, and enclosed by hills on all sides, one lost here the rays of the late afternoon sun.[1] Washington at that date, and about two years after his marriage, came very near his death gasp, as he wrote his friends, but was presently on the road to recovery. Had he passed away, how sadly different might have been our country's record for the last twenty-five years of that critical century.

[1] 2 Washington's Writings, 180.

XIV

COMMON SCHOOL EDUCATION

IT has long been a cardinal maxim in America—and posterity should cherish and proclaim the fact— that education of the whole people is the fundamental condition of our civil progress, the palladium of our liberties. Knowledge of the truth that makes free promotes in any commonwealth or nation the practice and discipline of freedom. Coeval, therefore, and almost coincident with the earliest of these trans-Atlantic settlements, developed the deep and pious purpose, cherished by their earnest founders, of making each citizen here a unit of intelligence and usefulness in his community. Not, as in the Old World, were the concerns of culture and learning to be confined to a privileged class or order, while leaving society in the mass to wander in the bogs of superstition and ignorance, or to sink into pauperism and crime, the hopeless dependents if not the reprobate foes of society.

This great idea of a general social intelligence germinated in the minds of these British colonizers, and perhaps it found abroad an inspiration in Holland and Protestant Germany. There popular education had been widely favored; yet our Anglo-American ancestors moulded their institutions for themselves. The best and speediest fruition of such a scheme in colonial times was found, perhaps, in the New England 'commonwealths, Massachusetts Bay leading in that respect, and

originating a plan for her neighboring provinces to
emulate. For Massachusetts was settled and colonized
by men of the middle class of England—by that sturdy
set to which belonged the great Milton and Newton
in the mother country; and their homogeneousness at
the start, their congenial views in problems of Congregationalism—"a church without a bishop and a state
without a king"—all tended to make them denizens of
a republic, vigilant and inventive for the common good
and zealous to promote a civilization of the highest
order consonant with the shortcomings of human
endeavor.

Those eastern colonies were proud of their common
educational system by the time that separation from
the mother country was at hand. In 1771 we see a New
England press proclaiming "the glory of our public
schools, the foundation of rising youth." The public
school system of our twentieth century—a concern, still,
for separate commonwealths of America to build up and
foster locally, but vastly developed in the new States
and territories of our broad domain through the generosity of Congress and the nation in endowments from
the public land—takes a scope far more comprehensive.
That system of the present age extends, in some Western State jurisdictions, to offering a free education of
sons and daughters from kindergarten to university,
open liberally, supported by public taxation, and
unsectarian. And now is inscribed the fundamental
maxim upon the massive and monumental walls of
some costly public building for posterity to ponder over,
"The State requires the education of the people as the
safeguard of order and liberty."

Grund, a wise and profound German, who travelled
in the United States about 1830, observed the differ-

ence which then distinguished the two great educating
countries of modern times, as a result of their different
systems of popular education applied to peoples differently governed. "Germans," he writes, "are the best
people in the world for collecting materials; but the
Americans understand best how to use them." And to
American text-books for pupils of one grade or another
he paid a deserved tribute for their excellence of preparation and adaptiveness. Then it was said, as perhaps
it might be to-day, that while Europe has trained pro-
founder scholars than the United States in one branch
of learning or another, not a European nation can exhibit such a multitude of common people who read,
write, cipher and show familiarity with the rudiments
essential to an intelligent, practical course of conduct
Of the American common school as we find it to-day
an accomplished writer and citizen of our own times
pronounces it "the most original and vital product of
the national life;"[1] and he adds, moreover, what is both
true and closely pertinent, that our common school has
had a profound influence upon the government and
order of society in America from the beginning of our
colonial life, and has been a formative power in the
development of our early history as a republic.

Probably the United Netherlands were the best
schooled population in Europe during the seventeenth
century. But New England and her English-speaking
colonists originated their own independent system in
that respect so far as posterity has the means of judg-
ing; and the real initiative came, not from the *May-
flower* pilgrims of 1620, who had sailed from Delft-
haven, and hence might have imbibed Dutch ideas, but
from those later and more liberal settlers who came

[1] A. D. Mayo, Report, 1893-94.

direct from home to penetrate the wilderness about Boston and the north shore of Massachusetts Bay. For in 1635 the people of Boston, in town meeting, enacted a law establishing a public school "for the teaching and nourishing of children." In 1636 the General Court of Massachusetts took initial steps toward establishing the earliest college founded in America. Next after Harvard's safe foundation, and while the various towns of that colony were providing for their separate grammar schools as they might, the Massachusetts General Court by various enactments, and particularly that of 1647, outlined a complete system of popular education for the colony—with (1) the elementary or district school, (2) the grammar or secondary school, and (3) the college for higher learning—all as creations by and for the general benefit of the people, to be supported by the contributions of parents, the gifts of private benefactors, and grants made by the public, all together. Connecticut in 1650 made a similar provision. At the dawn of American independence, a century and a quarter later, Connecticut had advanced its standard for general education even beyond that of Massachusetts; and these two colonies led all the thirteen in the general enlightenment of its youth.

In short, except perhaps for Rhode Island, the scheme of popular education was constantly fostered throughout colonial New England. Under the example of Massachusetts, towns were here laid out after a general pattern, which brought the populations compact and close together, with the common right of choosing deputies to the legislature; and the agreement of fifty or sixty families to build a church and support a minister and schoolmaster made the basis of their incorporation into a town. A town with a hundred families or more was bound to set up a grammar school and engage an instructor competent to fit youths for college. A town with fifty families should, at all events, appoint one to teach the children to read and write; and in this latter provision originated the familiar district school.

Dutch settlers of New York, then New Amsterdam, had received injunction from the states-general of Holland "to find speedy means to maintain a clergyman and a schoolmaster," and to lay a local tax accordingly. This was done about 1633, and the New York colony established accordingly its free school. Latin was publicly taught under the rule of Peter Stuyvesant. But the British Government, which succeeded in 1664, gave to the system of that colony a setback; the more so since a cardinal point was now to supersede a Dutch language and Dutch civil and religious influences by loyalty to the British Crown and to the doctrine and discipline of the Church of England. In Pennsylvania, the Quakers interested themselves in free education, and wealthy Philadelphians left money to aid in appropriate endowments. But the want of a homogeneous township system, as in New England, which compacted the inhabitants and stimulated local pride and the local interest—the incongruous character of these middle settlements—interfered practically with all such establishments while the colonial condition lasted. To a similar want of towns and a closely combined population was added as a drawback in our Southern colonies the aristocratic structure of society among the planters, and the disposition, even in county matters, to keep down the common concerns of taxation to the lowest point. Here, as among the English-speaking people of that day everywhere who kept to the ideas of the mother country, parents were permitted to bring up their children after their own discretion; and the education of youth, religious or secular, each head of a household was expected to impart for himself after his separate means and ability. Governor Berkeley's famous ejaculation, which has come down to us for ridicule through the centuries— "Thank God, there are no free schools nor printing" in Virginia—befitted an age when English nobles reasoned that the common people ought first of all to submit themselves to their betters, and that all general spread of knowledge meant the diffusion of heresy in the church, disloyalty to the king and perverse disobedience. Even among intelligent planters themselves in the South was felt the dread of levelling distinctions between rich and poor.[1] But Jefferson and the Revolutionists of this Southern section promoted more liberal views among their fellow-citizens; and as part of a charitable establishment, at least, the education of the poor and humble became extended.

Both in the Middle and Southern colonies, however, down to the era of final separation from England, and so long as the influence of the Crown lasted, schemes of education for the people partook to a considerable degree of the nature of almsgiving and patronage, so far as the poor man and his children were concerned. For their so-called "free school" was one in which the rich of the community or men of moderate means paid tuition for their children, while the offspring of poverty were admitted without charge, if at all. And such, to some extent, seems to have been the situation throughout our colonies. Gradually, however, in all America

[1] 2 Ramsay's South Carolina.

the standard of popular education was raised under the
instruction of teachers, public or private, whose support
came by one means or another. And the tuition of our
youth was practical in its scope, and what was taught
was taught well. "In science," wrote Jefferson in 1785,
"the mass of the people of Europe is two centuries
behind us, their literature half a dozen years before us.
We know books really good which sustain themselves,
but are meantime out of reach of that nonsense which
issues from a thousand presses and perishes almost in
the issuing."

Here, however, we should also observe that the education of youth in America as in Europe, during most
of the eighteenth century, was subordinate to the
supreme work of preparing the soul for an immortal
existence—for eternal salvation, in the hope of another
and a higher life beyond the grave. Learning was in
those days the recognized handmaid of religion; the
instructor, like the law itself, was our schoolmaster to
bring us to Christ; and Protestantism, though less
blindly submissive to its spiritual guides than in those
European countries which were still ruled by monastic
orders, was nevertheless exacting in its tenets and discipline. To catechize the children once a week—and
every Monday to go over the points presented by the
Lord's-day discourses from the pulpit—was habitual
in our New England public schools; nor throughout our
colonies in those days was it deemed a bias incompatible
with promoting free intellectual growth to habituate the
young when brought together to an opening prayer and
the reading of the Scriptures. All such instruction began, to be sure, at the home and the fireside, as it always

should; and in each family group, to the pious and conscientious zeal and devotion of those courageous Christian women who shared the hardships and privations of our pioneer life and who bore and brought up sons and daughters was greatly due that sturdiness in first religious principles which made America free. To render education compulsory in effect from the religious standpoint, so that children in families should grow up capable of reading "the Holy Word of God and the laws of the colony," was proposed in Connecticut as early as 1650; and both the Massachusetts and Connecticut codes set forth early the open Bible in English vernacular as the compend of liberal culture, opposed to the practice of the mediæval church; "it being one chief project of that old deluder, Satan, to keep men from the knowledge of the Scriptures, as in former times keeping them in an unknown tongue." And since the English system of parochial schools committed the work of popular instruction largely to the ministers of the Established Church, so in this country, without a church establishment at all, strictly speaking, did the local clergy of the ruling faith of each colony exercise in those early times a considerable supervision over the local common schools, whether as committeemen or pastors, though with a lesser influence than abroad, and liable to the offset of dissenting sects in the community.

Ere the present day, all this has been greatly changed. In our modern eagerness to avoid all possible charge of bringing religious prepossessions to bear upon a young child's mind, we tend to the opposite extreme of paganizing the offspring upon whom must rest in turn the full responsibility of sustaining or destroying the fabric of free government. Free will, free choice in concerns of the human soul, does not draw the present

line at sectarianism only, but often are our public educators forbidden to give a bias to Bible teachings or to
instill into the youthful mind a preference for Christian
institutions. In its effort to be liberal with common
school standards in matters of the conscience, the public
will dispense with prayer and the reading of the Scriptures when youth are gathered together for self-
improvement; so that among all great works of literature in our language, the one ancient, sublime and
indispensable to mankind of all books is studiously
avoided. This seems neither wise nor consistent on
our part. Is not the child biased in the secular studies
of life; in the discoveries and even the speculations of
modern material science; in human history, economics,
geography and the facts and deductions of liberal arts
and sciences? Do we hesitate to mould his plastic mind
in favor of his country, its flag and its political institutions and ambitions? Do we refuse to prejudice his
views as to the great theories of human speculation—
Newton's gravitation, Darwin's evolution, Spencer's
survival of the fittest? Do we refuse to display the
charts of the starry heavens, contrived for us by the
bold astronomer, who views that vast celestial domain
as through a glass darkly and not face to face? Ignorance in these intelligent times is in some respects far
more reprehensible than a possible secondary error;
and so is it, as it seems to me, with regard to that
knowledge which, rightly bestowed, should fit the soul
for a sweep of that immortal existence to which this life
is but the prelude—which should fortify mortality itself
against selfish and corrupt indulgence in the present life
and make it strong to endure whatever bodily ills, trials
and vicissitudes of failure or misfortune active adult life
may prove to develope.

True is it, however, that thus far in our national career an innate desire to live true, moral and upright lives seems still to impel youth forward in the right direction. How much of this impulsion comes from heredity and the religious force of former precedent it would be hard to say. But personal example counts for much with the youth of every generation. And much of the determining influence in life is unconsciously exerted for good or evil by those who are pursuing ideals and plans of their own, while manifesting, incidentally, their belief and aims to those about them.

With due provincial variation, the range of common education in America while royalty lasted was this: The education of the child began at home. But as to children past the age of tender nurture, neighbors grouped together and afforded, for some winter weeks at least, a training in the primary or district school. For this the town or district raised as it might by taxation, and beyond this, individual gifts or tuition charges supplied the needful. If an outside teacher came to conduct the school, he was paid to some extent in kind and not in money alone; the families would board him around among themselves. All such instruction was practical, being chiefly confined to the rudiments of reading, writing and arithmetic and to encouraging a taste and proficiency in the English mother tongue. In the Dutch schools of our New Amsterdam, the disposition had been to put boys early to business. In the great farming communities of our North-Atlantic slope children were busily employed for most of the year; and so was it with the sons of tradesmen and mechanics soon to be apprenticed out. But in the "free school" or "grammar

school" proper, wherever it might flourish, the scheme
of studies took a wider range; though all such liberal
tuition was rather for the children of those, prosperous
or ambitious for their progeny, who meant to send them
to college and fit them for a profession, chiefly for
divinity. This "grammar school" broadened consequently into classical instruction in Latin and Greek,
besides providing the higher English branches. There
were "free schools," so called, in the mother country,
the most notable among them supported by endowments
of one kind or another; but on the soil of this new continent sprang up these grammar schools, modern and
spontaneous in their origin, and maintained not by
single benefactors so much as by the people themselves.
Such creations, once more, were sustained by all the
means locally obtainable, public or private. Few if any
of such schools could rightly be called "free," except to
the children of the poor.[1] An American public school
at our present day is the possession of the whole people,
built and maintained usually by taxation alone; yet
children of the poor and untaxed attend it with no
designation apart from the children of the taxpaying,
and we say truly enough that it is free.

What "free school" meant in the seventeenth century
(observes that illustrious educator, the late Herbert B.
Adams) was free in the sense of teaching the liberal
arts preparatory to college training; and in England
and her colonies free schools were originally synony-
mous with Latin schools or grammar schools.[2] Con-

---

[1] Franklin took but one short term at the Boston Latin (or
"Grammar") school, and he lived to repay his native town a thou-
sand-fold. His bronze effigy looks this day upon the now vacant
lot where that school stood.

[2] See Educational Series: William and Mary, etc., H. B.
Adams.

sequently the high school or academy—the latter word
then held too sacred to come readily into use—was a
broadening of the American grammar school, so as
more immediately to prepare for college, the primitive
grammar school serving rather to round off the average
youth's education.[1]

Thus did our colonial Latin or grammar school become "the cornerstone of the college proper."[2] Some
of our American colleges carried on in these times their
own grammar or high school, which was in a sense
conjoined with the college itself, and served as a feeder
or preparatory annex to the college. Kings (or
Columbia) had such a seminary. Princeton was thus
supplied, and from the senior class of its grammar
school we see ten admitted in 1772 to the freshman class
of the college proper. Philadelphia's great institution
of higher learning, the University of Pennsylvania,
originated in 1740 in a charity school. From thence
sprang up an "academy," nine years later; from the
academy a college in 1755; and that college during the
Revolutionary War grew into a university, the first
to be incorporated in the whole United States by that
supremely dignified title. During the last years of
colonial rule, the Pennsylvania College and Academy
were in close alliance, and together asked gifts from the
public. Franklin, who in a sense was chief founder of
this noble and expansive institution, wrote of it in 1751
that the academy was flourishing beyond expectation;
that it had already more than one hundred scholars,
and constantly increased in numbers. It was served,

[1] The separation of "Latin" and English high school is of post-
colonial date.

[2] H. B. Adams. Besides religion and letters, education was to
be "in good manners."

he said, by excellent masters, who were paid good
salaries; by a rector, who taught Latin and Greek; a
mathematical professor and three assistant tutors. The
scholars paid each £4 (or $20) a year.[1] Old William
and Mary had also in colonial days a grammar school,
whose privileges became in some way confounded with
those of the college proper, much to the disrelish of
baccalaureate graduates. Jefferson, when governor of
Virginia during the Revolution, caused this grammar
school to be abolished, hoping that more dignity would
be given thereby to the college course.

The native bent of all cis-Atlantic education in those
days, so as to give to our settlers the rudiments of a
good English training, was clearly apparent. To make
vernacular scholars of the rising youth was strongly
kept in view, both as to composition and oral expression. Franklin wrote with pride of the proficiency
shown at Philadelphia's "academy" in English decla-
mation[2]—a practice always of great service to youth
in forming taste for eloquence and pronunciation upon
the best models. "We have little boys here under
seven," says one of his letters, "who can deliver an ora-
tion with more propriety than most preachers."

In proof of the universal uplifting sought by public
educators in our leading provinces, we should not omit
the pains taken—in Boston and Philadelphia, at least—
to set up night schools for affording the rudiments to
those whose days were too much occupied to yield the
usual hours for tuition. In 1769 the opening of a night

[1] Yet two years later he described the institution as considerably in debt, with a vacancy in the rectorship not yet filled.
[2] 2 B. Franklin's Works, 235, 242, etc. (1751-53).

school was announced in Philadelphia at the Friends' public schoolhouse, to instruct youth in "reading, writing and arithmetic;" and this, I presume, was provided at the common cost. In Boston, a tutor "in writing and arithmetic" was detailed in 1772 to attend every school at 6 o'clock in the evening. About 1733, Connecticut foreshadowed her later State policy of granting public lands as a permanent fund for education; and not only did this colony encourage public schools, but it discouraged private ones.

In America's instruction of the rudiments, the time-honored dame familiar to European countries seems not to have figured largely; but male teachers, young and progressive, imparted to pupils still younger the stimulus of their inspiration. College students, in fact, or young college graduates, wherever the sphere of collegiate influence might conveniently extend, taught temporarily in the rural district or grammar schools; and in so doing they helped out the needful expense of their own higher education. This by the eighteenth century was largely the case in New England, where Harvard and Yale long arranged the midwinter vacation so that needy sophomores, juniors or seniors might conveniently absent themselves for such a purpose, making up specially when they returned the overlapping studies of the year's curriculum.

As for the famous "district school" for the rudiments, it has travelled far and wide on this continent, as the tale of many a farmer's son or pioneer still living may remind us. The old red schoolhouse or log cabin, on a convenient lot, owned by the rustic community, and opened but a few weeks or months of the year, when home and farming work is dull and a child's labor may be spared, has given the mental start in life to

many a rural American ambitious of bettering his condition. In fact, the New England or Northern district
school, appropriate to our Revolutionary age, is still
reproduced in the rude wilderness beyond the Alleghanies or near the Rocky range and in the vast basin
of the Mississippi. Its type is still seen with more or
less variation and extension in the simpler villages of
New England itself, where, together with the town
meeting, they flourished a century and a half ago. The
primitive system may thus locally avail, with supplies
assessed among remote rural folk whose purses are
scant; these furnish fuel for the winter school from
their own woodpiles, while those board the teacher
round in turn; families with the largest number of
children to be taught bearing the chief burden of the
hospitality. The teacher himself goes early on a
winter's morning and makes the fire which is to warm
up the schoolroom, before the scholars arrive to take
their seats on the benches, with rude desks, green
painted, or perhaps mere boards, planed and pinioned,
as a table before them. Such schools could hardly be
graded; the teacher called up classes in turn as occasion
might serve him; and much of his time was spent in
setting copies for the writing books or in mending with
his so-called penknife the clumsy urchin's goosequill.
If wise, he armed himself with rod, ruler, switch or
ferule in token of his authority; and many have been
the stories among returned college students thus placed
in charge, of tussles with the older boys, bigger than
themselves, where some rebel, who made purposely an
issue of strength, had to be thrown upon the floor and
physically compelled before the new master could rule
his little realm respected. Girls and boys of neighboring families here collected day by day for their tasks,

taking their sports at recess apart; and the visit of the district school committee was a crowning episode of the term.

By the year of the Stamp Act, America had, besides her public schools, good corresponding means of private instruction, whether as preparatory to college or for completing the average youth's training for active life. In old Virginia and such other colonies as were loth to tax themselves for common education, parents of means and social standing patronized largely these private schools, whose masters were often Scotch or English clergymen, liberally trained, but without glebe or tithes for an adequate support. Jefferson, Madison and Monroe received their early schooling in this manner. Pursuing the fundamental English notion that every head of a household should teach his children according to his ability, the plantation lords made much, moreover, of private tutors in their own households. One Virginia gentleman we see advertising in 1774 for a person to teach Greek and Latin in his family. Another in 1772 announces his wish to engage some single gentleman who would live upon his plantation with the family; he desires five or six of his grandsons grounded in grammar, writing and arithmetic under his own inspection, and offers £50 a year, with board, not objecting to "standing in" besides for the cost of washing and slight repairs. Washington, while looking after the education of his young ward and stepson, Jack Custis (whom, by the way, he called "my son-in-law" in one of his letters of that date), followed the fashion of his province in putting out the boy at the age of fourteen to a church incumbent at Annapolis, who had

other pupils; having provided for the lad's earlier
studies under another clergyman, who was domiciled
at Mount Vernon.

There were at this time private schools of varying
merit at Philadelphia, New York, Boston and our other
chief centres, and the word "academy" came at length
to be shared by such institutions of the higher grade.
Besides managers and head masters, applicants for the
post of tutor in a school or private family made their
wants known widely through the local press. Thus in
1772, in the *Pennsylvania Gazette,* one offered to be
private tutor in a gentleman's family or to take a school
near the city; he had taught in this country several
years with approbation; he was sober and intelligent;
he could instruct in spelling, in "reading English with
propriety," in arithmetic, merchants' accounts, trigonometry and navigation. In New York City a private
teacher of Latin, Greek, science and mathematics
offered to provide pupils with a better knowledge of
English "than is common in the reading and writing
[or public] schools," and to teach the English tongue
grammatically. We see a boarding school opened in
1772 at Trenton, whose head master engaged to teach
the English language grammatically, and give lessons
in writing, arithmetic, bookkeeping after the Italian
method, geometry, trigonometry, mensuration, survey-
ing, gauging and navigation.[1]

The prominence given to the English rudiments in
such appeals is noteworthy; and the language, the literature of our mother tongue, was held the first essential

[1] "Those who intrust him with the care of their children," he
unctuously added, "may depend on his exciting so as to facilitate
their learning, instruct their morals and in every respect approve
his conduct to God and man. N. B. Proper care will be taken of
their clothes."

of secular culture. "English grammar, logic and composition," argues one advertiser of 1772, "are much insisted on in these days for making a figure in the lettered world, and enabling young masters and misses to write polite letters on business and friendship." Yet our best private schools and teachers were competent, besides, for grounding in Latin and Greek, and youths were well prepared for college and a classical course. French, however, which ranked as a polite accomplishment, was largely imparted by the music and dancing masters from abroad.

The strenuous exertion for self-improvement, nursed in New England life by both the public or compulsory system and that of private or voluntary enterprise, was already apparent. One hard-worked private teacher of Boston, whose day school was already a success, advertised to open an evening school, if sufficient patronage were offered him. Another in that town expressly conformed his time to those who attended the Latin school, besides carrying on a school at the usual hours, for spelling, writing and arithmetic—8 to 11 in the morning and 2 to 5 in the afternoon; and this special school occupied the space from 11 to 12 A.M. and 5 to 6 P.M. "Such pupils as choose to be instructed at home," announces another advertiser, "will be waited on there at such hours as may be most convenient." And here, finally, a private morning school was opened for young ladies or young gentlemen "who have a mind to become acquainted with "French, English, arithmetic, penmanship or epistolary writing;" and here the hours named were 5 to 7 A.M. "On morning's wings how active springs the mind!" adds this last competitor for favor, dropping into poetry. Many of America's private schools took then, as in later times, both day scholars and boarders as a means of support.

Co-education prevailed, of course, to a considerable extent in our colonial schools, and especially in rustic communities, where boys and girls grew up as acquaintances together, and each family supplied its quota of both sexes. In some of the high-grade private schools provision was thus made, though the more select among them educated the daughters in their teens apart. The training, however, for women differed considerably from that bestowed upon her natural protectors, and found perhaps its outer bounds in pleasing accomplishments; there was, of course, no college for women thus early, nor could a careful outfit be afforded in the classics and liberal sciences. At a private school for young ladies in Boston, conducted "by a lady," we see announced French, English and needlework as the chief branches. At Williamsburg, in 1774, a "female boarding school on the English plan" offered reading, tambour and other kinds of needlework; while dancing and writing masters were supplied, and lessons given on the guitar. Another Virginia school for young ladies in 1772, besides reading, writing and arithmetic, set forth Dresden tent work, shell work and all kinds of needlework. In fact, the skilled product of woman's peculiar weapon was much insisted upon, with its technical details, in all our young ladies' schools—point, Brussels, Dresden, embroidery and all kinds of darning, French quilting, marking samplers, plain work and knitting being minutely set forth in many a school prospectus. Even milliners undertook to teach specially all kinds of needlework "in the most genteel and elegant taste."

Select schools for young women, and particularly the boarding schools, were conducted by persons of their own sex; propriety and good manners were treated as matters of careful attention, not less than the fundamental morals; and then, as always, the tone and select companionship promised by such establishments counted for much with parents in their selection who had daughters to bring out or push forward in society. Most likely the choicest of such institutions did not have to advertise in the papers at all; but we see one which in 1774 offered, among other inducements to patrons, to introduce the young ladies "to genteel company" at very moderate expense. While French and dancing lessons were often provided as an extra in such schools, immigrants from France gave special tuition of their own outside the seminary. "These two branches," observes a French refugee in 1776, who had set up schools of his own for these accomplishments, "are now becoming more necessary as the means how to behave in fine company."

The true aim in all education of the young—and especially in training the children of a whole people—should be to fit them for their probable vocation in life, so that they may go forth into the world better equipped to sustain the duties of a useful and responsible career. And hence, while average Americans of the sterner sex are trained to become good farmers, merchants, mechanics or professional men, skilful and prosperous each in his own sphere of activity, so far as may be, and withal good citizens for all possible concerns of peace or war, besides competent heads and founders of a family, woman's sphere may still be regarded as

secluded and subordinate by comparison, influential
most of all in the household and conventional society,
with marriage and the nurture of children as the destiny
most likely to assure her best fruition in positive influence and activity. Hence at this era her domain was
accepted as essentially that of the human heart and her
empire as founded upon gentle submission and devotion—the best possible discipline for inspiring man's
devotion and love in return. Both sexes blended into a
common purpose. The patriot sons and sire went forth
with sword and musket to win free government; while
the mothers and daughters at home sewed shirts or provided blankets for the soldiery; and the spinning-wheel
parties of our earlier non-importation days bore witness
to the self-sacrificing loyalty to liberty's cause of which
the women of our Revolution were capable in the time
of trial. And so has it been at every crisis of a people's
freedom wherever that freedom is fought for.

One should not assume to prophesy or forecast what
changes in human life and conditions our new century
is destined to bring forth. That science and discovery
will add much to the world's sum of human knowledge
and capability is certain. As to human government and
intercourse, two great problems remain for our better
comprehension and solution. One involves the ulti-
mate relation of the different races of mankind and the
test of their fundamental equality or inequality. The
other concerns the relative position in the several races
that man and woman shall occupy toward one another.
If the different races of mankind cannot live in peaceful
union and equality with one another, the black or the
yellow skinned may seek their destiny apart from the
Caucasian, and, achieving the best that is in them, make
institutions separate, and so preserve with dignity on

separated domains their separate independence. But man and woman, of whatever race, were made for one another, and their independent separation for permanent companionship is morally impossible. Sooner or later, if they have not already done so, the sexes must adjust themselves to one another in their lives and fortunes; and in any true adjustment which deserves permanence, it will not be that what one sex does the other does likewise and equally, or not quite so well, but that each shall supplement the other and both grow' into a better comprehension that ministration, comfort and support are mutually needful to man and woman, and that in sight of God and nature an equally high, honorable and essential mission awaits them, not in merging so much the identity of the one sex or the other, but rather in their lasting mutual love and cooperation, as offspring of the highest types of a Divine creation.[1]

[1]The simplicity of common school education in those earlier days as contrasted with the complexity of our present school studies has been noted by some leading educators of this day.

XV

COLLEGES AND THE HIGHER EDUCATION

EIGHT important establishments of the higher learning flourished in these colonies prior to the Revolution—Harvard, William and Mary, Yale, the Academy and College at Philadelphia (since expanded into the University of Pennsylvania), Princeton, King's (since Columbia), Brown and Dartmouth, this being the order of their separate creation.[1] Only three out of the eight—Harvard, William and Mary, with Yale, whose foundation dates at 1701—were ushered into existence prior to the eighteenth century. Brown and Dartmouth, both organized after the French and Indian War, were the youngest of them all.

These eight institutions, none of which bore in those days a more imposing title than college, had each its own distinct provincial origin for provincial needs, its own local environment, while its educating influence beyond such confines was potent only in a subordinate sense. To train up specially men of learning for the ministry of the religious sect which its own colonial settlers and inhabitants favored was a prime object in the original foundation of these colleges, and more particularly in the three oldest. Yet, as we shall see, great lawyers, great statesmen, as well as great divines, gave lustre to the rolls of their alumni as time went on.

[1]Besides the above, Washington and Lee in Virginia dates its foundation at 1749, and Rutgers in New Jersey at 1766.

The founding of Harvard, in 1636, the first institution of them all, was as unique and impressive an educational fact in the settlement of our Massachusetts colony as that other contemporaneous one I have already described—the training of all youth in the rudiments as a fundamental duty of the commonwealth.

Benefactions and gifts, great and small, public and private, were sought and obtained in every direction within the Massachusetts jurisdiction to sustain and build up this earliest of America's higher institutions of learning; and so was it with the later colleges of our colonial era in other commonwealths. Sturdy Connecticut, likewise emulous in the cause of education, profited by so pious an example; aiding generously, however, in Harvard's success by sending students to her sister colony until the time came, in 1701, when, with the aid of benefactions from among her own people, another and a home experiment of the kind might propitiously be undertaken. In both these colonies, in fact, the legislature led off with its own grant of endowment, the British Crown showing no special interest. But appeal was made, besides, for private gifts of the faithful. In Massachusetts, the timely benefaction of a young dying clergyman, a dissenter from the Church of England like his fellow-citizens, came in place of royal bounty and patronage, assuring life to the new-born enterprise. In Connecticut, a rich London merchant and an ex-settler of the colony, who had lately amassed a fortune in the East India trade, was destined, through his generous and repeated gifts, to have his name, Elihu Yale, bestowed by baptism upon the new college, and so be identified forever, like gentle John Harvard, with the cause of advanced education in this new world. Both these New England establishments, fairly indig-

enous in origin and owing little of pecuniary encouragement to the British Crown, developed healthily
into seminaries of American independence.

With William and Mary, intermediate in origin, and
planted, far remote from New England, in the Old
Dominion colony, the conditions of birth and early
growth were quite different. This institution, as its
name imports, was chartered and endowed in loyal
recognition of the new accession to the British throne
which followed the final expulsion of the Stuarts. And
it is notable that the same Governor Berkeley of Virginia, whose bigoted denunciation of free schools and
printing has been so often quoted against him in our
own enlightened age,[1] was by no means disinclined to
patronize, among the privileged of his colony, the cause
of higher learning which they strove in his day to
obtain. For the Virginia province was not wanting
in ideals of education, but to raise a suitable fund
by public taxation was the practical drawback. In the
present instance, patronage from abroad removed the
initial difficulty, and good William and Mary, the
world's only notable sovereigns in the duality of husband and wife, started the proposed college establishment with the means of a public support, and granted
a liberal charter besides. Its charter passed the seals
at London in 1691, and by 1693 the college was organized and set in operation at Williamsburg, bearing in
gratitude the joint names of its royal patrons.[2] Unlike
our other colonial colleges, the toil and tribulation of

[1] *Ante,* p. 199.
[2] This charter proclaimed broadly the establishment of a seminary for youth in a perpetual college of divinity, philosophy,
languages, and other good arts and sciences. One condition
of this charter required the college authorities to furnish to
England's ruling sovereign yearly, on the 5th of November,

William and Mary came late, instead of early; for it started its work with a money gift from the Crown of £2000, and with the further substantial privilege of certain taxes and perquisites. We see great institutions of learning in our day sustained by steel or standard oil; but the prime source of original support for William and Mary was tobacco, by a levy upon the export of that staple. The higher education thus made available in Virginia was intended for Maryland's benefit, besides, and the little candle at Williamsburg threw its beams, to speak metaphorically, over the whole region of Chesapeake Bay. A peculiar tie of affection bound this college to the mother church of Protestant England.[1]

My main purpose here is to picture these three earliest of American colleges—and those, besides, of eighteenth century origin—as they appeared and operated at the time when the bonds of colonial allegiance loosened and dropper apart. And first, to recur to Harvard, the oldest and proudest of them all. Under the wise and temperate administration of Edward Holyoke, who died in office in the non-importation year, 1769, at the age of eighty—the longest incumbent of the presidency in official term, save its present head,[2] that

two copies of Latin verses; and this—intended, I apprehend, rather as a token of safe allegiance than a proof of consummate scholarship—was regularly furnished while Virginia remained a British province. See H. B. Adams, in 1 Bureau of Education Reports (1887).

[1] The Bishop of London was the first chancellor of this institution, and the Virginian Bishop Madison, in after years, made here the connecting link of an American episcopate in Virginia.
[2] Dr. Charles W. Eliot.

Harvard has ever known—this institution prospered and advanced steadily in the confidence and affection of Massachusetts, despite the disfavor or indifference of Crown and Parliament. Native statesmen and men renowned in science, law and medicine graduated here, as well as noted divines of the Congregational faith. Hutchinson, the accomplished lieutenant-governor of this province, who served his king too faithfully to please his own fellow-subjects, was a Harvard man of the period; and more famous alumni, because famous rebels, were Samuel and John Adams, John Hancock, Jonathan Trumbull and Timothy Pickering—bright stars of our patriot constellation. Nor was it strange, considering the traditions of this college and commonwealth, that when Boston's long-smouldering discontent burst out into a blaze of opposition to the King and Parliament, Harvard should have espoused in sympathy the cause of the Massachusetts people against all oppression from over the seas.

Yet Harvard's authorities were wary during the first years of collision, and sustained the courtesies and dignity of their peculiar station. When in 1769 the Massachusetts legislature protested against sitting in Boston's old State House, with British redcoats stationed outside and a cannon pointed at the door, Governor Bernard ordered its sessions to be changed to Cambridge. To this the college corporation acceded, giving the use of Holden Chapel to the people's representatives. But when afterward the royal governor began issuing writs for convening the legislature at Harvard College, the corporation excepted to such sovereign infringement of its rights; and governor and council yielding the point, a formal request for the use of the college buildings was preferred and granted.

So then the General Court met and organized at the college, and after a sermon at the church, a dinner was served at Harvard Hall. In 1771, Hutchinson having by this time been made lieutenant-governor, the college sent him an address of congratulation, felicitating Harvard upon the honor shown by the Crown to one of its alumni; and Hutchinson made presently a public visit to the college with military pomp, when a beatific anthem was sung, a sermon preached and Latin orations pronounced. Laudation of the King had been avoided in the corporation address, but not in the lieutenant-governor's reply; and this whole demonstration offending the downright opposers of royal policy, Harvard changed presently her tone, as the logic of swift-moving events required. Classes of her zealous students had on various occasions since the Stamp-Act year passed resolutions to wear clothes of American fabrics on commencement and to withdraw their custom from a certain Boston bookseller known to be a rabid Tory. Even the theses in 1768 were printed vauntingly on paper made in the Massachusetts town of Milton. Afterward, when Cambridge became the highway of forcible resistance to the King's troops, and then headquarters of the American army, the college shifted its quarters; from the year 1775 commencement was omitted for some years, and Concord became for a brief spell Harvard's temporary seat of learning. Then back once more came students and faculty to Cambridge, whose buildings had been damaged by our Continental troops while occupying them as barracks during the siege of Boston.[1]

[1]It is a controverted point whether Burgoyne's officers, after the surrender of that general, were quartered in these college buildings. See XI Harv. Grad. Magazine, 50.

Meanwhile, the judicious Holyoke had been followed in the college presidency by Samuel Locke, a clergyman, who held office only four years, and resigned suddenly in 1773 for some unknown cause, his tender of office being accepted without formal regrets. To him, in 1774, succeeded Samuel Langdon of Portsmouth, New Hampshire, after others had declined, and this divine served through the most exciting years of the war. It was he who, at Cambridge, in cap and gown, on the lawn near the college grounds where Prescott's men were drawn up on their march to Bunker Hill, prayed for their success in the coming fight.

During the epoch I am describing, and shortly before Revolution, a rivalry sprang up between Yale and Harvard; and while the college at Cambridge was already thought lax in religious tenets, Yale was rigidly orthodox, and appealed accordingly to rural New England. This New Haven institution kept the main purpose of training for the ministry still in view, yet more than half her graduates were already laymen. The zealous but obstinate Clap and the affable and easygoing Daggett carried Yale's presidency to 1777 and the climax of Revolution; and there were brilliant tutors in those days, Jonathan Trumbull, Timothy Dwight and Joseph Buckminster being of the number. After our struggle for independence had once begun, Yale received little aid from the State for twenty years. The college stood high by this time in reputation, and was perhaps the highest in all British America for numbers and good scholarship; but its students were thought lacking in good manners, gentle amusements and polite accomplishments.[1] Revolution, while it lasted, severely crippled Yale, as it did our other col-

[1] Education Reports, No. 14, B. C. Steiner.

leges, disturbing the customary influx of young men, some of whom would go forth to fight for their country, while others came in meanly under the academic wing to avoid conscription. Nathan Hale, whom the British executed as a spy, was a Yale graduate, and so were General Wooster and that distinguished war governor of New Jersey, William Livingston. Connecticut, we should recall, escaped the worst ravages of war, except for Tryon's raid in 1779; yet Yale, like our other colleges, had a hard struggle for existence in those years of war and distress, though Dr. Stiles, installed as president in 1778, supplied an able administration.

At William and Mary, before Revolution developed, a good understanding was kept up in Virginia's capital between the college authorities and the Established Church of the province. The Episcopal clergy held their conventions in its buildings, and so did Virginia's House of Burgesses before their own edifice was erected. A representative of the college sat regularly in the Virginia legislature down to the Revolution. The faculty of instruction, here as elsewhere, preserved the old classical fundament of an English liberal education. Scholarships were established, and the annual revenue of the college before the outbreak of Revolution has been estimated as high as £2300. The establishment prospered throughout the colonial age; it was patronized by Virginia's influential families; it supplied to the patriot cause besides Jefferson, its most distinguished graduate, strong patriot leaders like Ben. Harrison, Thomas Nelson, George Wythe, Peyton Randolph and John Tyler, the elder. Washington and John Marshall, though not regular students or undergraduates, owed each something to William and Mary for the credentials of his civil profession. When

America's fight for independence began, far away in Massachusetts, there were here seventy students, more than half of whom joined speedily the Continental army, James Monroe being of the number.

But for years previous to 1775 complaints had been made that, notwithstanding its rich resources, superior, in fact, to those of any other college in the land, William and Mary fell behind the times in fulfilling its ends; that its discipline was lax; that both curriculum and strict tuition were wanting; that students elected chiefly their own studies, were allowed to go and come as they chose and gained their degrees too promiscuously.[1] For these or other reasons Madison took up his own course at Princeton in preference; while Washington himself, after encouraging the son of a personal friend to make a like choice of the New Jersey college, put his young ward, Custis, in King's (or Columbia), New York City.[2]

A few passing words with regard to the five new American colleges of the eighteenth century, born prior to the Revolution—Pennsylvania, Princeton, Kings (or Columbia), Brown and Dartmouth. Of the origin and rapid development of Pennsylvania I have spoken;[3] and this institution, which in ante-Revolutionary times was usually styled the Academy and College "of Philadelphia," made boast of its liberality in having a provost (or chief executive) of the English Church, while its

[1] V. G., 1774.
[2] II Washington's Works, 262, etc. Part of the undergraduate equipment of this young Virginia lad of independent means consisted of two horses, with a young colored boy to wait upon him.
[3] *Ante*, p. 205.

vice-provost belonged to the Church of Scotland. Pennsylvania started the earliest medical school in this country, with courses of lectures and the award of professional diplomas, long before the Revolution. Chastellux, attending its college commencement near the close of the war, found leaders of Congress, the president and executive council of the State, General Washington and the French minister among platform dignitaries with himself. Declamations in Latin and English by the graduating students impressed him very favorably. But in natural science this college seemed backward; "almost the only book of astronomy studied at Philadelphia," he observed, "is the almanac." The institution had sought in colonial times to stand well with the mother country. At the June commencement of 1765, "before a numerous and polite audience," as we read, that famous provost, William Smith, of Scotch importation, expressed in an elegant speech his warmest gratitude for the kind patronage of his sacred majesty and for the noble English benefactions already received for placing the college on a secure foundation. Dr. Smith made here a capable and energetic head, long in useful service, despite some vicissitudes. We see him in 1772, while soliciting funds in South Carolina, claiming with pride that Pennsylvania had already sent forth "a succession of patriots, lawgivers, sages and divines."

Princeton was even more fortunate when she secured Rev. Dr. John Witherspoon for president in 1768, an exotic likewise from Scotland, where he had gained distinction for learning and piety. In war times, when college work was for the time suspended, Witherspoon served acceptably in our Continental Congress. Imparting to his institution the spirit of liberty, he signed his

name both to the Charter of Independence and Articles
of Confederation. Chastellux, in his tour, met this
accomplished educator and held easy converse with him
in French. He found him ambitious for his college
and disposed to claim its rank as that already of a complete university, with a capacity for two hundred
students, besides the outboarders. About the time of
Witherspoon's instalment at Princeton, the college
trustees entered upon a new scheme for making the
necessary living there as moderate as possible, at the
same time goading parents and guardians of the students to greater punctuality in their remittances.[1]
They also made a post-graduate provision, encouraging
those who had completed their regular college course
to come back and pursue advanced studies, "whether in
divinity, law or physic, or such liberal accomplishments
in general as fit young gentlemen for serving their
country in public stations." Madison, the most famous
of Princeton's alumni in that era, availed himself of
these post-graduate opportunities. Yet in the year
1772, when Madison and Freneau took their degrees
here as bachelors, Princeton had a graduating class of
only twelve; and we must suppose that Dr. Witherspoon's grand schemes for his college, like those of some
other contemporaries, discounted considerably the aus-
picious future.

King's (now Columbia) College in New York City
was founded and administered as an institution of the
Episcopal faith, though broadly conducted in educational respects. This, like Pennsylvania, boasted the
special favor of the first three Georges, and some handsome gifts came from abroad for the Philadelphia and
New York colleges jointly. Here, too, somewhat later

[1] William and Mary had likewise to dun its debtors. V. G., 1771.

than at Philadelphia, was started by 1767 a medical school. King's sent forth her patriot sons, Jay and Hamilton among the rest, in the day of patriot resistance; yet the political atmosphere of that college was somewhat equivocal.[1] In 1776 its books and apparatus were stored, and under direction of the provincial Committee of Safety, its buildings were devoted to hospital uses; and when this college reopened its portals at the close of the war, a State charter changed its name permanently from "King's" to "Columbia."

Brown (the "Providence" or the "Rhode Island" College, as styled at first) was founded in the Roger Williams, or Baptist, faith, so widely prevalent in the Rhode Island colony. At the commencement of 1771, six seniors received their parchments; and one feature of the previous year had been a piece from Homer spoken by a boy of the grammar school only nine years old; for Brown, like other colleges of that day, had her preparatory department.

Dartmouth originated in Dr. Wheelock's transfer of his Indian school from Connecticut to Hanover, New Hampshire; and no little jealousy was aroused at Yale when this new seminary announced its readiness not only to teach Indians, but to train white missionaries for their conversion; nor this alone, but, under license of its liberal provincial charter, to exercise the functions of a college by instructing all who might apply, red or pale-faced, in humanities, the arts and sciences. Young men, especially from eastern Connecticut and the region of Wheelock's earlier labors, went consequently to Dartmouth in preference to Yale itself during the seventies.

[1] Lord Dunmore and General Gage were prominent in critical years at King's commencement exercises, which purposely left political subjects out of the programme.

In 1772 both of Dartmouth's graduates were from Connecticut; in 1773, five out of six; and so it continued for several years. John Phillips of Exeter was prominent among the eastern benefactors both of Dartmouth College and of Exeter Academy.[1]

The usual degrees in course were conferred by our American colleges in these early times, but not, as a rule, the honorary doctorates. Seniors, when graduating, were made bachelors of arts, and three years later advanced to masters. The usual grade of medical honor was bestowed upon those who took full courses at the schools in Philadelphia or New York; so that America had her M.D.'s. As to degrees purely honorary, Harvard, far back in 1692, had made Increase Mather a doctor of divinity; but that case stood as exceptional for nearly eighty years, during the long period of submissive allegiance to the mother country. Smith, of college presidents, had been made a doctor of divinity in 1759 by Oxford University; Witherspoon brought over a Scotch degree of similar grade. In 1770 Oxford conferred its D.D. upon two eminent clergymen of the Established Church in these colonies, William Peters of Philadelphia and Mather Byles of Boston; whereupon the latter, who was equally renowned in that day for his witticisms and Tory politics,

[1]Dartmouth celebrated her second commencement, in 1772, after a strenuous fashion. The governor of New Hampshire was present at the exercises; and to the people present, numbering some hundreds, there were distributed by his order an ox roasted whole, bread and a hogshead of liquor. The press relates that these common folk partook of the executive liberality with a decency and decorum that astounded the gentlemen present—so unlike the populace of other countries. M. G., 1772.

remarked, àpropos of the rising passion for non-importation in his vicinity, that he expected soon to find degrees turned out in America as a home product. He was not mistaken; for Harvard, at its commencement the very next summer, revived audaciously the sacred doctorate, bestowing it upon one of its own Congregational faith, Nathan Appleton, pastor of the church at Cambridge. Nor was this all, for at the commencement exercises in 1773 two more doctors of divinity were announced, Locke, the new president, and Rev. Samuel Mather; besides which Professor John Winthrop of the faculty, a man renowned for learning and liberal attainments, was made an LL.D., the first person at Harvard, and probably the first in all America, to receive such native distinction. Revolution and independence relaxed the conservatism of other colleges in this respect; though when Yale first conferred an honorary degree the General Assembly of Connecticut thought it a usurpation and unwarranted by the college charter. Washington, it is well known, was made by Harvard a doctor of laws in 1776, soon after the British evacuated Boston; and Chastellux mentions with pleasure eight years later a like conspicuous honor that he himself now received from William and Mary.

In soliciting benefactions, the heads of our several colleges bestowed something of that same assiduous ingenuity which in our own day is imposed upon such executives, though with more pitiful results. Smith of Pennsylvania and Witherspoon of Princeton kept up a lively competition in this respect, each making frequent appeal through the press in aid of his personal efforts. The one, after a successful trip to the mother country for funds, called, in 1772, for popular gifts from Pennsylvania's neighboring colonies. The other, in 1769, made a begging tour of Virginia and the South; and we see him in October preaching at Williamsburg to a good congregation and taking up a collection for Princeton after his sermon. Brown's executive the same year canvassed South Carolina for a similar purpose; and the fervid appeals made by Smith, Witherspoon and some other of our college presidents extended in that epoch not to our thirteen colonies alone, but even to British Jamaica and the remote West Indies.

Harvard, whose sons and grandsons set in the Massachusetts province the grand example of systematic filial remembrance—which, after all, is the most desirable in the long run—and to whose treasury individuals at home or abroad had by 1780 contributed about three times as much in money, land, produce, plate, books and apparatus as government had ever granted in the aggregate, framed, in 1773, a deliberate scheme for coaxing legacies and other donations into its treasury. A special book was to record the names of such donors, and their gifts were to be reported at each commencement. A further proposal—that of inscribing their names in gilt letters upon the walls of the college chapel—was not adopted.[1] Large benefactors of the college were further commemorated by having their pictures hung at Harvard Hall. When, in 1772, handsome bequests came to the college under the wills of Ezekiel Hersey and Nicholas Boylston, the corporation,

[1] Chastellux observes that in his time (1780-82), in order to reach the college from Boston, he had to take the ferry for Charlestown, and, in fact, to travel by sea and land, and pass through a former field of battle and an intrenched camp. He notes that each benefaction to the college library occupied its special place apart.

besides voting its formal thanks and giving to each professorship a commemorative name, asked the heirs of each donor for his portrait, to be painted at the college expense. Seven years earlier was installed a Hancock professor of the Hebrew and Oriental languages, through the liberal bounty of the late Thomas Hancock. At the commencement exercises of 1770 the audience were edified with a dialogue carried on in the Chaldaic tongue, "the first of the kind ever exhibited in America," and wholly the product of this generous foundation. Again, in the programme of 1771 was inserted a Samaritan dialogue, and in 1773 one in Arabic. John Hancock, the nephew, was immensely popular at Harvard in these ominous years by reason both of his late uncle's munificence and his own. He was chosen treasurer of the college with great applause; among his general gifts to alma mater were books for the library, carpets and wall paper; and he received in 1771 the distinguished honor of a standing invitation to dine at the college on all public occasions, taking his seat among the dons—"an extraordinary honor," observes President Quincy later in his history of Harvard College, "and without a parallel."

Co-education was a feature of Pennsylvania's academy and college in this eighteenth century. "Over two hundred of both sexes," announced Dr. Smith in 1770, "are constantly educated here on charity." And two years later he advertised that the board, lodging and washing of the average student was about $64 a year, while the cost was but $12 a year for education and firewood. Harvard and Yale competed in this era for students, and Yale seems sometimes to have outstripped her elder institution in numbers; yet in 1768, as we read, over forty seniors took the baccalaureate degree at Harvard, while at Yale the number was only twenty-nine. Emulous zeal, moreover, for astronomical research was shown. Yale had an excellent refracting telescope, and did good work on the meteors; but while Harvard, in June, 1769, studied the transit of Venus, Yale, not apprised of the planet's approach, lost her chance.

As to modes of higher education, America patterned largely upon those of England's best collegiate schools; and the prevailing distinction among men of higher culture in those days was founded upon proficiency in Greek and Latin. Orators in their speeches and literary men in their prose essays loved dearly to crack a Latin quotation for academic listeners or readers to enjoy as the mystic passwords of an exalted brotherhood. Matriculation needs at Harvard seem to have been somewhat increased in the time of President Locke; yet translating Cicero and declining perfectly the paradigms of nouns and verbs in Greek was the usual standard for admission. In Harvard's code, Christ was proclaimed the foundation of all sound knowledge and learning, and each student was expected to read the Scriptures twice daily and show his proficiency therein. At Yale, while Latin was pursued through standard classic authors, no Greek for a long time was regularly taught but that of the New Testament. Forensic disputations with syllogistic argument were in vogue both at Yale and Harvard—at first in Latin, but with English allowed later by way of variety. At Yale, President Clap developed the curriculum so as to give to natural philosophy and mathematics part of the time formerly bestowed upon logic; and he interested his students in the Newtonian philosophy, besides giving public lectures of his own on topics of civil government. Both forensics and disputations at the leading colleges in those times, whether as in course or for commencement parts, took up abstruse points of theology, though problems of civil government also received attention. As colleges gained in years and experience, tutors, professors and even presidents were chosen by preference from among the alumni.

The usual rules of academic discipline have been preserved in old college codes, which were engrossed at first in Latin and afterwards in English. To redeem the time, to avoid profane language, to attend all lectures and recitations, and never to leave town and the college environs without permission—these were standing requirements that explained themselves. Attendance upon morning and evening prayers and the Sunday services was also enjoined; and besides the spiritual good thus afforded, the daily prayers served as a conventional roll-call and counting of the students, an incentive to promptness and regularity for meals and rising and a powerful stimulus withal to the ideal of a full collegiate brotherhood—classes and faculty all united in devotion. Great reverence and respect to the faculty was inculcated, though not actually rendered without that respect of persons which buoyant youth, keen observers of their elders' weaknesses, will manifest to the end of time. All undergraduates were to doff the hat when their governors were about, never seating themselves first nor speaking to them except with uncovered head. Upon freshmen most of all did the rules of college behavior bear thus early with stringency. No freshman, as Harvard's laws enjoined, was to wear his hat in the college yard unless it rained,

hailed or snowed, provided he were on foot and had not
his hands full. Freshmen were to consider students of
all other classes as their seniors and accost them with
all the outward signs of deferential respect. Yale's
rules forbade freshmen to play with members of an
upper class without being asked or to be familiar with
them, even in study hours. At both institutions, and
probably among our other colleges, as in the great
English schools, fagging prevailed to a considerable
extent; and youths of the class last entered were expected to run errands for the upper students. Moreover, as Harvard's rules expressed it, when any one
knocked on the door of a freshman, he should immediately open it without calling out, "Who is there?"

Against oppression, stern discipline or inflicted hardships, rebellion will break out in college precincts as in
the commonwealth of adults. Harvard men, in 1766,
indignant over the poor bread given them in the commons, sought board in private families. At Yale, in
1771, the greater part of the students "eloped from
the college" (as newspapers of the day expressed it)
because of some dissatisfaction; but many of them soon
returned to duty. Private reprimand, public admoni-
tion, suspension or expulsion might serve for a graded
college discipline of dignity, though fines were to some
extent imposed. For the old arrangement of placing
students according to their social station, the modern
alphabetical order was substituted at Yale only a few
years earlier than at aristocratic Harvard, whose privileged sons of the quality continued to secure the best
chambers in the college and to help themselves first at
commons until 1773. Sports were not in those days
so organized as to monopolize time or divert the youth
from serious studies; but while match games were per-

haps unknown here in the eighteenth century, students took simple recreation, such as running long foot-races around the college grounds. Football, in its season, was already a game in which the sons of Eli were thought highly accomplished, though simply and fairly conducted, as compared with the present day. Hazing prevailed at most colleges, and other such outrages of remote origin; ingenious tricks were played upon members of the faculty, and especially the unpopular ones; while at Harvard disorders became so frequent on quarter days, with the breaking of tutors' windows, that the observance of those dates was finally discontinued. Commencements, too, with the leave-taking of classmates, engendered lawless riot and drunkenness; hence at Yale, in 1760, each candidate for a degree was restricted, by a faculty vote, to two gallons of wine for his parting entertainment. Plum cake is said to have done students much harm at festive entertainments of this character.

Commencement day was in all our collegiate towns at that era a sort of public occasion. Its celebration was marked by a great display and liveliness among the common people such as we nowadays seldom witness. Booths were erected along the sidewalk, and a disposition was shown, even among the industrial and illiterate of our college towns, to enjoy a general holiday. The governor of the commonwealth, escorted by soldiery, came out to participate in the exercises, as he still continues to do in some States; and the march of the students, gowned dignitaries, public men and invited guests for academic exercises and the bestowal of degrees at the church was of a unique character, as it very largely continues to this day. Inside those sacred walls the programme differed very little from that which graduates still living can recall. Innovation, in fact, upon the old curriculum or upon old customs and ceremonies of our collegiate life came very gradually in America until a new and vigorous sweep of the besom began some thirty years ago. In colonial times, much more than now, commencement dinner, with its toasts and speeches, interested outsiders and the general public; and sometimes, as at Cambridge, a vocal and instrumental concert rounded out a memorable holiday.

So once more the sacred insignia of academic authority were brought into view whenever a new college president was inducted into office; seal, keys, books and charter were handed over to him on the platform as he was formally placed in the imposing but highly uncomfortable chair of state. In short, the Old-World ideals of ritualism, so jealously prohibited by our New-World Puritan and dissenter in matters of religion and the church, found still a considerable expression where scholastic and secular dignities alone were concerned.

XVI

THE vivacious Chastellux had little fellow-feeling for the Sabbatarians of this New World. "You cannot," he writes, "travel in New England on Sunday but the deacons will stop your horse and take you to a magistrate." And he contrasts French observance of that day as a gay and joyous holiday, with the wretched idleness and listlessness, as he terms it, of a Sunday passed by the people of the United States.

In vain has been such criticism. As well seek to uproot the palisades along the Hudson as to persuade Americans to celebrate the Lord's day after Parisian fashion. Not all the laxness of religious faith, the atheism and agnosticism, the reactionary impulse from intensity of work to intensity of recreation, which these last hundred years have wrought in American life, has greatly changed the prevalent disposition to keep the Lord's day holy, in a sense—to make it, at least, a day of rest and outward sobriety rather than of boisterous pleasure-seeking. When in Rome we do as the Romans do, but when in America, American opinion sets the fashion. More than a quiet desecration of the Sabbath is scarcely tolerated.

The motive for a strict Sunday observance among our colonial progenitors is traceable to the Christian and Protestant character of America's early settlements.   It was not the quest of gain or the love of adventure that brought them over in bands to these Atlantic wilds so much as a deep desire to escape the bonds of church and state, which defined their humbler condition at home, and to solve in this New World great problems that interested them.   Colonization here was coincident with Reformation in Europe, and the popular struggle was for greater individual freedom in matters both of religious and secular rule.   If not tolerant themselves in all respects, our fathers sought toleration for what most deeply interested them; if nonconformists in a sense, they wished conformity to their own dissent.   Puritans, who gave much stability to the political forces developing here, felt deeply themselves the seriousness of human life and endeavor.   Gayety or light-heartedness, such as befits a people for enjoying recurring holidays, goes rather with a fixedness of inferior social caste, monotonous toil for a living and the absence of all broad opportunity for bettering greatly the conditions of birth.   Most of all, it involves a childlike irresponsibility for the direction of affairs.   Who can estimate how greatly man is indebted for his happiness in the chance occasions of life to the consciousness that the operations of the weather, which help or mar a projected plan, must go on without his intervention or conclusive forecast?   Hence in Continental Europe was seen a joyful holiday abandonment on the part of a populace, such as Americans had far too serious a task to share.   Like Sancho Panza's wife, who gave all her big words to the priest, they of contemporary France, Spain or Italy cast their cares upon their temporal and spiritual masters and confessed their own littleness.

"Merrie England" herself, in the age before

America was discovered, was more of a child in popular pastimes than it has ever been since the days of the Protestant martyrs. It was a tale often told during the era we are considering,[1] that when in the mother country Charles I. issued his proclamation authorizing sports and amusements throughout the realm on Sundays, as in the olden times, he required the royal mandate to be read in the churches. Many of the reluctant clergy complied with the order, some refused, while others hurried through the document in tones as inaudible as possible. But one minister, whose congregation had expected no such compliance, did, to their great surprise, read the proclamation through distinctly. He followed it, however, with a reading, equally distinct, of the fourth commandment, "Remember that thou keep holy the Sabbath day," and so on. "Brethren," he then proceeded, "I have laid before you the commandment of your king and the commandment of your God. I leave it to yourselves to judge which of the two ought rather to be observed."

Life here was no bagatelle for jesting. It required courage enough to take ground against prevailing tenets, however reverently. Outside Pennsylvania, a Quaker or a Papist in these colonies had hardly a safe refuge against persecution. In Virginia, very close to the Revolution, Baptists were imprisoned for their nonconforming extravagance, and preached from grated windows to those who gathered outside. "What!" said Patrick Henry in his maiden plea as a jury lawyer on their behalf, shaming the prosecution, "that these

[1] IV Franklin's Works, 435.

men are to be tried as for misdemeanor for preaching
the Gospel of the Son of God!"

Thus, then, did society rest from secular toil,
while religious worship and meditation marked the day.
Even Saturday night was one of Sabbath preparation
as far as possible—a "tub night" for the young children, with subdued amusement, if any, for their elders;
while Sunday evening, though it might be argued that
the Sabbath ended at six o'clock, was the favorite time
for sparking or family visits. And for these latter
purposes it availed not a little that cleanliness had preceded godliness, and that the best Sunday clothes were
in evidence. Riding was chiefly to church or meeting
in rural communities, and the bright Sabbath stillness
was broken only by the church-going bell. To meet
once a week as neighbors in the great congregation was
of itself inspiring.

> "How sweet a Sabbath thus to spend,
> In hope of one that ne'er shall end."

Over the irreligious minority of their own inhabitants
the native press held constantly the rod. "They who
drive their carriages on the Lord's day," it was laid
down,[1] "must at least walk gently their horses when
they pass a meeting-house; otherwise we shall complain
of them as a nuisance."

The Congregational Church, which thus early
formed the establishment of the Eastern States or
colonies, was rigid, for the most part, in its Calvinism.
Presbyterians flourished among the Middle and South-

[1] M. G., 1771.

ern colonies, the Scotch-Irish settlers in rural and mountainous regions furnishing the sturdiest element of that faith. Virginia had modelled early a church establishment upon that of the mother country, the Bishop of London having a perfunctory oversight; and so, too, after the expulsion of the Stuarts, had Maryland, rejecting the broader tolerance proposed by Lord Baltimore. The old parish subdivision of counties, in preference to the New England town system, obtains in Maryland and Virginia to this day. For Congregational and Presbyterian supply in the ministry, the several provinces provided as far as possible in their local colleges; but our Episcopal churches came under the nominal supervision of the Bishop of London, and every one of their clergy was examined and ordained in England at a considerable personal cost. Populous Pennsylvania, under the wise direction of her great founder, encouraged churches of all denominations; and there alone among our colonies Quakers themselves made a respectable show in point of numbers and influence. Among the other Protestant bodies of those times were the Baptists, whose chief strength, perhaps, was in Rhode Island; the Dutch Reformed of New York and the French Huguenots in South Carolina.

For powdered heads and grandeur of costume as displayed in the city churches, Episcopalians and Presbyterians (or Congregationalists) took the lead. Few wigs or velvet suits were to be seen among the Baptists; while Quakers dressed in the plain drab of their order. How many evangelical ministers, churches and communicants were in America at the outbreak of Revolution cannot be determined, but the proportion they bore to the population was far less than in later times.[1]   Nor

[1] Baird's "Religion in America."

should this seem strange when the sparseness of those broad settlements is considered. Methodism with its itinerant preaching had hardly yet taken the field, and as remote homes were compelled to dispense practically with the physician or surgeon, so, too, did they bear privation in gospel privileges. But the Bible was daily read at the hearth and fireside. The earnest parish clergyman extended far his visitations, and people journeyed miles by chaise or on horseback to attend an occasional public worship.

I have spoken of an evangelical or Protestant ministry in the thirteen colonies. The Roman Catholic Church, so powerful in our own day, with its historic unity, its immense organism, its devoted hierarchy and an adaptation far better to the tastes and exigencies of American life than formerly, was almost literally outlawed during colonial times, except in Pennsylvania. And the inspiration of intolerance in that respect came from England herself, after the accession of William and Mary. Liberty of conscience, "except to Papists," was the expression of the Massachusetts charter of 1691. Jesuitical influence, a pompous ritual and ceremonies, the Bible in an unknown tongue and the priestly control of laymen's consciences were all hateful to the Protestantism which peopled our wilderness. On each recurring 5th of November a stuffed image of the Pope was borne about in effigy and burned; and in the Stamp-Act riots, Pope, devil and the obnoxious minions of the Crown shared popular execration alike and were consigned to the flames together. When Samuel Adams held forth to the people of Philadelphia on the steps of Independence Hall, just after the Declaration had been adopted, he denounced Popery and monarchy together as the twin foes of popular freedom.

Many of us still living have seen spasmodic returns of such popular odium, with Roman churches and clergy assaulted in our chief cities, and Roman convents burned to the ground by mobs whose rallying cry was "Americans to rule America." And among our forefathers, in the age I am describing, the opinion strongly and constantly prevailed that there was something foreign, outlandish and tyrannous in Rome's ecclesiastical methods. A scorching sermon, printed about 1767, set forth "the idolatry and damnable heresies and abominable superstitions and crying wickednesses of the Romish Church;" and Harvard included that topic of denunciation among its annual Dudleian lectures. We see the Virginia *Gazette* complaining in 1775 that the imported British soldiery sought to force these colonists to submit to "Popery and slavery."

It is estimated, however, that at the date of the Revolution there were about fifty Roman Catholic Churches in all the colonies, and about half that number of Romish priests. Most worshippers of that faith were humble Irish, who could afford but little outlay. Strange did it seem to tolerant Philadelphia to behold, by 1737, a chapel whose doors stc od open not only upon church fasts and festivals, but every day in the week. Our French alliance aided Romanism in Baltimore. When Count Rochambeau returned northward with his French troops from victorious Yorktown, he left one of his legions in Baltimore until the close of the war. An unfinished Catholic chapel was here opened for their benefit, and mass was celebrated on occasion, a French

military band accompanying the service with their
music.[1]

Not only was Rome's hierarchy dreaded in colonial
America, but to a large majority of the inhabitants
even the moderate name of Bishop was obnoxious.
Happily for the public peace, our Episcopal clergy were
moderate and evangelical for the most part. They
shifted the surplice before mounting their preaching
tubs, and wore in the pulpit that black Geneva gown
with which so many of our dissenting clergy liked to
adorn themselves. They disregarded the church calendar, observed Sundays only, avoided mediæval practices and made of our English liturgy a service bald
and tedious to prolixity. When the project of sending
over an American bishop was broached about the
middle of the eighteenth century a large number of
that clergy, particularly in Virginia and her neighboring provinces, were found indifferent or averse to the
project, as well as were the laity. The Virginia House
of Burgesses voted in 1771 their thanks to the clergy
of that province who had opposed this "pernicious
project." Meanwhile our colonists at the eastward had
taken up the discussion. Such divines, on the one side,
as Apthorp, Cutler and Chandler were stoutly con-
fronted on the other by Mayhew, Chauncey and others.
There were pamphlets of "appeal" and of "appeal
answered." One popular objection put forward was
that colonists would be obliged to maintain bishops,
when they could hardly maintain themselves, still less
the churches and clergy of their own faith. Prejudice
was inflamed, moreover, against any strengthening of

[1]Scharf's "Baltimore."

ranks and orders; "no lords, spiritual or temporal," was the cry. Yet it was not only the lords spiritual who might have been feared in a religious establishment. Blackstone, the recluse who was found on Boston soil when the Puritans came to settle there, received invitation to attend their Congregational worship. "I came from England," he replied, "because I did not like the lord bishops; but I cannot join work with you because I would not be under the lord brethren."

The Methodists, so strong a body in our own century, had not yet fairly organized. But the Wesley brothers had visited America; and their eloquent young associate, Whitefield, who first came over in 1740, travelled north and south for years as an itinerant preacher and missionary, dying in Massachusetts in 1770, while in the plenitude of his fame. He and the "new lights" school of evangelists to which he belonged—for the Church of England, to its later regret, had suspended him and the Wesleys from the ministry because of their non-conforming modes—preached earnestly in our churches, of one denomination or another, on individual work for individual salvation, and raised dormant and complacent congregations to new zeal and new effort in personal religion. Dancing schools were discontinued and balls and concert rooms shut up, while thousands thronged eagerly to hear Whitefield discourse of the higher life at church or in the open fields. He was a prodigy of eloquence, and devoted to his work; not a leader, perhaps, in theological thought or discussion, but unquestionably the greatest pulpit orator of his times in the English tongue. He did not hold camp meetings, however, nor apply lay stimulants to a popular excitement, but inspired and entranced by his own fervent preaching.

Jonathan Edwards, New England born and pastor among the Congregationalists, must not be forgotten; nor the powerful revival he accomplished during that era in Connecticut and Massachusetts. His exposition of God's wrath and the impending terrors of the second death made sinners quake and tremble before him. "Fond, impious man," whose doom he pictured, seemed to him like some bloated black spider, hanging by his thread of self-sufficiency, whom a repulsive Deity would cast into the depths of a bottomless abyss. Edwards was something of a naturalist, scrutinizing the visible signs of the lower creation about him; and the sketches of sermons, still extant, which he used to carry with him into his pulpit, at first written upon fair sheets of paper, but in later life upon the blank pages of old letters and scraps, cannot well be read by the average eye without the aid of a microscope.

As to our clergy generally in the Revolutionary age, we find them differently regarded for temporal functions in different jurisdictions. New York, Delaware, Virginia, the Carolinas and Georgia each showed in framing its independent State constitution a real dislike of clergymen in politics. To be sure, chaplains in the military service or for public secular occasions were generally approved; but as to having ministers sit in a legislature or hold civil office, that was another matter. Dr. Witherspoon of New Jersey (and he a college president, not settled over a congregation) supplies the exceptional instance of one, ordained and enrolled in the ministry, who sat as a delegate in the Continental Congress. But some of our thirteen colonies, Massachusetts notably, took a different view.

Her constitution of 1783 drew the line rather against Harvard College and its instructors; it was these who were forbidden to sit in the General Court. In truth, the influence of the New England clergy in public affairs at that day and long after was very great. The town-meeting system favored a settled parish minister in that respect, for in such gatherings he had a voice and vote with his fellow-citizens; and as a townsman of superior talents and education, stable and fixed in his domicile, the rearer of a large family with the rest, and a ready speaker besides, he was often put forward in politics to give strong direction. In this eastern section we see the ambassador for Christ chosen frequently to serve as a town delegate in convention or the legislature. But his chief political influence was in his own pulpit; for there he had abundant opportunity, which he improved, to discuss the affairs of the day and give his own bias to public opinion. His fast-day sermon discoursed of political sins and shortcomings; that of Thanksgiving recounted political blessings. Civil magistrates, and representatives both civil and military, sought their chosen clergymen to gain inspiration and guidance for the work before them. At New England celebrations the sermon was a chief feature. In Massachusetts, for spring "election day," the preacher was chosen in rotation, by the people's representatives one year and by the royal governor the next.

The fervent recognition of a Divine intervention on the popular behalf marked the age I am describing. "It is the Lord's doing," proclaimed the clergy as independence approached. Sermons, like other pamphlets, were kept constantly on sale or offered for subscription. Among both clergy and the laity we see in the letters and diaries of this age, as well as in the press, a strain of pious ejaculation, with moralizing upon passing events. The churches, among other public bodies, would proffer their congratulations to temporal rulers, expecting formal response. Listeners at church took down sermons in shorthand. Among Presbyterians the custom prevailed, as we still see it observed in the Church of Scotland, of keeping Bibles in the pew and carefully verifying the text and scripture citations of each Sunday's discourse. Sermons were lengthy and to a large extent ranged under consecutive heads for developing the idea of the text, after which came corresponding heads for application by way of improvement. Many a preacher inverted his hour-glass as the discourse proceeded.

Congregational clergy were settled locally by the local congregation, and the New England theory was that of independent churches and independent ministers of the faith. Presbyterians yielded more to a governing supervision, and held synods in Philadelphia, which considered the general advantage of the body in various colonies. The Episcopal Church, we have seen, had no resident bishop, and hence no positive local supervision. Yet the Episcopal clergy of adjacent provinces (probably without lay representation) met at seasons for mutual counsel and encouragement; as in 1768, when those of New York, Connecticut and New Jersey assembled in New York City.[1] Consecration abroad and an English common prayer made a bond of union. There were no ecclesiastical courts in America; but Presbyterians were guided by Scottish precedents,

---

[1] That gathering, however, was largely for uniting efforts to procure the appointment of a bishop by the Crown, and no general church convention for the colonies seems ever to have taken place.

while Methodists, as they developed, took their rules from John Wesley. Quakers and Baptists made little acknowledgment of external influence or dictation. Among the Congregationalists of Massachusetts there was a fraternity of the churches, but it disclaimed all exercise of authority.

In working out, much later, a general toleration and the voluntary system of support, the religious bodies I have described combined in the various commonwealths according to circumstances. Episcopalians, as well as Baptists, felt the burden of supporting Congregational ministers and churches in New England; while in Maryland and Virginia Baptists and Presbyterians united against the favoritism of tithes and glebes which the transplanted mother church had enjoyed. Congregationalism in its religious polity wove admirably into the New England pattern for temporal affairs, since local self-government was its essence.

For the support of aged and infirm clergy and the widows and orphans of such as died in the service of the English church, missionary provision was aided in the mother country; but in our churches of independent tenets such relief was precarious, and varied with the local regard in such matters. Clergymen of advancing years were assisted by colleagues, or "partnership clergymen," as they were called, who, like the young coadjutor of a church bishop in our day, might look forward to a full succession whenever a final vacancy should occur. The tenure of colonial clergy in New England towns promised great stability for each pious incumbent who could keep down dissension and strife. Pastors were known to serve here for fifty years or more over one congregation, and such was the strength of social and family ties that the old pastor not unfre-

quently handed over his charge to a son or son-in-law in
the faith. In old Virginia, parish vacancies were seen
advertised, which set forth the salary as something
exclusive of perquisites. Preachers, as a rule, were
males, of course, in those days, and a sedate and educated ministry was preferred for the most part. Boy
evangelists were unknown; and the inspired tinker or
cobbler was most likely a Baptist innovation, for congregations made up of simple folk. Among Quakers,
or Friends, however, men or women arose in the meeting, as the spirit moved, and there was a noted woman
preacher of this faith, Rachel Wilson, who went about
between New Haven and New York as an itinerant.
Whenever a new church was "embodied" in a town and
a pastor installed, all was conducted (as the press of
the day would phrase it) "with the greatest decency
and order."

Anything like the calendar of the mediæval church
Americans of this age inclined, as Protestants and re-
formers, to disregard. Christmas day itself had been
constantly under the ban in Massachusetts. Nor even
among our churchmen could the Lenten season find yet
a Protestant observance, nor Good Friday and Easter ·
bind Christian hearts together. For merriment and
good cheer, so far as permissible, New Yorkers fixed
upon New Year's, while New England set up a November celebration of its own named Thanksgiving.
Church feasts and fasts were condemned and controverted by Presbyterian and Congregationalist alike;
while Episcopalians themselves reduced such celebration to a limited standard. To attend divine service on
week days was not to be thought of, save for bald
observances which had not church tradition back of
them. Notable, however, in this latter respect was

Boston's Thursday lecture, which had been observed
there from the first settlement of this town until the
British occupation. After Washington raised the siege
here, in 1776, Bostonians gathered once more to renew
that sacred institution, our grave commander-in-chief
lending his own devout presence to the occasion. He
was met, with his general officers and the invited guests,
at the council chamber, attended by the sheriff with his
wand, the councillors, the selectmen and others. The
whole procession marched to the old brick meeting-
house near by, where Rev. Dr. Eliot preached from
Isaiah 33 : 20.[1]

A few words may be added touching our church edifices and their arrangements in our Revolutionary age.
Of church architecture at that date in America we may
fairly judge by the specimens still left in our older
States ; among the best of them, and the most characteristic, being King's Chapel, the Old South and Christ
Church in Boston, St. Paul's Chapel in New York and
Christ Church in Philadelphia. In remote New England towns, moreover, we may still see the big, painted,
wooden sanctuary perched in a commanding place and
guarding its old cemetery, while in the Middle or
Southern colony stands its rural contemporary of more
durable brick, inspiring equal reverence. Such temples
of worship were severely plain in outward and interior
aspect, with singers' gallery opposite the pulpit, great
side galleries for boys and indentured servants, and
pews (a modern institution), high backed, supplied
with doors and fastenings and severely exclusive in ap-

[1] N. E. C. A dinner at the "Bunch of Grapes" followed at
the public expense, with appropriate toasts of joy.

pearance, in which gathered severally the large families of the locality for public worship.

Only the Church of England houses of worship imitated Catholic Christendom in those times by applying names like Christ, St. Paul's or Trinity, to designate the society; and most commonly congregations in a town or parish were distinguished as numerically the *first* or the *second,* and so on, of a particular faith. In the early settlements of New England it often happened that the local house of worship served for town gatherings besides, where politics were discussed; and hence the familiar term "meeting-house" as applied by the common folk, with the phrase "going to meeting" to attend the Sabbath worship. Many a patriotic gathering took place in such houses of prayer and praise. In the Old South orators denounced standing armies on each recurring anniversary of the Boston massacre. And in Virginia, too, it was the parish church at Richmond where Patrick Henry made his immortal appeal for "liberty or death."

To the reforming, protesting spirit of our evangelical religion a century and a half ago churches or cathedrals of the mediæval pattern with ornate interior were offensive. Church edifices still to be seen in London of the Wren pattern furnished models for our religionists of the New World. Favored by the needs of England's metropolis after the great fire, Sir Christopher rose to pre-eminence there by the new buildings of modern styles which he introduced, and most of all by the new St. Paul's Cathedral, with its massive dome, which rose from the ashes of its predecessor upon historic Ludgate Hill. Yet that costly and magnificent church—the largest Protestant temple of worship in the world to this day—expended its chief resources upon

outside grandeur, and until about thirty years ago its
blank gray walls and interior seemed to repel emotion.
Still more so was it with the image-breaking spirit
which inspired our stern Protestant worshippers of the
thirteen colonies. Imposing effects, if there were such,
were chiefly displayed outside, for within the walls
pictures, sculpture, high altars, ritual processions and
ceremonies were strenuously forbidden. Such adornment as might at all consist with the orthodox spirit
of the day did not extend beyond tablets of the com-
mandments with letters in flourishing script, plush
velvet pulpit cushions, cherubs' heads and wings, a pipe
organ in the loft or a glass chandelier at the centre of
the broad aisle. Nor were even such ornamental ap-
pendages common. Churches on bleak sites, which had
been kept closed all the week, were not easily warmed
for the Sabbath in winter time by the moderate stoves
and heating apparatus then in use.[1]

With the mediæval tower less in vogue, current
ecclesiastical taste favored sharp steeples or else the
round-topped belfry, these running to a height which
would well rear the sacred 'pile above the ordinary
abodes of home and business. Old Trinity in New
York, a parish already wealthy for its real estate possessions, had a steeple 175 feet high and ornamental of
aspect. Old Christ Church in Philadelphia paid, by the
proceeds of a lottery, for erecting a steeple, nearly
twenty years after the body of the church was built.
Copper-plate pictures of Boston at this period show the
buildings of that town surmounted by pointed steeples,

[1]Progress had been made with stoves for keeping one's extremities warm during the long hours of worship; but Franklin,
in 1773, still found occasion to commend foot-stoves and bear-
skin cases for the legs, *more majorum*.

picketed close together, as though ready to impale the host of Lucifer should such adversaries fall once more from heaven.

As silent guide and monitor to the inhabitants of the sober little community, the church with its lofty topping undertook three general functions: (1) Its bell rang out for fire and the curfew, or to summon and celebrate on public occasions; it sounded for joy; it tolled for funerals or for public sorrow; and all this in addition to the Sunday summons. (2) Its vane, perched on the pinnacle, pointed the direction of the wind and aided man's forecast of the weather; and were the device a cockerel, a grasshopper, an arrow or something still more fanciful, the eyes of mankind grew used to watching it. (3) Its clock at the belfry's base, though as yet a feature for America somewhat uncommon, regulated the daily life and rounded out a wholesome influence through the week. In the push and turmoil of modern life we open our hearts less readily to impressions for good such as moved the imagination of our sober ancestors amid more simple surroundings. Religion in our own day has to arrest, if it may, by more sedulous endeavor, the alluring schemes of worldly indulgence or ambition which tend to absorb men's souls and draw them from contemplation of the life hereafter. Steeples themselves dwarf into insignificance in our noisy and crowded cities, overtopped, as we so often behold them in recent years, by the high Babels of finance and business.

XVII

LIBRARIES AND CLUBS

A FEW words as to libraries, those life-long educators of the young and old of both sexes, whose opportunities in our own later times are large and constant. Each of the colonial colleges I have described[1] had its own library, more or less ample, besides scientific implements; chiefly, however, for the immediate use of its students and faculty for the time being. It is said that America's best library and philosophical apparatus of the age perished in the flames when Harvard Hall was burned down in 1764. But that hall was rebuilt substantially, as it still stands, shortly before the Revolution; and Massachusetts bestowed upon the college in 1778 hundreds of books confiscated from Tory refugees as an outfit for the future. Princeton's library and philosophical apparatus were much depleted while New Jersey was the seat of British hostilities.

Public or general libraries as we have them so abundantly to-day, the offspring of local taxation or a rich person's munificence, had no existence in America in colonial days; but they whose means and tastes permitted it filled their shelves at home with such books as personal gift or purchase might bring together, and loaned to their less favored friends and dependents. Except, indeed, for the Bible and the almanac, people pored over print far less than they do now; and the

[1] *Ante,* p. 216.

books they read were more for self-improvement, self-
edification or for storing the mind in the practical pursuits of divinity, law, medicine or politics, than for
any mere recreation or light amusement. But there
were already co-operative or subscription libraries in
the leading colonial centres; and chiefly to the public-
spirited Franklin we owe the origin of such establishments. Out of the club, or Junto, of young mechanics in
Philadelphia, who had brought their private books together in a single room for mutual convenience, grew,
in 1731, the primitive scheme of an organized subscription library, such as first developed in Franklin's
adopted city and thence spread rapidly to other chief
towns and provinces. Its fundamental idea of support
was that of a solid sum paid to constitute full member-
ship; with a yearly subscription, besides, by way of
current assessment for the annual privilege of taking
out books.[1] No better plan was ever devised for stimulating reading and self-culture in a community which
finds no wealthy benefactor and is itself too poor to
levy a tax for such purposes.

General circulating libraries were also maintained to
some extent in this early age, and such agencies, to be
self-sustaining, were naturally the enterprise of individual booksellers. John Mein, a Boston bookseller,
undertook in 1765 to loan books in this manner; "a
scheme," as he advertised it, "hitherto unattempted in
New England."[2] This circulating library was chiefly
for Mein's fellow-Bostonians; but persons living in the

[1] The Philadelphia library began (as Franklin relates in his
Autobiography) with fifty subscribers of forty shillings each, to
start with, and ten shillings a year while the term of association
should last.

[2] The rate he proposed was £1, 8s. a year; catalogues were
issued at 1s. extra; and subscribers were requested to send a

country might pay double and get two books at a time; being, moreover, at the special cost of conveyance, whatever that might be. Philadelphia in these years had also a bookstore, kept by a man named Nicola, who advertised 700 choice books for hire, of the most approved authors.[1]

Books and a good library have supplied the chief or, indeed, the only means of education of many a man struggling upward in life with the weight of early poverty and privation to encumber him. But more than this, such silent aids to knowledge and self-improvement avail many a college or university man whose routine opportunities have somehow failed of their full results. We discuss, sometimes, the question whether the higher education for active life should be longer or shorter; whether one, two or three years ought to be taken away from the period of college undergraduate work, to be tacked on to a person's high-school course at one extreme or to that of his professional school at the other. But it is not, believe me, the higher training of a few years, more or less, that fits one for a really useful career. At the college, the university or the professional school the youth of talent and promise gains choice and stimulating companionship at the plastic period of life, measures himself against great contemporaries while he and they are young, and masters the various schemes which may enable him to choose and steer his course over the wide sea of human endeavor and achievement. And yet, for real success and ac-

list of six or eight books at a time, so as to be sure to get some one of the books wanted. ' M. G., 1765.

[1]His terms of subscription were $2 per year, to be paid half-yearly, and no credit given. But credit was actually given, and general duns for payment were sometimes advertised in the local press.

complishment, the labor before him is that of a well-
bestowed lifetime, beginning with his youth; and not
only does the strong incentive to study come to many
of us at some stage of experience after the brief college
years have actually ended, but all study and all higher
education should, in order to produce perfect fruition,
continue as long as one's mental powers are capable
of production and exercise at all, and until death comes
or the collapse of that intellectual capacity to which
nature sets a limit, but no definite one.

Among the maxims inscribed upon the marble entrance hall of that noble library building in Washington
which confronts our great temple of national legislation
on Capitol Hill, is this: "The true university is a collection of books." To a statement so broad we may not
readily subscribe; but, at all events, it may well be said
that books remain our permanent tutors and instructors
long after the university or professional school, with its
curriculum, has been left behind.

Distinct from those private organizations of which
we find so many nowadays for objects religious, political or philanthropic, is the club proper, whose chief aim
is good fellowship. Exclusion, segregation is here the
vital principle; and however far-reaching may be associate aims for the general good, it is mutual improvement alone or mutual pleasure that is more directly
sought; while the admission of outsiders to the con-
fraternity becomes a matter of strict patronage, selection and favor. This very idea of keeping out the
common herd gives zest to the personal and piquant
enjoyment of a club, somewhat as in the closely drawn
circle of home and family or the cliques of fashion,

Everything in our present age tends to organism and the co-operation of individuals wherever something grand is to be accomplished; but it was far less so in the days of our Revolutionary forefathers. Then the first strong bond was that of one's own household, and next came the fraternity of congenial neighbors. Lines of travel were circumscribed; wives gossiped at the back door of each other's houses, and men who sought easy companionship in the hours of idleness drew up their horses on the road to discourse, or lounged in the inn bar-room, or sat about the stove together at some country grocer's. Of social clubs, such as we find them nowadays in our chief cities, with costly buildings and sumptuous equipment, all for privacy and pleasure—homes, in a sense, for the homeless few and favored, but rather disintegrating in their influence upon the domestic and married life—of these there were none whatever in America at that early period. For, first of all, we had not communities rich enough or populous enough to support such style. Men were busy, simple and domestic in their tastes, and the idle and pampered sons of luxury were wanting.

Yet at one stage of development or another the club principle, which combines choice spirits for the common pursuit of some desired end, selfish or unselfish, indoors or out-of-doors, is as old as mixed society itself. It may be a literary junto or a beefsteak club or a jockey club; it may hire a room for meetings, patronize an eating-house or build a cheap rustic lodge for sporting convenience, if no more. What Dr. Johnson defined as "an assemblage of good fellows, meeting under social conditions," may have combined early for various elevating objects which develop incidentally a personal companionship, or it may have proposed simply those coarser delights of eating, drinking, gaming or hunting. In Great Britain, from times quite remote, was the industrial guild, with funds available for objects fraternal, not the least of which was an annual banquet for the feeding and guzzling of the elect. But the primitive club met usually in temporary quarters; and whether in Europe or America, the permanent and independent club-house with its own restaurant did not appear until after the wars of the first Napoleon.

Table gatherings, with eating, drinking and conversation, took place at intervals, however, in these more simple days, at some tavern or coffee-house, whose host supplied the solid fare. Toasts and speeches were an incident of banquets more formal. Dr. Johnson's famous Literary Club was founded as late as 1764, though there were other London clubs for wit and gastronomy of earlier date; and what a gathering of immortals must that have been, with Goldsmith, Garrick, Burke, Gibbon, Sir Joshua Reynolds and the sage dogmatizer himself at the head of the table! Here, as often in such masculine associations, domestic loneliness was an inspiration, and widowers or bachelors predominated. Less characteristic in that respect, but better suited to the atmosphere of contemporary America, was that cis-Atlantic Club of Philadelphia, known as the "Junto," and founded by that other humbly born philosopher, Franklin, as far back as 1726; it was made up of simple mechanics, who gathered their books together in a room of their own and fostered a civic spirit.

Various other social clubs, less conspicuous historically, were formed in our provinces in those late colonial days; the word "club," however, being then applied in a somewhat promiscuous sense. For out-of-door sports, men of congenial tastes and habits, who were blessed with means and good social standing, used to get together on occasion to enjoy some favorite pastime appropriate to the locality. From 1732, Philadelphia had a Schuylkill fishing society, whose members angled together in the warm months for perch and rock, and at their club-house held meetings, chose officers and spread a sumptuous table. To the southward, the landed gentry met socially together for fishing, shooting or fox hunting, organized after a fashion to maintain the expense of their favorite sport. Among these men of leisure in days before the Revolution we see Washington of Mount Vernon, with his Potomac friends and neighbors, fishing for the river sturgeon or gunning, or leaping fences on horseback, booted and spurred, like a squire of the old country, in pursuit of the fox or squirrel. On one occasion, as he relates, his party ran down a fox with a bob tail and cut ears, after a seven hours' chase, in the course of which most of their dogs were wounded. When, in 1773, the predestined "Father of his Country" (a term used, by the way, in our press before it was ever applied to him) took a journey to New York to place his young ward, Jack Custis, in college, he dined at the "Jockey Club" in Philadelphia, and then at some other club (as he styled it) in New York; passing, furthermore, a short evening at the "Old Club" at Hillis's in the latter city. He makes further record of a club which he once attended at Philadelphia while serving in the Continental Congress. These facts we gather from the brief diaries which he used to keep in the leaves of his annual almanac.[1]   [1]II Washington's Writings, 230.

But the word "club," as Washington thus frequently applied it, here and in the course of his political service at Williamsburg or Richmond, and while a delegate in the House of Burgesses, had rather an indefinite sense. To him and to others ranking as American gentlemen it often signified the mere gathering together of friends for some occasional spread. Moreover, the term was much applied to the mess of one's own set in the legislature at some private boarding house. Club messes, in fact, of this latter description became quite common in the early Congressional life at Washington City, which began with the nineteenth century, and members of the Senate or House living at the capital without their wives or families would monopolize some landlady's table for their own exclusive set, admitting no fellow-diner to the mess except by common consent.

At our more populous centres small congenial sets gathered for winter entertainments at one or another's house in turn or partook of the special hospitality of some host, their accepted leader. Thus originated the "Wistar parties" of Philadelphia renown during the Revolution; and similar gatherings, for cards or conversation, were held in other towns and commonwealths. Even rural neighbors might modestly meet for some stated purpose once or twice a month to relieve the humdrum of home life. Informal happenings of a social character lead often to plans for a continuance and interchange, and something of a permanent establishment.

Nor were societies of more ambitious scope wanting in America thus early, to promote learning and the liberal arts and to bring the cultured and those aspiring to culture into sympathetic relation. We read in 1773 of a Virginia society for the advancement of useful knowledge, whose headquarters were at Williamsburg. More notable, as well as more permanent of duration, was the Philosophical Society of Philadelphia, or Academy of Sciences, the earliest institution of the kind still extant in America. Chastellux speaks of its meetings, held once a fortnight, one of which he attended in the course of his travels; and he comments upon its scrupulous gravity, after the manner of the French Academy, in the election of new members, passing upon foreigners of distinction as well as residents, for its roll of honor. Founded in 1769 by the union of some earlier literary societies, Franklin and Rittenhouse graced in succession its list of presiding officers. Some fifteen dignified men in powdered wigs and embroidered small-clothes met in solemn conclave and listened gravely to the reading of some scientific paper by one of their number upon electrical experiments or the use of the orrery. Jefferson was a benefactor of this society; and about 1780, while yet our Union was a Confederation, the plan was broached among its members of co-operating with similar learned bodies to be formed in other States. New York, too, had a Society for Promoting Useful Knowledge while still a British province. This, in 1768, was seen commending through the press a new automatic machine for pumping vessels at sea; and the Philadelphia society pursued a like plan of public announcement from time to time of ingenious native inventions.

America, furthermore, maintained in colonial times fraternities of a more popular and gregarious kind, whose aims were good-fellowship and benevolence, with a touch of ambition in political direction besides.

Tammany flourished at that period in our middle colonies as an Indian sachem, the patron saint of America; and Tammany meetings were held, with a Tammany dinner and public ball, at prominent provincial centres, such as Philadelphia, New York and Williamsburg. British immigrants, besides, gathered into societies, according to their English, Scotch or Irish antecedents, to practise philanthropy and the art of self-enjoyment; for, strong in their kindred ties, our foreign born would enroll as the Sons of St. George, or St. Andrew or St. Patrick.

Freemasonry, with its sacred bond of brotherhood, established on this continent its provincial lodges about the middle of the eighteenth century, following Great Britain's espousal of that ancient institution. A worldwide affiliation, dating back ostensibly to the founding of Solomon's temple, commended this order, which originated in handicraft, to a constantly widening class of our common people, attracting them by an ancient and solemn ritual, the imposition of oaths of secrecy and the symbols of a mysterious public influence. Equal brotherhood was the spirit suffused by this ancient organization, at the same time that graded offices in its management with high-sounding titles incited the individual ambition for conspicuous posts of honor. Freemasonry in those days aroused strong opposition outside; yet despite the printed sermons and tracts of our clergy, which denounced the institution as a device of Satan, citing Scriptural texts or claiming to expose its base practices, the order spread steadily through these thirteen colonies as over Continental Europe itself. There was a right worshipful grand master for North America, symbolical of our tendencies to union; and lodges were instituted in leading colonies shortly before the drum beat to arms and independence

Notwithstanding some famous Revolutionists, such as Washington and Joseph Warren, enrolled themselves in America's Masonic fraternity, it is not likely that an order of such international scope should have lent itself clearly and decidedly to colonial schemes for severing Britain's empire. Secrecy under oath, with its grips and passwords, infects profoundly the average imagination, and too much individual advantage may be hoped for. I can myself recall how, at the time of our Civil War, local lodges in my native State did their proselyting work extensively among uniformed officers about to leave for the front, urging that in a grand fraternity of this kind brethren of one section of the Union who might fall by capture into the hands of brethren in another section would surely find herein a peculiar guaranty of life, comfort and personal safety. Such assurances proved, however, of little real avail where passions had divided men deeply; and so, too, Freemasonry in the eighteenth century counted probably for little in that earlier emergency of bloodshed. Yet some of our lodges took on the patriot hue as the range of local sentiment favored. The Boston lodge changed, in 1775, its gathering-place from the house of a Tory landlord to that of another esteemed "a friend to his country."[1] In 1777 the Freemasons of Philadelphia met to celebrate St. John's day. Thirteen members happened to be present; so for thirteen regular toasts they ordered thirteen bottles of wine and thirteen bowls of toddy; their reckoning was £13, and they spent thirteen hours in social companionship—all this in especial honor of the thirteen United States of America.[2]

[1] M. G., 1775.
[2] I. C., 1777.

The real political workers of our land, who conspired in secret to resist British policy and promote the cause of independence, affiliated as "Sons of Liberty." Beginning with the Stamp-Act resistance, the men of this famous order aroused opposition in their respective provinces to the British troops sent over by the King. They organized chiefly in 1765 and 1766 to nullify, first of all, the Stamp Act and cause its discontinuance; maintenance of order and the protection of American liberty being their declared objects. Their emblem was the liberty tree or liberty pole, which latter they would plant in token of a definite defiance; while Loyalists and the red-coats as eagerly destroyed or removed it. A riot arose in New York during the year 1769 over a flagstaff set "in the fields,"[1] which the royal troops cut down. Forbidden by the authorities to erect another pole upon public ground, the Sons next bought a private lot of land and there planted a high mast, which bore aloft a gilt vane inscribed "liberty," first drawing the pole through the streets in procession and then dedicating it formally to freedom. And so by their attitude toward such mute symbols of a rebellious spirit were Tories and Whigs in these Northern colonies largely distinguished.

[1]Since City Hall Park.

XVIII

THE origin of industrial pursuits among mankind is shrouded in a mystery as great as the origin of the human race itself. The labor of subduing this earth and utilizing its products for the needs, the comforts, the luxuries of life, begins and continues with the development of the typical man whom God made, at length, in his own image and placed in dominion over the brute creation. Rudeness everywhere precedes the refinement of civilized life. To quote the late Phillips Brooks, the great Book which reveals the birth and final destiny of man begins with a garden and ends with the celestial city.

But in the settlement of America, so modern and so fully chronicled, we trace out fairly well the progress of human industries upon a virgin soil which has to be reclaimed from primeval wildness and solitude by a new race of settlers. America began with agriculture as the chief and basic pursuit of its population in each of our thirteen provinces; Revolution was fought out by a union of "embattled farmers." Farming and stock-raising flourished by the latter third of the eighteenth century in all colonial America, and the native forests supplied whatever was most needed for fuel and industrial pursuits. Such simple products of the soil as lumber, potash and pearl-ash, tar and pitch were exported hence to Europe. More important still

for commerce, and more essential to the Old World,
were the cereal products of our soil.

"Agriculture," wrote Burke in 1775, "they [the
Americans] have prosecuted with such a spirit that,
besides feeding plentifully their own growing multitude, their annual export of grain, comprehending rice,
has some years exceeded a million pounds in value."
"At the beginning of the century some of these colonies
imported corn from the mother country. But for some
time past the Old World has been fed from the New."[1]
Nor should the export of tobacco from Virginia or of
rice and indigo from South Carolina be overlooked in
such a connection. South Carolina's rice, then her chief
staple, was reckoned the best at this time in all the
world. Yet while the trial culture of cotton only began
after the peace of 1783, our extreme Southern colonies
so favorably inclined earlier, that South Carolina's first
Provincial Congress in 1775 advised the people to raise
that plant.

Northern farmers differed already as landholders
from the great plantation lords of the South; and those
differences have affected the social growth of the two
sections ever since, notwithstanding the common existence of slave institutions when America first rebelled.
Throughout the North, and notably in New England,
the farmer tilled an enclosure of moderate extent, aided
in the rougher work by the sons of his numerous family,
while wives and daughters attended to the dairy and
other farm pursuits. None were drones in such a hive,
and with poverty went at least a livelihood and an
honest independence. In our eastern section, withal,
improvement of the soil went on in a regular way,
every new village touching on an old one and new

[1] II Burke's Works, 116.

settlements growing in regular order and progression. In Pennsylvania any one could buy the land he wanted for improvement, binding himself to pay a small annual ground rent. Here, however, houses and farms were widely scattered on the borders, and the advantage of a compact and contiguous growth for mutual help in need was lost. In the middle colonies the hunter or pioneer would often clear his wilderness, make the rude beginnings of garden, meadow and field cultivation, erect a log hut and then sell out to some other settler the half-improved farm, emigrating to borders still more remote.

By the Revolutionary age many of our freeholders let their farms to be worked on halves and confined their personal attention to other pursuits in life. Stock raising was diversified; yet many outside the closer population of the cities raised on their own ground, besides flowers, the family vegetables. Gardening, as a special vocation, is of quite modern date, for in those early times men, women and children lived and worked much for themselves in the open air. Orchards, too, were tended with care as a personal industry; and in New England hay and cider were important products. The maxims of the almanac were memorized by our hardy husbandmen. Thus, when summer opened,

> "He that by the plough would thrive,
> Himself must either drive or guide."

Or again,

> "He that now neglects the hoe,
> Must in winter suck his paw."

Southern planters, though living more idly, with servile toil at full command, took pride, like true sons of

Adam, in agriculture. Jefferson chose always to reckon himself among our farmers. Washington, one of the chief landholders of his times in all America, while ordering from London silks and satins for his wife and costly suits of velvet and broadcloth for himself, with shoes (to be patterned on a specified last), procured also from abroad the needful materials for his servants' clothes; he had the latest farming manuals sent him, along with pictures and playing cards. Great interest was taken by Virginia in cultivating new products, and her Burgesses in 1772 voted an annual bounty of £50 for five years to encourage experiments in raising grapes for wine in the mountain highlands of that province.

Little progress was made in colonial times respecting mining or metallurgy. Soft coal, offered for sale about the James River; stone, quarried casually in a Northern province to build some solid edifice near by; iron, rudely smelted in small quantities for the needs of an immediate neighborhood—these complete the native record of the era in that respect.[1] In emulation of Spain, the British Crown put a clause into our charters during the seventeenth century which reserved specifically one-fifth of all such gold and silver as the unexplored soil might yield. Such talliage, however, amounted to little or nothing; and still less did the fifth of all precious stones, of which the second Massachusetts charter also made mention. Coal was little searched for at a time when forests were close at hand and wood fuel abundant. But Appalachian America's real mineral wealth lay in the homelier yield of coal, iron and petroleum, whose

[1] At an early date, in Virginia, Master Berkeley is supposed to have found a lead mine, whose secret perished with him. Cooke's "Virginia."

best secrets were locked up all the while that royal supremacy lasted.

In fishing and hunting, however, these colonies yielded abundance, nor was it in vain that charters of New England had enjoined it upon the inhabitants to pursue "the trade of fishing" and "the business of taking whales." Burke's splendid tribute of 1775 to America's fisheries, and particularly to the whale fishery of our eastern colonies, will not soon be forgotten.[1] Cod fisheries off the Grand Banks, near Newfoundland, also engaged the hardy mariners of Massachusetts Bay. Whales in those days came sometimes near the coast and were captured easily; one forty feet long, discovered off Marshfield in 1769 and attacked by sharks, became the prize of a fishing schooner; others were seen occasionally near Philadelphia and off Cape May.

The general commerce of these colonies was brisk, active and diversified, whether foreign or coastwise. For not to speak of other ports, we see, in 1765, vessels clearing or entering Boston from Connecticut, New York, Philadelphia, Virginia and the James River; from various West India islands; from Greenock, London and the ports of Continental Europe. But there was little native capital embarked in such business, and the policy of the mother country was to confine all her colonies as much as possible to agriculture and the simple kindred pursuits of hunting and fishing, while she kept both commerce and manufactures for her own profit in this distant market.

Dwelling upon the monopoly feature of England's commercial policy toward her colonies—that policy which contrives a "home market," so called, out of a distant and subservient population—Burke further

[1] II Burke's Works, 116-118 (1775).

observes that Americans, and particularly those of the
Northern provinces, imported ten times as much from
Great Britain as they sent back in return, and that a
great part of their foreign balance was and had to be
remitted to London.   True was it, as others had observed, that American seas were covered with ships and
their rivers floating with commerce; "but it is with our
ships," he explains, "that these seas are covered, and
their rivers float with British commerce."   Americans
were not rich, as a whole, nor were there really rich
men among them; for in some of their most considerable provinces, such as Massachusetts and Connecticut,
not two men could be found who could afford, as
absentees, to spend a thousand pounds a year.   "The
American merchants are our factors," says Burke; "all
in reality, most even in name.   The Americans trade,
navigate, cultivate with British capital—to their own
advantage, to be sure, for without these capitals their
ploughs would be stopped and their ships wind bound.
But he who furnishes the capital must, on the whole,
be principally benefited; the person who works upon it
profits on his part, too, but he profits in a subordinate
way, as our colonies do," or, in other words, as the
servant of a wise and indulgent master.[1]

In trade, to speak broadly, social distinctions are
fostered by the demarcation of wholesale and retail.
"Raw wool," writes Douglas Jerrold, "does not speak
to half-penny ball of worsted; tallow in the cask looks
down upon sixes to the pound, and pig iron turns up
its nose at ten-penny nails."   Yet wholesale and retail
in a community are always relative terms, and in the

[1] Burke's Works, 375, 392-394.

days of our forefathers, whose capital was so meagre, even the largest dealers among the inhabitants did what nowadays would be thought rather a petty business. Importing merchants advertised consignments from abroad or coastwise of all the miscellaneous articles of wear, food or drink products that might suit the various classes of consumers in a new society. There were English, Scotch and Irish goods; broadcloths of scarlet, crimson, green, black, blue, chocolate, drab and mixed, from London, Liverpool or Glasgow; damask, brocade, lutestrings, satin, sarsnet and poplins; gold, silver and Brussels lace; fashionable silks, satin shoes, garnet or pearl necklaces and white or black beaver riding hats for the ladies; with muffets and tippets, besides, and a host of minor commodities "too tedious to mention," as the advertiser would close his enumeration. Besides sugar, Bohea tea, coffee, chocolate and spices, were announced imported raisins, currants, Turkey figs, olives, Cheshire and Gloucestershire cheeses, fresh and pickled limes, citron, sweet China oranges, Lisbon sweet oil, London porter and even orange juice for punch.

We speak as a novelty of department stores to-day, such as are carried on at our chief centres for the general public as individual buyers. But one reads of such an establishment, called the "Universal Store," which did business in New York City a hundred and thirty years or more ago, at the sign of the looking-glass and druggist's post. So far, too, as local trade might permit, such was, in fact, the character of most of our country stores in that eighteenth century, whose custom was drawn from a safe constituency, when travel to a metropolis was rare and mail and carriage facilities inadequate. The country trader in "dry and West

India goods," purveyor for the people and general factor in the exchange of farm supplies for miles about, was indeed a man of substance and held high his head; in town or county affairs, and perchance in the parish church, too, his influence was great, for he knew every one; and at his store, as in a tavern, men drew up by the fire to discuss politics and the local news, stimulated by the glass of liquor which he disdained not to measure out for modest coin.

The regular storekeepers of these provinces antagonized the auctioneers, whose sales at vendue, as they were called, embraced not only second-hand goods, but such at first hand, besides, as might need to be quickly disposed of for ready money. The sales of sheriffs and fiduciaries were at public auction. Men sharp and glib-tongued devoted themselves to this pursuit. We see one who opened his "auction hall" close by the town house, with a livery stable for his patrons conveniently opposite. Goods imported twelve months earlier were offered by him two days in the week. In large towns might be seen evening auctions, besides; there were horse auctions, book auctions and mock auctions; and prizes taken by our privateers during the Revolution were presently knocked off in this manner. Auctioneers, like other business men of our colonies, accosted the public in the third person when advertising. "Puffing is not his talent," announced one of these in the local press, content, as he declared, with a moderate commission; "but he begs to say that, as he is determined to exert himself and use his utmost endeavors to give satisfaction to his employers, so he humbly hopes that in point of fidelity, assiduity and dexterity they will find him to come out not far from the first three."[1]   [1]N. E. C., (1775-76).

Startling and spectacular modes of doing business, such as we witness at the present day, were not in vogue thus early. Men did not propose "large sales and small profits," but rather moderate sales with a moderate return. Sales at "immense sacrifice" were not proclaimed, as though the main effort of merchants were to escape from their ventures with the lowest possible margin of loss; but dealers meant to make ends meet, if no more, and said as much. There appeared no individual haste to get rich, no monopoly. One who was hard pressed offered to sell at lowest prices, which meant at somewhat more than cost. An enterprising dealer at one of our ports announced in 1771, as a novel plan, that he would hereafter sell by wholesale and retail, at "little more than the sterling cost and charges." He warranted, moreover, that the teas and indigo he sold were of the best kind, and if it proved otherwise, he would take back the goods and refund the money. In short, if our colonist offered to sell at actual loss, he would not say so; but when closing out a business hastily, he offered simply to sell at much under the customary advance.

The wide recognition of a credit system in these colonies bred difficulties which trade had constantly to cope with. Murray, a Scotch immigrant, found in 1736, when importing his first cargo to a Southern port, that in the Carolinas a twelve months' credit was regularly expected; and a large part of what he received for his merchandise was in North Carolina currency and in private debts floated by bills receivable, which he could not negotiate abroad. Not only did the plaintive duns of printer and carrier frequently appear in the press of this era, such as I have elsewhere mentioned, but those, besides, of business men, equally vague and equally deferential toward all delinquent patrons. The threat to sue was always a covert one, without mention of names, and usually, we may assume, that threat was not fulfilled. Several times (one of these forbearing creditors would say) he had given public notice to all debtors to settle with him, but little attention had been paid. So now for the last time he issued his notice, and those who disregard it "will be sued according to law, without respect to persons."[1] "Intending very shortly for England" was a favorite plea as Revolution approached, and he who was thus winding up his American affairs "begged the favor of all persons indebted to make immediate payment;" for delinquent debts long standing he would certainly leave in the hands of an attorney. Many an advertiser had debts of his own that must be paid, and hence he begged leave to press for the payments due himself. "Cash or short credit" was the mode favored in Philadelphia by 1772; or perhaps "cash or short credit or barter." One would sell his cheapest if paid for the goods in cash; and he sought security where he sold on long credit. By 1773 some declared publicly that they had suffered great inconvenience of credit, and would sell hereafter for ready money only.

Of course, in our primitive state of society the barter system had largely prevailed. Farmers exchanged at the country store their meat, their grain, cheese and butter and their garden truck for household groceries and clothing. The miller who ground corn took his toll from the meal. Due bills from a dealer were payable out of his stock in trade. Car-

[1] M. G., 1773.

penters and painters made good what they owed by jobbing their services. During the momentous seventies of the eighteenth century one rum distiller offered to sell cheap for cash or molasses; another consented to take "good merchantable potash," and a third tobacco "and other articles that sell." It was not uncommon thus early for men to play one trade into another, as where a cutler who sold knives and razors took in exchange the skins of otters, foxes and wild cats. Paper makers gave out new paper for old rags. Coppersmiths or pewterers would offer the highest price for old copper, brass, pewter or lead. A brushmaker took hogs' bristles for his wares. A general grocer, disposing of his stock of goods, first offered to give long credit on security; and this failing to stimulate custom, he proposed further to take "rum, sugar, molasses, coffee, chocolate or cotton wool" in payment.

Tobacco was long used in Virginia with great satisfaction as a medium of exchange, and it served the people well in the War for Independence. Provincial bills of credit, however, were a constant source of confusion, mingled with the Continental loans and currency; and the paper emissions of our thirteen States during the exhaustive strife with the mother country brought such disastrous results that the framers of our Federal Constitution prohibited absolutely the issue of State bills of credit. Provincial paper money, poorly printed, had circulated locally in these colonies in place of coin long before the Revolution.[1] Great perplexity arose in changing permanently our money denomina-

[1] Among things stolen from him, a Philadelphia advertiser announced, in 1769, 2 six-dollar bills in Maryland money, 3 fifteen-shilling bills, and 3 ten-shilling bills; also a five-shilling bill, Newcastle money, with a person's name written on its back. P. C.

tion from pounds, shillings, pence to dollars and cents. Many used the latter mode of counting while yet they were British subjects; but the custom varied in different provinces, and it was long before our people, as a whole, could get out of the old way of reckoning.[1]

With shops, as with dwelling houses, in colonial times, there was no precise numbering or lettering, even in the cities, but one's situation on a street was identified by other means of description. One advertised his place of business as "close by the town house," "nearly opposite" Judge C.'s dwelling or some designated meeting-house, "next to" D.'s bake-house, "corner of Winter Street and opposite the lane," "Strawberry Alley, third house from Market Street, and nearly opposite Mr. Luke's tavern," and the like. Shop signs were not common which gave the retailer's personal name, but emblems, rather, were used, as at an inn. One's pursuit was carried on at "the lion and glove," "the lock and key," "the heart and glove," "the blue ball" or "the gold ball," "the bell in hand," "the ship aground," "the sun," "the whale-bone," "the tobacco pipe," "the brazen head," "the lamb," "the golden cock," "the fan," "the naked boy," or "the three doves." Of such devices posterity has long been reminded by the tobacconist's "Highlander" or "Indian" and "the golden mortar and pestle" of the apothecary. The

[1]About 1765, the money used in New York consisted of silver, gold, British half pence (often called "coppers"), and bills of credit. Against the violence of a mob, which lasted several days, the leading business men of that city enforced a mutual agreement to require 14 coppers to a shilling, in place of the 12½ formerly current, so as to conform to the value of a shilling in neighboring colonies.

business designation itself was more specific and technical, in many cases, than we find it nowadays, for one described himself as a glover, a fuller, a dyer, a mercer, a draper, a haberdasher, a pewterer, to say nothing of other names in the vernacular which have held place better. The style of the pursuit clung closely to the individual, who, less cringing and obsequious in his pursuit, perhaps, than after the London fashion, gave, nevertheless, the impression of knowing his place, and not intending to get above his business lest his business should get above him. All this, however, was subject to disturbance by the new ideas of equal opportunity and rise in life which came in with the Declaration, stirring the old fixity of American conditions into a more emulous composite. Most shopping was done by day, and only grocers and druggists kept open in the evening.

One of the most striking characteristics of those times was the domestic association which trade presented, whether for town or country. In Philadelphia, as in our other chief centres of business, men kept shop in their own dwellings—a custom which still holds largely true of London and Paris. Such dwellings were usually two stories in height and only moderately spacious; the shop seldom occupied the whole depth of the first story, but was chiefly confined to the usual front rooms; while in the rear and overhead lived the tradesman with his family. Hence was it that wife or children waited much upon customers, and the widow not seldom continued the trade of her late husband. For if woman had not yet launched into that wider range of professional and clerical pursuits with which the present age is familiar, she took at least a considerable range of experience in those smaller industries which kept her at home. In shop-keeping the sex showed much business capacity, made a comfortable living for the family, and in their own sphere were respected. Other uses were made of the domestic premises as occasion might suggest; and in the pinch of hard times we see tradespeople, wholesale and retail, advertising for boarders or lodgers or to let their stables.

The same domestic and business combination, let us note, applied in most other pursuits of life at that period. Such, to this day, is a common mode of living with clergymen, physicians, dentists, literary writers and those who take private pupils for instruction. Hotels and inns are thus carried on. The farmer's life makes home and family its base of operations. Cobblers, tailors, dressmakers, milliners, small tradesmen and a host of those engaged in sedentary pursuits of the humbler kind live and carry on their work surrounded by wife and children, and enclosed within the wholesome environ of home. And so was it, far more positively and universally, in America during the simple colonial and Revolutionary age. They, even, whose pursuits were manufacturing or mechanical, requiring special workshops, built close to the homestead on their own private acres, and the sound of the saw-mill and grist-mill was heard through the kitchen windows. Even distilleries were thus carried on; the large country store, if not in one's own dwelling, was at all events contiguous to it; and many a lawyer and country squire to whom his fellow-townsmen came for consultation had a detached building, which he called his office, on the same lot with his residence, though closer to the roadside. Farmers, when landholders besides, are proverbially a sturdy race, lovers of freedom and virtuous;

and a people whose individual homes and business grow up together are the last of mankind to be enslaved or subjugated by a foreign oppressor.

Of the learned professions in those days, divinity took precedence; and the college-bred men who expounded the tenets of the provincial Christian faith and set a godly example to their parishioners had an abiding influence. But medicine and the law, despite some practical drawbacks, found their votaries here among the rising generation. Medical schools in Philadelphia and New York opened the way for our native-born to practise, while other young men of talent and ambition in the chief provinces sought distinction at the bar. "In no country, perhaps, in the world," wrote Burke in 1775, "is the law so generally a study. The profession itself is numerous and powerful, and in most provinces it takes the lead. The greater number of the deputies sent to Congress were lawyers." And so, we may add, did the later exigencies of Revolution keep our patriot lawyers at the front. For the study of the law, as Burke has observed, "renders men acute, inquisitive, dexterous, prompt in attack, ready in defence, full of resources," and with their innate love of freedom, men of this intelligent profession prove powerful when assailed.[1]

Architects, surveyors, bankers, brokers pursued their several callings in those times after the prevalent fashion. Our bankers and brokers dealt chiefly in loans at interest upon mortgage, bottomry or pledge, and discounted the bills, bonds and notes of private individuals. The term "intelligence office" was used in those days to

[1] II Burke's Works, 125.

denote a general brokerage in goods, wares and merchandise, such as merged readily into pawnbroking, with its secrecy and despatch. But by 1773 we see set up at Boston a general register office "to meet a great inconvenience of masters and mistresses," and out of this grew, probably, the "intelligence office" as we understand that term at the present day. Scriveners, conveyancers and scouts were found on the outskirts of the legal profession; and we read of a notary in Philadelphia who offered to translate or draft any French or Spanish writing, and eked out his income by carrying on a reading and writing school.

Besides the home or domestic attribute of which most callings in that early era partook, we should recall the personal and individual character of trade and the professions alike. Joint-stock companies or corporations had hardly yet a footing in England or America, and chartered monopolies, even for banking, were almost unknown, save in a rare connection with public operations like the Bank of England. Whether a business was conducted in the name of factor or principal in those days, the capital was commonly furnished and risked by some individual, and individual liability as well as individual enterprise embarked in it. Men pursued their plans of life with a moderate capital. Whatever one placed in trade or finance, he managed or supervised himself. The added capital furnished by an outsider was simply borrowed money, for the most part, with or without security, and one was bound to repay it like his other obligations. He might associate with him a partner; but partnership and single pursuit risked alike all that one had in the world, and both self-interest and the dread of imprisonment for debt or of bankruptcy kept one sedulous to protect his credit.

Successful, on the one hand, or failing disastrously, on the other, our merchant was swayed to the side of moderation; he sought a moderate business, a modest competence, moderate profits. There might be competition, but no one in the community was strong enough to drive out all rivals and engross the opportunities for himself. Partnerships, too, consisted largely of family relations, and the father meant to hand down his business to his son, as in the European days of fixed conditions in life.

In manufactures, at this age, American progress was that of an active and ingenious though undeveloped population. Needful construction from the trees and soil products about them was the settlers' first concern. Nothing shows better the stage reached in comforts and luxuries at any time than the style of a people's habitations. Saw-mills came early into vogue. From rude huts and dwellings our colonists gradually advanced to buildings, public and private, of fair architectural pattern; though for doors, window sashes and the finer products of the joiner they relied mostly upon master workmen in the mother country, who dressed imported lumber and sent it back fashioned for its uses. Shipbuilding was another early occupation of our colonists, fostered by the universal zeal for fishing and cruising; and this may be pronounced the first great manual industry established on this coast, being recognized, in fact, as highly important, a whole century before we declared our independence. So, too, in carriages and furniture of the common and simple pattern colonial America made rapid progress. Our use of metals was primitive. Native iron was worked up into kitchen utensils and the simpler implements of farming. The art of native pottery was turned to good account. But the better sort of table outfit, good axes and steel hardware were mostly imported. In short, American industry catered to the common wants of our common people, and essayed little to attract the custom of the high bred and fastidious.

But in textiles, more particularly, our colonies were kept dependent on the mother country by the artful policy which British manufacturers had impressed upon the King and Parliament for their own constant advantage. For all fabric-weaving machines, as well as for fabricated goods, the rule of the mother country was to make and keep her colonies in this new world dependent upon her to the utmost. Our colonists brought over with them early the spinning-wheel and hand loom; and the weaving of homespun clothing was one of those farm occupations which, like knitting and sewing, engaged the female members of a family and wedded each small manufacture so long to the household. For the primitive home market of a people is the individual home. We had also the fulling-mill for felting and compacting woven fabrics.

Down almost to the very date of American independence the machinery for clothing our inhabitants was nearly as simple as that of the feudal ages. Rude water-power turned our saw-mills or ground the miller's corn; rude hand-power or horse-power accomplished most other work of the mechanical kind. Not until about 1775, or the battle of Lexington, was the Watt steam engine first set in successful operation in Great Britain; so that steam motive power—that giant force which has changed completely the material operations of modern society—post-dates, in reality, our colonial era. Moreover, as we should recall, it was the decade 1760-70 which first brought out in Great Britain the new inventions in textile weaving; and so jealous were English manufacturers of those years over their novel experiments that all export of the new machines to America was strictly forbidden, nor was even the migration of workmen who knew how to construct and operate them permitted. In various other ways trade in these colonies had been hampered from time to time by stringent acts of Parliament, with the like intent of enriching home merchants and manufacturers at our expense. Hence it may be fitly said that America's Revolution was a parallel revolution, both political and industrial, in point of time.

As an instance of colonial enterprise in that century, a coarse but comfortable hat had come into fashion, of native make, for which a market was opened in the British West Indies. But Parliament stopped that trade short by a prohibition; and the Crown in 1767 issued strict orders to watch all vessels arriving from New England, New York or Philadelphia in the West Indian ports, and to detect all attempts at selling American hats and enforce the penalties of the law. In the earlier days of peaceful submission America's profit had been not so much in any fostering care exercised by the mother country as by what Burke styled "a wise and salutary neglect," which had allowed intelligent industry in these colonies to take its own way toward perfection.

The non-importation leagues formed here in 1767 were a fitting response to the new policy now entered upon by the King and Parliament. Such retaliating

combination was not alone for increasing our corresponding trade and manufactures, but largely for
alleviating by self-denial the inevitable distress of our
people. The New England and middle colonies, which
chiefly practised the new policy, were greatly in debt,
and economy was needful. They had no great staples
to export, like Virginia and South Carolina, for maintaining their resources and soothing the oppressor. A
resolve passed by the Massachusetts General Court
early in 1768[1] carefully avoided all expression offensive
to royal authority, and urged as leading considerations
for a non-importation policy the great decay of trade in
that province, the scarcity of money, the heavy debt
contracted in the French and Indian War, which was
still unpaid, and the great difficulties to which our
people were reduced. Yet the production of home
manufactures was kept likewise in view.

Our Northern colonies, indeed, suffered great depression at the date of Parliament's fatal experiment
of taxation; and it is only just to add that England
herself was similarly impoverished, not only because
of that same war, which had involved the struggle of
France and Great Britain for supremacy in the New
World, but through temporary embarrassments, besides, of her East India venture, which threatened home
bankruptcy and failure. Once aroused, our native zeal
and energy turned sedulous attention to the development here of a home market. The breed of native
sheep was encouraged, and the people passed local re-
solves not to buy lambs nor to kill early, so that native
wool might be grown and the poor employed. A New
York society "for promoting arts" voted premiums to
such as should spin the most linen yarn in course of

[1] See I M. G., 1767, 1768.

a year, knit the greatest number of stockings, keep the neatest beehives or make the best cheeses. Patriots of the middle colonies voted not to buy foreign beer, but to patronize the breweries of Philadelphia and Baltimore. Among ingenious experiments of those times was one of preparing flax so as to resemble cotton in whiteness, softness and coherency; and another of making cloth out of hop stalks. Pennsylvania stimulated by bounties the cultivation of mulberry trees for rearing the silkworm; and for Pennsylvania's emulation, Franklin held up China to notice as a country whose prolific people went about cheaply and durably clad in silk clothing.

It must be conceded that our colonial Whigs, in their earnestness to make effective their own plans of resistance to the mother country, suffered not fools gladly, nor endured with patience the indifference or noncompliance of Tory fellow-citizens. Sons of Liberty published the names of those who chose to import in violation of the public agreement, and denounced the social excommunication of such offenders, or, as we would say in our own day, declared a boycott against them. Methods of compulsion practised by one hostile class of the community against another vary not radically from age to age. But the non-importation principle had broad justifying grounds aside from all present intent of retaliation. And in all ages of tyranny and coercion on the part of a parent government, the refusal of the oppressed to buy or consume the wares and products of those at whose greedy instigation the dangerous policy of commercial monopoly has been entered upon is the simplest, safest and one of the surest means of effective resistance.

XIX

PROVINCIAL POLITICS

L ET us now inquire what free political parties, if any, existed in America in the latest colonial years, popular in their scope and open in their appeals for public support. Party divisions originate in human nature and grow with the free expression of self-government; party spirit flames brightest and hottest in a commonwealth or community where open patriotic concert may achieve an efficient direction in affairs. During the earlier period of our colonization, and while the mother country either neglected her offspring or was distracted by her own civil tumult over the Stuarts and Cromwell, American politics developed daringly, and the body of settlers in each colony gained from the set to whom chartered privileges had first been granted various popular concessions in the direction of equal political rights. In Massachusetts, without any express royal license, the people chose their own rulers. It was after the compact of Crown and Parliament which settled the line of William and Mary that our politics sank into a placid and subsidiary condition, under an astute management from abroad, which kept the colonies locally disunited for over seventy years, and until the Stamp Act experiment aroused strong opposition.

Roundheads and Cavaliers had, meanwhile, given place on British soil to the national party division of

"Whigs" and "Tories." The latter distinguishing terms were long in vogue there; and so, too, following the parental fashion, were they in these cis-Atlantic provinces. "In every colony," writes John Adams in 1812, "divisions always prevailed. In New York, Pennsylvania, Virginia, Massachusetts and all the rest a court and country party have always contended. Whig and Tory disputed very sharply before the Revolution, and in every step during the Revolution."[1] This positive statement is corroborated by other testimony of our Revolutionary fathers. Yet narrow and crooked enough were the channels through which coursed native politics while our provincial interests were kept apart, and the grand ideas of an independent Confederation, of a union irreconcilable with British sovereignty, remained in embryo.

We at this day, who vote freely and frequently together without requirement of rank or property for exercising the right, and who elect our chief magistrate, our chief executive subordinates and even our judges, as well as representatives in both branches of the legislature, and the local county, town or city functionaries, should recall that the elective franchise in those early times was far more restricted in its exercise. For, first of all, with negro slavery nominally existing to 1776 or later in all the colonies, and white bondage, besides, to a considerable extent,[2] the voter, a male inhabitant twenty-one years or more in age, must have been a freeman or "free white man," at the least. More than this, only "freeholders," or those

[1] X John Adams's Works, 23.
[2] See Chapter II.

owning real estate, possessed the suffrage at all in various Middle and Southern colonies, while Massachusetts and Maryland each fixed a property qualification in lands or personalty as indispensable. Only Pennsylvania, Rhode Island and Connecticut—colonies treated by British kings with marked favor in their respective charters—bestowed the suffrage liberally in those times upon freemen, or at least free taxpayers. In these and some minor respects colonial laws varied.

Nor as to the rulers to be voted for was the method at that day a liberal one. In most of these colonies, as in Great Britain, the range of a voter's choice was confined to officials of his own town or county, and to sending, moreover, from among neighbors and fellow-citizens such as might represent his little community annually in the legislature. This meant scarcely more, in practical effect, than local self-government, pure and simple. Municipalities governed by mayor, aldermen and councilmen scarce existed, but selectmen and the petty local officers down to hog-reeve comprised the usual list. This was about all. In only two colonies out of all the thirteen, Rhode Island and Connecticut, had chartered voters the right to choose all colonial officials, the governor and council included. Massachusetts had once exercised such popular functions by forcing the phraseology of her original charter; but that from William and Mary which replaced it gave only a modified right of choosing the governor's council, through a selection by the legislature itself, then styled the General Court. In Pennsylvania and Maryland, under proprietary grants, were hereditary rulers of the Penn or Calvert families, who, as overlords and absentees, drew an income from the inhabitants and appointed each his resident lieutenant-governor with the royal sanction. In all but four, then, of these thirteen colonies the royal government was really provincial, and the governor himself, the King's vicegerent, was appointed and recalled at pleasure by the Crown. Nor did the colonial legislatures (except for Rhode Island, Connecticut and Massachusetts) represent the subject people, except in a single branch, such as Virginia's House of Burgesses. For the council, so called, that germ of our modern State Senate—with functions, then secretly exercised, which blended executive and legislative authority—was a royal or proprietary adjunct of British rule like the governor himself. Members of this council or upper house were generally selected, under royal sanction, from among influential persons of the colony, legal, financial and military, and were held bound by fees and salaries to regard the local interests of the Crown; their approval, with that, besides, of the provincial governor, was indispensable to give measures of the popular house the force of laws. Nor this alone, for the King usually reserved a final veto upon all the legislation of each colony. Judges held their commissions by executive appointment, or in some instances were chosen by the legislature; but never in those times were they elected by the people.

Even for the legislature itself representation was not popular, in our modern sense of the word, but the town or county unit supplied, as such, its whole delegation. By this means was fostered local pride rather than the numerical rule by a census. Less than a century later the colonial charters of Rhode Island and Connecticut, so much vaunted for their democracy in this earlier age that they were long kept intact in place of independent State constitutions, were denounced and struggled against almost to the point of rebellion, not only be-

cause the voter's franchise became antiquated in its
limitation, but by reason of the travesty upon popular
consent which ensued by the time that great growing
cities and dwindling rustic hamlets became classed
numerically in the same rigid category for representative vote and influence. Equality of political rights is
the ideal of every advancing commonwealth in a country like ours; but as years roll on the liberality of the
past becomes the irksome exclusiveness of the present,
and all true republics tend to the rule of numbers.

And so, once more, in contemporary modes of
suffrage, the age I am describing favored strong
families and the ascendancy of an upper class in society
to an extent which in our own day American States
would not tolerate. Bribery and coercion were the
open accompaniments of election in the British Isle,
especially when members of Parliament were to be
chosen, and though little prevalent on this side of the
ocean, such abuses were closely incident to the polling
methods then prevalent. In our own day, great stakes
at issue in patronage and great corporate wealth and
social complexity foster corruption; yet the better regulation of the suffrage supplies a corrective. The ancient
hustings, the show of hands, the open declaration of a
voter's preferences, amid pugilistic confusion, coarse
ribaldry and the rowdyish marshalling of party ad-
herents we seldom witness at an election nowadays;
but ballots, officially printed and furnished, voting lists
and the well-guarded ballot-box protect in our day the
voter's secret and personal choice.

The old English method of oral or *viva voce* vote
prevailed in America during colonial times, and New

England's town-meeting discussion or the open-air stump speaking and joint debate in Virginia favored such courageous assertion of one's civic preference. But voting by the ballot had come gradually into vogue in America, first for religious congregations and next for secular gatherings; so that our commonwealths by 1776 were found discordant in preferences on this point when forming their several State governments. Massachusetts, New Hampshire, Connecticut, Pennsylvania and Georgia pronounced at once for the ballot, while most of the remaining colonies showed their adherence still to the ancient oral method of their forefathers. So strenuous, indeed, did Virginia continue, with the child of her loins, Kentucky, for the old method of standing up like men to be counted, that as late as 1850 those two commonwealths announced in newly drafted constitutions, dramatically and somewhat humorously, that in all elections, whether by the people or the legislature, "the votes shall be personally and publicly given *viva voce,* provided that dumb persons entitled to suffrage may vote by ballot."

In provincial New York the oral mode of voting had prevailed from the earliest times; but by 1770 a strong popular current set toward substituting the ballot, and controversy became heated on this subject. Many voters complained that they were intimidated at the polls by employers and those of superior influence in the community, with whom it rested to favor or oppress; and hence they wished to vote secretly. "Many of the poorer people," they contended, "feel deeply the aristocratic power, or rather the intolerable tyranny, of the great and opulent, who openly threaten them with loss of employment and arrest for debt unless they give their votes as desired." But opponents argued that to dare and choose to speak their minds freely was "their birth-right as Englishmen and their glory as freemen." At a public meeting called that year in New York City to discuss this question, the ballot mode was voted down, and those present pronounced by a large majority their approbation of the old mode of *viva voce*—this, how-ever, we should observe, by taking their vote after the very method objected to. Resolutions of instruction to the provincial legislature followed, which declared: (1) That the ballot was a dangerous innovation, di-rectly contrary to the old laws and customs of the realm and unknown to any British government on this con-tinent. (2) That its use was an implicit surrender of one of the most invaluable privileges of Englishmen—that of declaring one's sentiments openly on all occa-sions, instead of by secret and clandestine expressions. (3) That the argument of delivering the poor from the influential rich is delusive and fallacious, since no honest man will sell his birthright. (4) That the right of ballot opens doors to fraud, and that in Pennsylvania and Connecticut, where elections have constantly been by ballot, frauds are more and more complained of which scrutiny does not detect. (5) That ballot will destroy the right of the majority and introduce con-fusion; for no one will offer himself as a candidate, nor can there ever be a determinate number of candidates where whim may guide the choice. (6) That it will encourage hypocrisy and deceit and prevent laudable zeal. (7) That thereby too much is intrusted to the scrutiny and count of some returning officer.[1] But while those who stood for keeping the old colonial cus-tom unchanged prevailed on this occasion—"the mighty, the rich, the big-wigs and square toes," as it

[1] M. G., January 18, 1770.

was said—controversy would not down; and voting reform made such progress with other Revolutionary ideas that the framers of New York's State constitution in 1777 concluded to try the written ballot, simply as a novel and experimental substitute, and subject to the final discretion of the legislature. "Among divers of the good people," observes that notable instrument, the opinion is prevalent that voting by ballot "would tend more to preserve the liberty and equal freedom of the people" than the oral mode.[1]

We are to conclude, then, that in our Revolutionary era American politics, so far as the common voter was concerned, took a narrow range, and consisted mostly in local home rule. In that particular the New England town meeting for town government afforded the most admirable epitome of a democracy which the world had ever witnessed; coequality among fellow-citizens here prevailing, so far as coequality could consist at all, and the idea of practical co-operation in local public affairs being strongly presented, while at the same time was supplied a school for politics where public discussion, public oratory and public influence might mould political leadership in earnest. The county grouping of the Middle and Southern colonies gave far less political directness. Our development westward, over the surface of a continent, has since somewhat modified the original type in a civilization which commingles the blood of the primitive settlers and infuses foreign elements besides; and nowadays we have to confront the

[1]We may note that our early ballots were written, not printed, and that upon the penning of the voter's choice were based some lesser objections to the new method.

swarming of our composite population into great
hives of industry, whence issue those monstrous
municipalities, hard to regulate, whose problems of
self-rule are difficult and whose administrators slip
too easily into the mire of misgovernment and
corruption. But the New England town meeting
serves still the choice American model for self-rule
by the people, wherever communities are not too
vast or too incongruous to apply it, modified or
unmodified.

Beyond and outside the circumference of local home
rule, all was representative for the individual citizen
in these early times, except in fortunate Rhode Island
and Connecticut. The voter took part in choosing the
person or persons who should represent his town or
county in the legislature, which generally meant in a
House of Commons; for where, as in Pennsylvania,
there was no governor's council at all, the colonial legislature had not two branches. All elections were annual,
for "where annual elections end tyranny begins," as
our ancestors used to say. Here the voter's discretion
ended; and whatever of official patronage the King, the
royal governor or the proprietor might not control, the
legislature absorbed for itself. When, therefore, our
commonwealths expelled, in 1776, all royal prerogative
and authority, governors, judges and the rest received
in most States their new commissions not from the
people, but, directly or indirectly, from representatives
of the people. Even delegates to the Continental Congress were chosen by the several State legislatures.
And thus came it about that when the Federal Constitution was framed for our more perfect union, and
an executive established for the first time for all these
States combined, delegates in the convention of 1787

thought the selection of a President of the United States by the people would be like referring the choice of colors to a blind man; and after barely escaping the alternative of a choice by one or both Houses of Congress, they congratulated themselves when the expedient of electoral colleges was brought forward. This, they thought, would lift the momentous choice of a nation's chief executive above both people and Congress. It was not, therefore, in the eighteenth century, as now, public opinion or the manifested will of the people which was trusted to dominate in the broad affairs of government so much as the people's representatives at their own delegated discretion.

Under such conditions, political parties, such as we know them in our own times, could have had but little range for combination or discipline among those who lived still earlier the tame colonial life. Parties, at all events, were local in scope, or, at the most, provincial. Conventions played an active part in Revolutionary times; but these were bodies of delegates fresh from the whole people, with fundamental credentials for making fundamental changes. They, too, were representative bodies, and for Continental matters the legislature usually chose. Of party conventions for nominating party candidates America knew nothing then, nor for a long time later. Political conferences, whenever held, bore rather the style of caucus; such conferences were usually secret and close; and of caucus clubs and king caucus, political leaders in our several colonies were made aware long before the fateful year of the Stamp Act.[1] It was a legislative caucus that largely led in provincial politics. More than this, Con-

[1]See *e. g.*, John Adams's Diary, 1763.

gressional caucuses nominated Presidents and Vice-Presidents of the United States for more than thirty years after this Union was set in operation, and until the people would submit to such tutelage no longer.

XX

WITH the great Revolutionary struggle of our eighteenth century confined to Britain's thirteen provinces on the Atlantic seaboard, from the Maine district of Massachusetts to Georgia, and with the whole British occupancy north of that extreme boundary or southward among the tropical islands of the Caribbean Sea destined to continue as before, we behold in this rebellious area extending westward toward the Alleghanies, provincial traits, originating in a separate colonial experience and a separate immigration; yet blending speedily into a unified concert of action, to which common blood, for the most part, common language and lineage, a common consuetudinary law, and common systems alike of religion, education and politics, gave strong impulse.

The homogeneousness of our Eastern section is memorized, not only by that familiar synonym "New England," still largely applied to it, but in the term "Yankee," which British redcoats at Boston, we are told, used in derision toward them before the fight of Bunker Hill. For while "Yankee"—a corruption, perhaps, of "English," as the Indians or Indian-French pronounced that word—was used in colonial times by New Englanders themselves by way of compliment to their own talents, it was the jeering strain of "Yankee Doodle" (or the "Yankee fool"), riding to town on his

improvised war steed, a mounted and ill-dressed min-
ute-man, that flouted him in contrast with the king's
officers, well equipped and uniformed in gorgeous red.
The real "macaroni," by the way (or fine fellows), of
our continentals, whose dress befitted a martial occasion, were in a Maryland regiment, which came to the
succor of these brethren.[1] America's Revolution bred
certainly a new turn to the song, and they who were
once ridiculed by a nickname made it their title of distinction. Men have won, before and since, in religion
and politics by such a sign. "Yankee Doodle" was
played in triumph by New England musicians at Burgoyne's surrender. The name "Yankee" overspread
later this continent, in the western sweep of New England's keen and aggressive intellect, until in another
century the name became applied by America to the
whole free North that fought in our Civil War, and
by Europe to the whole United States as a nation.

Such, then, were the northeastern commonwealths
when colonial vassalage was shaken off, albeit they had
their own minor distinctions from one another. But
the middle section, though defined apart, was too hetero-
geneous in its European elements for a corresponding epithet to fit; while the English-settled South,
homogeneous once more, chiefly by reason of its peculiar plantation and labor systems, showed local varie-
ties of type—the proud Virginian predominating,—
with names and epithets apart which have not well
lasted.

America's thirteen colonies in 1776 kept within

[1] Yet some have opined that both air and the style of words
antedate our Revolution by more than a century, and that the
original "Nankey Doodle" riding on a pony was in derision of
Cromwell himself, "Nankey" being changed in later times to
"Yankee." II Lossing's Field Book, 683. This we may doubt.

practical reach of the Atlantic Ocean. To lands in the Mississippi Valley, both north and south of the Ohio River, claims ill-defined were made—by Virginia most notably, and by other British colonies besides. But beyond the Alleghanies, save for some rough-and-ready pioneers from Virginia to the Kentucky territory on the south bank of the Ohio, little had been done under sanction of the mother country for reclaiming the vast interior wilderness. That whole great "country of the Ohio," as it was termed, on either side of the saffron river to its junction with the still more turbid flood of the Mississippi, had, to be sure, been confirmed in 1763 to Great Britain, by the peace of Paris and the surrender of French dominion therein; but little attention was paid to populating this extensive valley while England's hold upon her colonies remained. Tracts of bounty land had, however, been promised to American officers and soldiers, loyal co-operators in the French and Indian War; and in 1772 we see General Phineas Lyman, who had procured a Crown patent at London after much lobbying and delay, organizing at Hartford his "company of military adventurers," and preparing to set out with his comrades for a remote tract of land at the southwest.

Yet, while that French and British struggle was in progress, Americans had foreseen the advantage that would redound from peopling the remote interior of this continent. Franklin wrote to George Whitefield, that pioneer of Methodism, in July, 1756, the next year after Braddock's defeat: "I sometimes wish that you and I were jointly employed by the Crown to settle a colony on the Ohio. . . . What a glorious thing it would be to settle in that fine country a large, strong body of religious and industrious people! What a security to the other colonies and advantage to Britain by increasing her people, territory, strength and commerce!"[1]

Touching the idiosyncrasies of these thirteen distinct colonies, whose independent confederation, followed by a more perfect Union, was the most pregnant event of the world's history during that eighteenth century, I may recall that Virginia, with her high-born pioneers of colonial times, was largely influenced by a lofty pride—by the sentiment of honor, generosity and the desire to lead—when she espoused a quarrel with the mother country, far off in Massachusetts, which touched her own concerns but lightly. It was Virginia who pressed upon her sister colonies the maxim that wrong and oppression committed upon any one of the thirteen colonies was a wrong to them all, and should be resented unitedly. More passionately, but with a like chivalrous sense of honor, did South Carolina engage in the common conflict, though of all these British dependencies the most acceptable, commercially, at that time to the home government. With greater ardor than Virginia, and hence less fitted for leadership than inspiration, she threw herself into the Revolutionary struggle, uncalculating, as she has always been, in self-sacrifice and devotion. South Carolina was one of the younger and less populous of our colonies, while Virginia was the oldest of them all, and had then the most inhabitants.

With Massachusetts, on the other hand, as with her near New England neighbors generally, rebellion was the result rather of reason and calculation—of long

[1] II Benjamin Franklin's Works, 232.

irritation under commercial and industrial constraints decidedly injurious to her native interests; and of that innate dislike, moreover, of Crown and Parliament, which had sent Puritan roundheads, dissenters in politics and religion, so many out of caste and favor in their old homes, to work out their salvation in the remote wilds of a new world. For New Englanders had crossed the ocean, not from love of romance or adventure, not to amass riches, but rather to wrest a living from stingy nature, while experimenting in civil and religious institutions after their own ideals of life. With a sterile soil to cultivate, they added to agriculture the pursuits of fishing and navigation; they developed an extensive commerce, upon their own capital or as factors, and were pushing and persevering. Though Britons, and rural Britons withal, in many traits; in disposition tenacious each of his own; jealous, perhaps encroaching; not easily adaptable to those whose ways and habits of life differed from their own; they tended strongly among their own set to civil and religious equality. Massachusetts, for her own part, never forgave the mother country for cancelling her first charter and reducing a commonwealth, once almost independent, to a province ruled by a royal governor and carefully watched. Connecticut and Rhode Island—the latter founded by the man whom Massachusetts had harshly banished in those earlier days—enjoyed self-government largely by the king's favor, and chose executives, such as Massachusetts herself had been deprived of choosing. New Hampshire was a junior Massachusetts, with less of the urban polish, less capital.

With the middle section of United America, colonial growth and founding had differed much from either

New England or the South. New York and the
Jerseys were early settled by Dutchmen, Swedes and
others from Continental Europe; and here, in prosperous provinces, with the British element at length predominating, was seen in course of time a promiscuous
population, always, on the whole, more immediately
interested in their own personal advancement and family fortunes than in politics, and somewhat lacking in
public spirit, save under the stress and special direction
of external leaders. Pennsylvania, too, had rapidly
grown in numbers as a great feudal or patriarchal
province, whose Quaker proprietor aimed to attract
medley crowds of settlers, from Continental Europe
as well as Great Britain; and there, once more, private
and plodding schemes of life and personal aggran-
dizement were more apt to interest the average
citizen than public affairs or the right to participate
in them.

Englishmen of the best culture and polish at the
present day, whatever may be one's innate sense of
superiority, are found courteous and affable in general
intercourse; and in that respect their present king sets
them a good example. But the typical Englishman
of the eighteenth century has not yet vanished from
earth; and racial characteristics were reproduced
among our British-American settlers of purer stock
while the colonial condition lasted. Men we still
meet with in the United States who draw out in rigid
lengths like a telescope, according to the presumable
range or importance of objects within the field of personal vision. A well-bred Britisher of the eighteenth
century would carefully adjust himself toward those

with whom he came in external contact; with a formal
bow to this, a chilling indifference to that one, trem-
ulous and effusive warmth of devotion to a third—
great sticklers, all of them, for form and proper etiquette, on occasions, and insistent upon exacting from
inferiors their own individual due. At the root of
such behavior was a rigid regard for the proprieties of
life and a self-respect tending to pomp and disdain.
The English church catechism, admirable in its compend for the common folk, lays great stress upon Christian behavior: "My duty towards my neighbor is to
love him as myself and to do unto all men as I would
they should do unto me"—the golden rule first of all,
as it ever should be, and admirable for all times and
conditions. But what follows in specification is for
inferiors, and inculcates a submissive deportment—
to honor parents and the civil authority, "to submit
myself to all my governors, teachers, spiritual pastors
and masters," and "to order myself lowly and reverently to all my betters." But how shall betters com-
port themselves? How far ought a lord to condescend
toward those of low estate? On that point the catechism is silent. Perhaps the average man who must
reverence reaches his own selfish solution by exacting submission and reverence from those who
look up to him, and who cannot disdain his station
in life.

In practice, each Briton took his recompense as he
might. The fresh collegian who played the fag to his
elder was the petty tyrant in turn with another class.
In Sheridan's "Rivals," a play first brought out in
London during the famous year of Lexington and
Bunker Hill, the master abuses his valet, while the
valet consoles himself by kicking the buttoned boy of

all work. Novelists who describe English life and
manners of that era—Fielding and Smollett as contemporaries, Sir Walter Scott in the retrospect, and the
rest—seem not far out of the way, when they show
their fellow-countryman ready to browbeat and treat
with insolence any stranger who crosses his path; but
if the latter but stands his ground, fights with fists,
sword or cudgel, and gets the better of his antagonist
in a close encounter, he wins respect, and from that
vantage-ground may gain, perchance, a life-long friendship. For surly and overbearing as old John Bull
might show himself on a first and casual acquaintance,
purpling with pride, and mottled over with prejudices
like pimples against him who bore no letters of introduction, he appreciates success, especially when he may
himself profit by courting the successful; and he learns,
however awkwardly, to become gracious, friendly,
flattering, if only he may hold his lead. Such, at least,
was the typical Englishman in the age of our Revolution and the eighteenth century.

But America, as I have suggested, was complex,
composite—its nature dashed in destination with the
blood of many other Caucasian peoples, despite a pure
Anglo-Saxon lineage. Here in the broad wilderness
of this new world was ample field afforded for new
and varying manners, for a new political experiment;
and if this earlier colonizing age still kept somewhat to
social inequalities, as in Europe, anything indigenous
like monarchy or a settled nobility with ranks and
titles had long since proved impossible. Sooner or
later in aboriginal America the crown and sceptre must
have disappeared as symbols of public authority. For

in each of these thirteen colonies the lower House, or legislature, and popular representation had burst forth for a local ascendancy; in more than one colony the people chose their own executive, while in others jealousy of home rule was strong, because a corresponding right of choice was denied them. To be sure, there was aristocracy in America, in that eighteenth century, and much of it; but the milder British type of Whig had more real influence here than that of Tory in such a set. Yet Toryism ruled then in Great Britain for the most part, and, indeed, while George III. survived; and as late as 1815 an Anglican bishop said before an assenting House of Peers that he knew not what the mass of the people of any country had to do with the laws except to obey them.

It was characteristic of our colonial age that, at all events, decent people, even in a large town or city, had a speaking acquaintance with one another, whatever might be the constraint upon a familiar social intercourse. A stranger on the streets was at once pointed out. And people in the same social set mingled unceremoniously in company, with their herds of sons and daughters. Yet the line of social demarcation was pretty strongly drawn while America lived under the king; and even in the smaller towns and rural neighborhoods each household knew and kept its place, with little, comparatively, of that envious rivalry which set in afterwards with the Republic. Patricians took largely the social lead and their sons inherited an influence. Even in politics, while families were so large and united, as well as localized, family connections and influence must have counted for much, and the voters and managers showed their sense of the fact.

Tradesmen were identified in most of these communities by their dress and submissive manners, though self-respecting and strongly disposed to self-improvement. To such applied the saying, "It is better to be well-remembered than well born;" for men in many of our thirteen colonies rose from humble beginnings to be public leaders in the great constructive work of the age; and it was to the lasting renown of their social patrons that men of such sterling worth and character were encouraged to work their way upward as good citizens and co-operate in plans for the public good. Yet, as a general rule, fathers and sons accepted alike the condition to which they were born, and for the present were content with the dress and manners belonging to it. Such a state of things must have tended to free, simple and unconstrained intercourse on matters of mutual interest, without the fear of compromising one's visiting acquaintance or family alliances.[1]

Historians tell us that only one-fifth of the people of all these colonies had in 1775 some other language than the English for their mother tongue.[2] Under such a condition, British ideas and British institutions must have strongly prevailed among the sires of our Revolution. But with the Union of our own times it is far different; for this broad country long since became the general home and refuge of the oppressed of all

[1]Mechanics, we are told, wore almost everywhere their leather aprons on week days; and the red flannel jacket and cheap plush or leather breeches were other accepted badges of inferiority. "Leather-apron Club" was a term applied by Philadelphia's upper class, perhaps to Franklin's Junto, and certainly in scorn of upstart commoners emerging into influence.

[2]Immigrants from France, Sweden, Holland and Germany, in relative order.

Europe; and a most competent authority lately estimates that at least one half of our population to-day,
instead of one-fifth, were born where a language not
English was spoken.[1] The twentieth century will
hardly run its course with the United States rejoined
to Great Britain, in any race alliance against the other
powers of the earth.

America, earlier even than the Revolutionary War,
had attracted the attention of seers and sages in the
Old World, and omens abounded of its coming greatness. In such books as Charles Sumner's "Prophetic
Voices," we may see quoted, nearly a century later, the
choicest of those predictions of rising glory and illustrious empire which Saxon denizens of a new world
were destined to fulfil. The verses of Cowley and
Bishop Berkeley are still to us an inspiration, as they
were to our forefathers. Very close, moreover, to the
date of our momentous struggle, the versatile Lord
Kames of Scotland wrote, in 1774, in one of his volumes of speculative prose upon the history of mankind:
"Our North American colonies are in a flourishing condition, increasing rapidly in population and opulence.
The colonists have the spirit of a free people and are
inflamed with patriotism. Their population will equal
Britain and Ireland in less than a century; and they
will then be a match for the mother country, if they
choose to be independent." This passage was among
those cited by Americans as an incitement to fulfil the
presage. To be sure, the contest for independence,
here prophesied as though far off, was actually quite
close at hand; nor did Lord Kames forecast rightly the

[1]U. S. Labor Report, 1901 (Carroll D. Wright).

result of revolution to these colonies. "They will not incline," he predicts, "to a kingly government; but neither will they unite, like the Dutch or Swiss, since each colony is already prepared for its own republican government by merely dropping the governor who represents the Crown." There was, indeed, such an element here at work, the centrifugal of State pride; but a countervailing force operated to combine when common grievances and a common danger roused colonies so happily alike in customs and institutions. American independence became worth achieving, because with independence came a lasting and comprehensive union.

Whether our illustrious Scotchman drew his inspiration from immediate observers in these distant dependencies I shall not inquire, but certain it is that a native-born American no less famous than Franklin had imparted to him his own ideas more than ten years earlier. "I have long been of opinion," writes he to Lord Kames in 1760, "that the foundations of future grandeur and stability to the British Empire lie in America; that those foundations are broad and strong enough to support the greatest political structure that human wisdom ever yet erected."[1] These words were penned while Franklin was at heart a loyal Briton and planned for America's development in full allegiance. Six years later, when he visited Germany with a friend and made a hasty tour of its chief cities and universities, he met at Gottingen the Biblical expert Michaelis, who in course of a dinner conversation expressed a belief he had lately stated to some London friends, that the American colonies would one day shake themselves loose from England. Franklin an-

[1] III Benjamin Franklin's Work, 39.

swered earnestly, "Then you were mistaken; the Americans have too much love for their mother country." "I believe it," responded the German professor, "but almighty interest would soon outweigh that love or extinguish it altogether." Franklin could not deny that this might be, but he still pronounced a secession impossible.[1]

It is thus that men, the most profound and broad-reaching of all ages, live, after all, from year to year, unaware of the broad undercurrent that bears them onward in logical consequences to the destiny they somehow comprehend, but cannot yet recognize as approaching. Interest was the great irresistible force that must in time have detached us from the mother country, to gain ascendancy in this continent for a new lead and new ideas of government. Hence, the pressure of compulsion by the King and Parliament, at a time highly opportune for resistance, made England's conquest from France a conquest in effect for American benefit. The revenge of France, in aiding children to rebel against the parent, impelled us onward to freedom; and so was it with French influence, a quarter century later, when Napoleon, with a new hatred of England, sold us Louisiana, and so advanced our dominion of this continent another stage, to the base of the Rocky Mountains.

Though the strongest of political bonds, the filial one, united these colonies with Great Britain in early times, it was fatal to the maintenance of British sovereignty here that British people at home were indifferent to

[1] J. G. Rosengarten's "Franklin in Germany," citing from the "Biography of Michaelis."

the welfare of these colonies, while, with British rulers and ministry, the interest and wishes of a few London merchants and financiers had more influence than thousands of colonial subjects could muster, so far away. It was thus that the African slave trade was kept up in these colonies, supplying a labor market for the sake of plantation products, quite in disregard of all humane disposition here to check it. Once, when a jail distemper was brought over and spread through Virginia by the ships transporting convicts, so that many innocent people died in consequence, Virginia's House of Burgesses passed a law obliging vessels that arrived from Europe with the distemper to go into quarantine. But two merchants in London, contractors in that importation, objecting that such a requirement would increase the expenses of their voyage, the Virginia law was disapproved by the home government and failed of effect. If such is sovereign power exercised from across the seas, where children and colonists have been largely indulged with representative assemblies of their own and with suffrage and self-rule in local affairs, what must that sovereignty be when the millions ruled are of a different race, deemed inferior?

It is not so much from any general intent to oppress, as from the innate covetousness of a few and the heednessless of the many, that distant dependencies are ruled despotically, not having a voice or a vote in the home government which lays imperious burdens upon them. Without steam appliances for travel by land or sea, without the ligature of electric cables or telegraph wires, our thirteen subject colonies were in 1776 farther, much farther, in effect, from Europe, from their sovereign King and Parliament, though close to this Atlantic shore, than are dwellers across our continent at the present day who border the Pacific. But practical distance in any case makes indifference even among the well disposed of an external empire. Franklin, while in London in 1773, noted as the great defect of the British people he met a want of attention to what was passing in so remote a country as America—an unwillingness to read about them, and a disposition to postpone even what they would at last have inevitably to consider. And with all this ignorance and indifference went, as he observed, a purblindness of comprehension among the ruling set; they failed to comprehend that America would act except from a sordid self-interest; and a mere threepence on a pound of tea—a beverage of which one consumed perhaps ten pounds a year—seemed to them an imposition too trivial to be resisted. Yet, as Burke clearly perceived, a love of freedom was the predominating feature of these far-off Americans, scions of the Saxon race, and hence these colonies would become suspicious, restive and intractable, whenever they saw efforts made at home to deprive them of freedom by force or chicancery. "I think the Parliament of Great Britain," wrote Washington in 1774, "hath no more right to put their hands in my pocket, without my consent, than I have to put my hands into yours for money." Samuel Adams advanced the same idea; and he added, in 1780, "when a whole people say we will be free, it is difficult to demonstrate that they are in the wrong."[1]

Whenever, then, it came to compulsion of these colonies distance would prove a constant thwart to despotism. "With three thousand miles of ocean between

[1] I Chastellux Travels.

you and them," said Burke, "no contrivance can prevent the effect of this distance in weakening government. Divine justice interposes to rebuke man's imperial arrogance and says, 'Thus far shalt thou go, and no farther.' "[1]

[1]II Burke's Works, 120.

INDEX